LATIN

Better Read Than Dead

Essential Latin for Beginners and Refreshers

G.D.A. Sharpley

Bristol Classical Press

First published in 1994 by
Bristol Classical Press
an imprint of
Gerald Duckworth & Co. Ltd
The Old Piano Factory
48 Hoxton Square, London N1 6PB

Reprinted with corrections 1995

A catalogue record for this book is available
from the British Library

ISBN 1-85399-410-3

Printed in Great Britain by
The Cromwell Press, Melksham, Wiltshire

CONTENTS

LIST OF APPENDICES

PREFACE

Better Read Than Dead is an introduction to the language and civilization of ancient Rome, intended both for students and armchair enthusiasts. It has evolved over several years of use by sixth-form, university and extra-mural students, all of whom wished to discover (or rediscover) Latin within the schedule of one academic year. Such a brief course has its limitations, but seeks to accommodate the broad range of interests and linguistic experience of adult beginners. The principal features are as follows:

i) all the texts are taken from the works of ancient authors, and students read authentic Latin from the first chapter onwards (translations are included);

ii) the texts are selected and arranged to illustrate the history, politics and society of ancient Rome;

iii) each chapter comprises grammar, vocabulary and exercises (with answers appended), and includes a study of English words derived from Latin;

iv) a cassette is available which contains readings of all the Latin texts.

The book is unusual in so far as it combines a Latin primer with a brief introduction to Roman civilization. After some years of teaching Latin to those who attended purely by choice, this seemed the best approach. Colleagues in modern languages have impressed upon me the need to bring the learning out of the classroom and place it in a practical context. Of course, conversational Latin will no longer buy us our daily bread or take us to the Colosseum, and the practice of writing Latin survives only to enhance reading skills. Above all it is the literature that we want to 'use', and to use it properly we need to study both the language and the historical context which frames it.

People have different reasons for joining Latin courses: the eccentric – to compile botanical lists; the cautious – to find out what *caldo* means on an Italian tap; the practical – reading historical sources; and the investigative – exploring the parentage of our own and other western European languages. The sheer variety of these aims, despite good intentions, has helped to marginalize Latin and to give it an educational priority on a par with watching trains.

If there is one overriding reason why Latin should remain within our experience, it has to be the literature. In the passage of time, the poetry, histories, letters and speeches have become part of our own tradition, our heritage, a family heirloom to look after and enjoy. With a little patience, those who now reject

Latin for being 'too narrow' or 'out of touch' will find in this absorbing old fossil such multi-disciplinary interests as most educationalists only ever dream about: European history, linguistics, politics, social organization, ethnic studies, religion, philosophy, oratory (self-assertion), drama and poetry.

Teachers' Note

Newcomers to Latin and its grammar should seek the guidance of a teacher. Teachers are advised to give plenty of help during the reading of the texts, so that enjoyment of the Latin is not impaired by too slow a progress. They are also asked to note that a few of the texts contain constructions and forms which are not explained in advance.

Traditional language courses tend to explain points of grammar and syntax before they appear in reading passages. The approach in this book resembles more modern methods, although the careful study of grammar and syntax remains as important here as anywhere else. It has simply not been feasible – whether or not desirable – to introduce students to all the linguistic forms and rules before they appear in the authentic passages. So when teachers meet ablative absolutes, jussive subjunctives or indirect statements, they should resist the temptation to explain these to beginners, or even to name them. A true beginner will be frightened away by too much linguistic jargon, though will settle for a simple translation, which will allow him to concentrate on those parts of the text containing linguistic points he *has* covered. As more advanced syntactical explanations are reached later in the book, previous chapters will furnish a ready supply of examples for discussion and comparison.

The above is meant as guidance rather than instruction, for course-teachers are the best judges of what their students want. Much will depend on whether the book is for beginners, false beginners or those seeking practice and revision. Adult education classes often mix true with false beginners (just to keep the numbers up), and when a student with rusty school Latin greets an **ut** clause like a long lost friend, a newcomer can be expected to raise an eyebrow.

Acknowledgements

I warmly thank my students who over the years have given their support and encouragement, some indeed witnessing both the outset and completion of the project. For their contributions I am very grateful to Richard and Timothy Beard, Hans Bürvenich, Heather Davis, Gilbert Drinkwater, Mark Espiner, John Fussell, Sheila Garden, Mabel Jarman, Michael Jennings, David Miller, Peter Rowley, Geoff Sharpe, Philip Smiley, Margaret Taylor, Jill Vaisey, Jane Walthew, Thomas Wiedemann and Jim Will. I am very much indebted to Niall Rudd for numerous suggestions and help with points of detail. For their careful co-operation I thank the cartoonist Andy Riley and the Bristol Classical Press. Most of all I thank Sarah, my wife, who has been unstintingly supportive throughout.

EARLY ROME 1

Grammar

Nouns: subjects and objects

agricola taurum fugat
the farmer chases/is chasing the bull

The Latin word for *chases*, **fugat**, appears at the end of the sentence. *The farmer*, **agricola**, comes first, and *the bull*, **taurum**, is second.

The farmer is the active one, the person doing the chasing, and so is the subject. *The bull* is the object, because he is on the receiving end, i.e. he is being chased.

agricolam taurus fugat
the bull chases/is chasing the farmer

Now *the bull* is the subject, while *the farmer* has become the object. To make this clear, the English words have been moved. The Latin words, however, have not changed their position, but their endings.

> The Latin for *farmer* as subject is: **agricola**
> and as object **agricolam**
> The Latin for *bull* as subject is: **taurus**
> and as object: **taurum**

English also has a few words which change according to whether they are subject or object: *she/her, he/him, I/me, we/us, they/them, who/whom*. These words are all pronouns, words which are used in the place of nouns.

Practice A

Like **agricola**		Like **taurus**	
nauta	*sailor*	**servus**	*slave*
puella	*girl*	**dominus**	*master*
dea	*goddess*	**deus**	*god*
femina	*woman*	**equus**	*horse*
poeta	*poet*		

With the help of the pictures, complete the words and translate:

1. **puell..... equ..... fugat.**   2. **serv..... domin..... fugat.**

2

3. **naut..... femin..... fugat.**

4. **de.....poet.....fugat.**

The cases

The technical name for these different endings of a noun is 'case'. Each case has a particular function: it may be to show that the noun is the subject or object. The subject ending is called the <u>nominative</u> case, and the object ending is called the <u>accusative</u> case. There are other cases too:

The genitive case

> **taurus agrico<u>lae</u>** *the bull <u>of</u> the farmer*
>
> **oculus taur<u>i</u>** *the eye <u>of</u> the bull*
>
> **equus puel<u>lae</u>** *the horse <u>of</u> the girl*

The word *of* is often used to translate the genitive case:
> e.g. **taurus agrico<u>lae</u>** *the bull <u>of</u> the farmer*

We might leave out *of* and use an apostrophe instead. This form goes back to the time when English had cases too:
> e.g. **taurus agrico<u>lae</u>** *the farmer'<u>s</u> bull*

The English genitive ending was once *-es,* but the *e* has been replaced by the apostrophe.

The dative case

> **agricola taur<u>o</u> faenum dat** *the farmer gives/is giving hay <u>to</u> the bull*
>
> **femina equum puel<u>lae</u> ostentat** *the woman shows/is showing the horse <u>to</u> the girl*

The dative case is used for the indirect object. Key English words: *to, for*.

The ablative case

>**agricola cum equo ambulat** *the farmer walks/is walking <u>with</u> the horse*

>**agricola a tauro videtur** *the farmer is seen <u>by</u> the bull*

>**agricola in equo est** *the farmer is <u>on</u> the horse*

>**femina equum faeno pascit** *the woman feeds/is feeding the horse <u>with</u> hay*

>**servus e villa ambulat** *the slave walks/is walking <u>from</u> (out of) the villa*

The most common use of the ablative is instrumental (*by, with*) or with a preposition (e.g. **in, e**). Key words: *by, with, from, in, on*.

Practice B

With the help of the pictures, complete the words and translate:

1. **agricol...cum taur... ambulat.**

2. **equus in vill...est.**

3. **puella tauri faenum equ...dat.**

4. **poeta agricolae taur... deo dat.**

Summary

Latin nouns change endings according to their function in the sentence. These endings are defined as cases:

CASE	FUNCTION	**femina**	**servus**
		woman	*slave*
Nominative	subject	**femina**	**servus**
Accusative	object	**feminam**	**servum**
Genitive	*of*	**feminae**	**servi**
Dative	*to, for*	**feminae**	**servo**
Ablative	*by, with, from, in, on*	**femina**	**servo**

Please note:

i) There are no Latin words for 'the' or 'a': the sense should indicate whether your English translation needs them.

ii) There is a traditional practice which encourages the reader to look for the verb first. This often means scanning ahead to the last word in the sentence, and should only be done if the sense fails to come naturally. As a general principle, you should read the words in the order that they were intended to be read:
    e.g. **agricolam taurus fugat**

agricolam	*the farmer* (object)
taurus	*the bull* (does something to) *the farmer*
fugat	*the bull chases/is chasing the farmer*

iii) Where there is no subject noun, the subject (in English a pronoun) is implied in the verb:
    e.g. **taurum fugat**   *he/she chases/is chasing the bull*

iv) Note certain points of pronunciation: **au** is similar to *house*; the Latin **v** is pronounced like our *w*; **i** (vowel) as in *lip* or *leap*; **i** (consonant, e.g. **Iulius**) as the English *y*; **ae** similar to the English *eye*; **c** and **g** are both hard, as in *cake*, *gate*, (not *gender* or *chalice*). There is more information in A Guide to Pronunciation on p. 185.

v) Latin sentences do not begin with capital letters, though proper names do.

vi) In the first few chapters you will be given the case of a word, from which you can determine the word's function. The names of the cases will be abbreviated to nom., acc., gen., dat. and abl., and pl. indicates a plural ending.

vii) The Latin texts in the following pages are taken from ancient authors. Very little of the original Latin has been altered, although in a few selections some words have been omitted, altered, or added to complete the context.

Myth, legend and history

Origins are often defined for us by the limits of what we can see. Rome emerges from obscurity as a collection of villages which grow together and become a satellite of Etruria, a powerful culture to the north. 510 BC is the traditional date of the expulsion of the last king, Tarquin, and the beginning of the republic. The king was replaced by a pair of leaders (consuls), whose length of office was restricted to one year. Clearly there was a fear of power concentrated in a single authority for any length of time.

This moment in their history had great significance for later Romans, since it embraced the end of Etruscan domination, the beginning of the republic and self-rule. Free from patriotism or nostalgia, we might say that it was a political struggle of a kind which frequently recurs, followed by a compromise of power-sharing between the leading families. But this perspective was too prosaic for Roman historians, who worked within a different set of conventions to those of the 20th century. Their readers had no novels, films, newspapers or television. They did not want a set of scant statistics or incomplete details marking the dawn of the Roman era. Today's historian might well wonder at the first two books of Livy's history of Rome, with all their biographical excitement and facts interwoven with myths and legends; but that was precisely what his readership expected of him.

A myth is literally untrue, while a legend has factual origins which are distorted in the telling and re-telling of the story. There is a clear difference in meaning, as a hapless newspaper editor once discovered when he published an obituary of a local dignitary and described the man's kindness as a 'myth'.

Myths, though untrue, are not always meant to mislead. They are valuable as symbols or moral paradigms, and are often an articulate if implausible way of perceiving the world. Greek historians had already borrowed the theatre's tendency to make a metaphor of life, not simply hold up a mirror. Much later Oscar Wilde was to say, with some mischief, 'the ancient historians gave us delightful fiction in the form of fact; the modern novelist presents us with dull facts under the guise of fiction' (*The Decay of Lying*).

Roman historians admired and imitated the standards of accuracy and impartiality set by the Greek historian Thucydides, who wrote an account of the war between Athens and Sparta in 5th-century Greece. Yet the more immediate legacy was that left by later Greek historians, who were as much interested in an episode's dramatic, literary and moralizing potential as in its historical importance. The story of Brutus condemning his sons to death (see no. 8) has both a moral message of unflinching and exemplary parental behaviour, and dramatic suspense.

Roman historians absorbed these Greek historiographical conventions, adding to them a taste for biography, with its natural inclination to extremes, and raised the moralizing element to the grander level of national interest, public duty and Rome.

1. The most famous of Rome's ancestors is the Trojan prince Aeneas. He escapes from Troy after the city has fallen to the Greeks, and after a perilous journey westwards he and his companions reach Italy.

urbem Romam condiderunt atque habuerunt initio Troiani.

(Sallust, *Bellum Catilinae* 6,1)

urbem [acc.] *city*
Romam [acc.] *(of) Rome*
condiderunt *(they) founded*
atque *and*

habuerunt *(they) had, held*
initio [abl.] *beginning*
Troiani [nom. pl.] *Trojans*

2. Formal ties are made with the indigenous Italians.

Lavinia Latini filia Aeneae in matrimonium data est.

(Livy I,1,ix)

Lavinia [nom.] *Lavinia*
Latini [gen.] *Latinus*
filia [nom.] *daughter*

Aeneae [dat.] *Aeneas*
data est *was given*

3. Romulus is equally well known to us as founder of Rome, and he is credited with being a descendant of Aeneas. It is Romulus who founds the city of Rome, after slaying his brother Remus. The name of Romulus is given to the new city.

urbs conditoris nomine appellata est.

(Livy I,7,iii)

urbs [nom.] *city*
conditoris [gen.] *founder*

nomine [abl.] *name*
appellata est *was called*

4. As leader of the new community, he appoints a group of advisers.

centum creat senatores. patres appellati sunt.

(Livy I,8,vii)

centum *hundred*
creat *he appoints*

patres *fathers*
appellati sunt *were called, given the title*

5. Facts begin to emerge from the fables during the 6th century with the expulsion of kings.

urbem Romam a principio reges habuerunt.

(Tacitus, *Annals* I,1,i)

urbem [acc.] *city*
Romam [acc.] *(of) Rome*
a principio [abl.] *from the beginning*

reges [nom.] *kings*
habuerunt *(they) had, held*

6. Tarquinius Superbus was the last of the kings of Rome.

Tarquinius Superbus regnavit annos quinque et viginti.

(Livy I,60,iii)

regnavit *ruled*

annos quinque et viginti *for five-and-twenty years*

7. In place of the king, two consuls were appointed.

**duo consules inde creati sunt, L. Iunius Brutus et
L. Tarquinius Collatinus.**

(Livy I,60,iv)

inde *then*

creati sunt *were appointed*

8. Brutus condemns his sons to public execution, after they and other aristocrats are discovered plotting to bring back Tarquin.

stabant deligati ad palum consulis liberi.

(Livy II,5,vi)

stabant *stood*
deligati ad palum *bound to a stake*

consulis [gen.] *the consul*
liberi [nom.] *the children*

9. The struggle with Etruria is remembered for the heroic deeds of individuals.

**pons iter paene hostibus dedit, ni unus vir fuisset, Horatius
Cocles.**

(Livy II,10,ii)

pons [nom.] *bridge*
iter [acc.] *route, passage*

paene *almost*
hostibus [dat.] *enemy*

dedit *gave*
ni *if not*

unus vir [nom.] *one man*
fuisset *had been*

10. Cloelia is one of several Roman girls taken hostage by the Etruscans. She helps her comrades to escape and leads them back to Rome.

> **Cloelia Tiberim tranavit sospitesque omnes ad propinquos restituit.**

(Livy II,13,vi)

Cloelia [nom.] *Cloelia*
Tiberim [acc.] *River Tiber*
tranavit *swam across*
-que *and* (to be understood <u>before</u> the word to which it is suffixed)

sospites [acc.] *safe*
omnes [acc.] *everyone*
ad [+ acc.] *to*
propinquos [acc.] *relatives*
restituit *restored*

Vocabulary

Text

Roma	Rome	atque	and
filia	daughter	et	
vir	man, husband (acc.: **virum**, like **servus**)	ac	
		-que	
annus	year	est, sunt	is, are (but with a participle: was, were, e.g. **est factus**: was made)
unus	one		
duo	two		
quinque	five	venit	comes, came
viginti	twenty	reges	kings
centum	hundred	urbs	city (acc.: **urbem**)
omnes	all, everyone		

Nouns

amica	*friend* (female)	**amicus**	*friend* (male)
nauta	*sailor*	**deus**	*god*
dea	*goddess*	**dominus**	*master*
agricola	*farmer*	**equus**	*horse*
puella	*girl*	**servus**	*slave*
villa	*villa, farm*	**taurus**	*bull*
femina	*woman*	**Augustus**	*Augustus*
poeta	*poet*	**Brutus**	*Brutus*
		Iulius	*Julius*

Verbs

fugat	*chases*	**dat**	*gives*
ambulat	*walks*	**habet**	*has*
est	*is*	**videt**	*sees*

Prepositions

accusative		ablative	
in	*into, on to*	**in**	*in, on*
ad	*to, towards*	**cum**	*with*
		a, ab	*from, by*
		e, ex	*out of, from*

The prepositions **in** and **ad** governing the accusative case imply some movement, whereas with the ablative they describe a location only.

> e.g. **in villam** [acc.] *into the villa*
> **in villa** [abl.] *in the villa*

The prepositions **a** and **e** are never used before a vowel (**ab** and **ex**).

Exercises

1. Identify the case of each underlined word and translate:
   a) **agricola <u>servum</u> fugat.**
   b) **<u>Augustus</u> taurum habet.**
   c) **Tiberius <u>feminam</u> videt.**
   d) **Iulius in <u>Britannia</u> est.**
   e) **poeta cum <u>nauta</u> ambulat.**
   f) **villa <u>Tiberii</u> est in Italia.**
   g) **<u>Tiberium</u> in Britanniam Iulius fugat.**
   h) **<u>deo</u> nauta taurum dat.**

2. Choose the correct alternative in each sentence and translate:
   a) **filia ad [agricolam/agricola] ambulat.**
   b) **dominus servo [equum/equo] dat.**
   c) **nauta Augustum in [Britanniam/Britannia] videt.**
   d) **Iulius cum [amico/amici] ambulat.**
   e) **filia [Augustum/Augusti] equum in Italia habet.**

3. What do the expressions **in memoriam** and **ad infinitum** mean?

4. The Latin word **duo** is similar to its English counterpart *two*: both words are derived from a common ancestor. What English words are derived from **duo**?

5. What English words are derived, or part-derived, from **annos**, **urbem**, **omnes**, **initio**, **unus** and **deligati**?

CARTHAGE 2

Grammar

Singular and plural

Latin nouns have different endings to indicate the plural (as do English nouns, e.g. *farmers, women*). Once again, these endings vary according to the function of the word in the sentence:

tauri agricolas vident
the bulls see the farmers

tauros agricolae vident
the farmers see the bulls

tauros agricola videt
the farmer sees the bulls

The verb **vident** loses the **n** in the third example, because there is a <u>singular</u> subject.

> A verb ending **...-nt** implies a plural subject
> A verb ending **...-t** implies a singular subject

Practice

With the help of the pictures, complete the words and translate:

1. **agricol..... taur..... vide.....**

13

2. **agricol..... taur..... vide.....**

3. **amici poetae taur..... non vid.....**

4. **naut..... de.... vide.....**

Neuter nouns

femina is a feminine noun, while **servus** is masculine. Most nouns which end **-a** (like **femina**) are feminine (**agricola**, **nauta** and **poeta** are exceptions). Nouns which end **-us** (like **servus**) are usually masculine.

A third category is the neuter noun, of which an example, **vinum** (*wine*), is added to the table below. Most of the endings of **vinum** are the same as those of **servus**.

Neuter nouns have the same endings in the nominative and accusative cases, and so you will not know from a neuter ending whether it is subject or object: the context will help you resolve any difficulty. All neuter plurals end in **-a** in the nominative and accusative.

14

Summary of nouns

	FUNCTION	SINGULAR			PLURAL		
nom.	subject	servus	femina	vinum	servi	feminae	vina
acc.	object	servum	feminam	vinum	servos	feminas	vina
gen.	*of*	servi	feminae	vini	servorum	feminarum	vinorum
dat.	*to, for*	servo	feminae	vino	servis	feminis	vinis
abl.	*by, with, from, in, on*	servo	femina	vino	servis	feminis	vinis

Some of the endings could imply a number of different possible cases:

   e.g. **servo**   dat. or abl. singular

   femina   nom. or abl. singular

Use the context to identify the right ending:

   e.g. **servus vinum feminae dat**

The slave	(subject: **servus** can only be nominative)
wine	(subject or object: here, probably object)
of/to the woman	(gen. or dat.; **feminae** could also be nom. pl., but we already have **servus**)
gives	(**dat** confirms the subject is singular)

The slave gives/is giving wine to the woman
   or
The slave gives/is giving the wine of the woman

Carthage in history and myth

Hannibal's arrival in Italy over the Alps took the Romans by surprise. The English might have experienced a similar shock had the Spanish Armada beached in Scotland and walked unannounced into Aberdeen.

Rome had experienced conflicts and crises before, but never quite on this scale. Much of the growth of her power had been gradual, the result of alliances, diplomacy and protection of smaller states. With Carthage, of course, it was different. This north African city had long been the established power in the western half of the Mediterranean, with strong trading links and a powerful navy to protect them. Carthage did not need Rome's protection, and certainly not her competition.

While Rome's aspirations were confined to the Italian peninsula, Carthage could ignore her. But in the early part of the 3rd century BC, Rome's sphere of influence reached the southern parts of Italy and from there to Sicily, and conflict became inevitable. The ensuing Punic wars lasted about a hundred years, and Rome's eventual victory could not have been easy to foresee. First she had to overcome her inexperience in naval warfare, and then much later the heavy morale-sapping blows inflicted by Hannibal. His eventual defeat signalled the end for Carthage; and Rome, now more powerful than ever, directed her ambitions eastwards to Greece. There were already cultural and diplomatic ties with the Greek city-states, which had been under Macedonian rule since Philip, Alexander's father, annexed them in the 4th century. At the end of the 3rd century, the Greeks sought help from Rome to gain independence and protection, a request she readily granted.

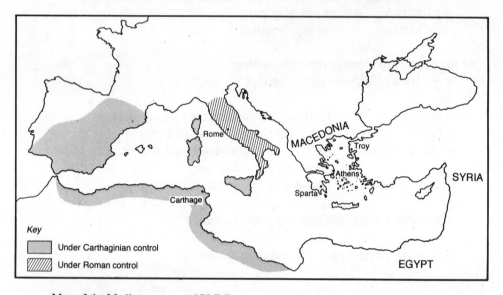

Map of the Mediterranean, c. 270 BC.

Virgil's story of Dido and Aeneas symbolizes the conflict and Rome's eventual success. Jupiter's desire for Aeneas to leave Carthage gives the seal of divine approval to Rome's destiny. It also lends a sharp edge to the story. Aeneas has to sail away because the gods wish him to, and we recognize this but cannot entirely condone it. Dido certainly does not. We can excuse him on the grounds of divine manipulation, but Aeneas is no puppet, for the gods interfere more to jog his memory than dictate behaviour. On another level the gods' behaviour serves as a metaphor, to enhance – not replace – human feelings and responses. Necessity (from the plot of the story) may be presented as a divine plan, but such is Virgil's art that the human characters always act in the belief that they are free agents taking their own decisions, often after

16

greatmoralstruggle.

There is nothing supernatural or odd about Aeneas' behaviour. The encounter in Carthage is a welcome relief after the perils of his journey, and he lets himself fall into a dreamy romance. In all too human a manner, he forgets himself and then does much damage in his waking.

Aeneas calls to mind the behaviour of other mythical heroes, such as Theseus' desertion of Ariadne, and Jason's treatment of Medea. These were characters whom Virgil had known from Greek literature, and the poet would have encouraged readers to make such an association. Greece gave Roman writers a cultural heritage, which they openly acknowledged by their deliberate reworking of Greek ideas.

1. Livy reflects upon the significance of the war against Hannibal's Carthaginians.

bellum maxime omnium memorabile erat.

(Livy XXI,1,i)

bellum [nom.] *war*　　　　　　　**omnium** [gen.] *of all*
maxime *most*　　　　　　　　　**erat** *was*

2. Hannibal reaches the summit of the Alps.

nono die in iugum Alpium perventum est.

(Livy XXI,35,iv)

nono [abl.] *ninth*　　　　　　　**Alpium** [gen.] *Alps*
die [abl.] *day*　　　　　　　　　**perventum est** *they reached*
iugum [acc.] *summit, ridge*

3. With hostile tribesmen and the extreme conditions causing acute difficulties, Hannibal tries to lift Carthaginian morale by pointing out the land ahead of them.

Hannibal militibus Italiam ostentat.

(Livy XXI,35,viii-ix)

militibus [dat.] *soldiers*　　　　　**ostentat** *shows*

17

4. The Romans were not expecting war in Italy. Several defeats cause confusion and panic in the city.

Romae cum ingenti terrore ac tumultu concursus populi in forum est factus.

(Livy XXII,7,vi)

Romae *in Rome*
cum [+ abl.] *with*
ingenti [abl.] *huge, great*
terrore [abl.] *terror, fear*

tumultu [abl.] *noise*
concursus [nom.] *rush*
populi [gen.] *people*
est factus *was made*

5. After an overwhelming Carthaginian victory at Lake Trasimene, Hannibal avoids a quick assault on Rome.

hac pugna pugnata, Romam profectus est, nullo resistente; in propinquis urbis montibus moratus est.

(C. Nepos, *Hannibal* 5)

hac pugna pugnata *after this battle*
Romam [acc.] *(to) Rome*
profectus est *he set out*
nullo resistente *with no one resisting*

propinquis [abl.] *neighbouring*
urbis [gen.] *city*
montibus [abl.] *mountains*
moratus est *(he) delayed*

6. Maharbal, a Carthaginian officer, urges his general to be bolder.

vincere scis, Hannibal, victoria uti nescis.

(Livy XXII,51,iv)

vincere *to conquer*
scis *you know (how to)*
victoria [abl.] *victory*

uti [with its object in the abl.] *to make use of*
nescis *you do not know (how to)*

7. Virgil's story of Dido and Aeneas symbolizes the destinies of the two cities. For a while the gods are unable to agree whether Aeneas should stay with Dido in Carthage or move on and found Rome. They contrive a thunderstorm, which scatters a hunting-party of Carthaginians and Trojans, and brings Dido and Aeneas together in a cave, alone.

speluncam Dido dux et Troianus eandem

deveniunt.

(Virgil, *Aeneid* IV,165-6)

speluncam [acc.] *cave*
dux et Troianus [nom.] *and the Trojan leader*

eandem [acc.] *the same*
deveniunt *come*

8. Jupiter does not wish the new city to end up on the wrong side of the Mediterranean, and sends Mercury to persuade Aeneas to leave Carthage and set out for Rome.

Ascanio-ne pater Romanas invidet arces?

(Virgil, *Aeneid* IV,234)

Ascanio [dat.] *Ascanius* (Aeneas' son)
-ne introduces a question
pater [nom.] *father*

Romanas [acc. pl.] *Roman*
invidet *begrudges*
arces [acc. pl.] *citadel*

9. Aeneas prepares to sail. Dido is enraged by his casual behaviour, and he tries to appease her.

Italiam non sponte sequor.

(Virgil, *Aeneid* IV,361)

sponte *by choice*

sequor *I follow, make for*

10. He fails, and Dido sends him on his way.

i, sequere Italiam ventis, pete regna per undas.

(Virgil, *Aeneid* IV,381)

i *go!*
sequere *follow! chase!*
ventis [abl. pl.] *wind*
pete *seek!*

regna [acc. pl.] *kingdom, land*
per [+ acc.] *across*
undas [acc. pl.] *wave*

11. Dido takes her own life – to the Romans, a proper and dignified end. Later in the poem Aeneas meets her spirit when he visits the underworld.

...Phoenissa recens a vulnere Dido

errabat silva in magna.

(Virgil, *Aeneid* VI,450-1)

Phoenissa...Dido [nom.] *Phoenician Dido*
recens [nom.] *fresh*
vulnere [abl.] *wound*

errabat *was wandering*
silva [abl.] *wood*
magna [abl.] *great, large*

12. Aeneas addresses her, but she does not answer.

tandem corripuit sese atque inimica refugit.

(Virgil, *Aeneid* VI,472)

tandem *at last*
corripuit sese *(she) hurried away*

inimica [nom.] *hostile, in an unfriendly manner*
refugit *fled back*

Vocabulary
Text

non	*not*	**urbis** [gen.]	*city*
quod	*because*	**duce** [abl.]	*leader*
Italia	*Italy*	**per** [+ acc.]	*through, across, by means of*
pater	*father*	**-ne**	*introduces a question*
dies	*day(s)*		

Nouns

filius	*son*	**Graecia**	*Greece*
populus	*people*	**bellum**	*war*
annus	*year*	**forum**	*forum*
Tiberius	*Tiberius*	**imperium**	*power*
Italia	*Italy*	**regnum**	*kingdom*
aqua	*water*	**faenum**	*hay*
filia	*daughter*		

Verbs

With a singular subject		With a plural subject	
amat	*loves, likes*	**amant**	*love, like*
ambulat	*walks*	**ambulant**	*walk*
audit	*hears*	**audiunt**	*hear*
bibit	*drinks*	**bibunt**	*drink*
capit	*takes,captures*	**capiunt**	*take, capture*
dat	*gives*	**dant**	*give*
dicit	*says, tells*	**dicunt**	*say, tell*
ducit	*leads, brings*	**ducunt**	*lead, bring*
est	*is*	**sunt**	*are*
facit	*makes/does*	**faciunt**	*make/do*
fugat	*chases*	**fugant**	*chase*
habet	*has*	**habent**	*have*
orat	*begs*	**orant**	*beg*
venit	*comes*	**veniunt**	*come*
videt	*sees*	**vident**	*see*

Exercises

1. Identify the case of each underlined word and translate:
  a) **Iulius in forum venit.**
  b) **filius in villa est.**
  c) **femina cum puellis est.**
  d) **Tiberius e villa ambulat.**
  e) **filius Augusti in Italia est.**
  f) **vinum servus bibit!**

2. Identify the correct form of each verb and translate:
  a) **puella aquam equo** [dat/dant].
  b) **dea poetam** [audit/audiunt].
  c) **Carthaginienses non Romam** [capit/capiunt].
  d) **dominus filiam** [laudat/laudant].
  e) **servus taurum ad aquam** [ducit/ducunt].
  f) **nautae poetam in foro** [videt/vident].

3. Translate into Latin:

> e.g.   *The master leads the slaves.*
> Answer: **dominus servos ducit.**

- a) The slave sees a woman.
- b) The farmer praises his sons.
- c) The daughter hears Iulius.
- d) Hannibal captures Italy.
- e) The slave begs the master.
- f) The girls love the poet.
- g) Augustus has power.

4. Exit and **exeunt** are used to describe action on a stage. What is the difference between the two?

5. The following words and expressions are all used today. Can you identify the cases of the underlined words?

in loco parentis, anno domini, in toto, via, ad infinitum, per annum

6. Identify Latin words in this chapter which are ancestors of:

> *video, suburb, transmit, rebellion, factory, bib*

GREECE 3

Grammar

Adjectives

Look again at the endings of **femina**, **servus** and **vinum** in the previous chapter, and compare the endings of the three nouns with the adjective **bonus** (*good*):

CASE	SINGULAR			PLURAL		
	masculine	*feminine*	*neuter*	*masculine*	*feminine*	*neuter*
nom.	bonus	bona	bonum	boni	bonae	bona
acc.	bonum	bonam	bonum	bonos	bonas	bona
gen.	boni	bonae	boni	bonorum	bonarum	bonorum
dat.	bono	bonae	bono	bonis	bonis	bonis
abl.	bono	bona	bono	bonis	bonis	bonis

The feminine endings of **bonus** are identical to those of **femina**, the masculine to **servus**, and the neuter to **vinum**.

Adjectives have equivalent case-endings to the nouns they qualify:
e.g. **femina <u>bona</u> servo vinum dat**
the <u>good</u> woman gives the wine to the slave

femina <u>bono</u> servo vinum dat
the woman gives the wine to the <u>good</u> slave

femina servo <u>bonum</u> vinum dat
the woman gives the <u>good</u> wine to the slave

An adjective is said to 'agree with' its noun. The adjective's ending must conform in three ways:

1. Case (nom., acc., etc.).
2. Number (singular or plural).
3. Gender (masculine, feminine or neuter).

23

LATIN *Better Read Than Dead*

est and sunt

1. The verb *to be* is followed by the nominative case, not the accusative:

     e.g. **Iulius est amic<u>us</u>**   *Iulius is a friend*
     Tiberius est ignav<u>us</u>   *Tiberius is cowardly*
     in foro sunt duo serv<u>i</u>   *there are two slaves in the forum*

2. **est** and **sunt** are sometimes used with a dative to show possession:

     e.g. **taurus est Iuli<u>o</u>**   *the bull is to Julius (i.e. Julius')*

Practice

Fill each gap with the correct form of **bonus-a-um**, and translate:

1. **vir .... vinum
    non bibit.**

2. **puella faenum equis
    .... dat.**

24

3. **servus........vinum videt.**

4. **Augustus feminas ....laudat.**

Please note:

i) For the next few chapters, the nouns and adjectives listed in the vocabularies will give all the possible cases an ending could imply, and the final choice is yours:

e.g. 'nom./acc.' means the word could be nominative or accusative.

ii) The gender of a noun (m., f. or n.) may be added to help you identify an adjective in agreement.

The legacy of Greece

The cultures of Europe and of many parts of the world have a debt to ancient Greece, and in particular to Athens of the late 5th and early 4th centuries BC. Democracy (*demos* = *people*, *kratos* = *power*) was first enjoyed by the Athenians, whose political participation amounted to much more than just occasional voting. The value they attached to public life can be seen in the etymology of the word *idiot*: *idiotes* means *a private man*.

Athens was infused with political, intellectual and artistic energies, which

25

yielded art, architecture, plays, histories and philosophy. In other eras and societies, consumers of such pleasures have been part of elite or eccentric groups, with a well-defined aesthetic distinction between highbrow and tabloid interests. This was not so in ancient Athens, where the 'good' and the 'popular' were one and the same. There have since been many imitations of Athenian styles, but few have succeeded in recreating the strength of her community, which both enjoyed the creative outpourings and breathed life into them.

At her most powerful, Athens controlled many of the smaller states in and around the Aegean Sea. Greece was not a single unified country, but a collection of separate city-states, of which the strongest were Athens and Sparta. These two came into conflict in the later part of the 5th century, and weakened each other enough for Philip of Macedon to occupy and annex all the Greek cities during the 4th century.

The conquests of his son, Alexander, had the effect of spreading Greek culture around the eastern Mediterranean and the Near East. His death led to a division of empire into smaller kingdoms, one of which was Egypt, where the Greek dynasty of the Ptolemies was founded.

From this fusion of Greece and the east arose the 'Hellenistic' culture, which was deliberately imitative of the classical period. Many of the Romans visiting Greece from the end of the 3rd century BC onwards developed an appetite for Greek culture, and inherited the Hellenistic criterion of good taste – that is, how something echoed a classical model.

Thus Virgil's story of Aeneas quite deliberately evoked association with the *Odyssey* and the *Iliad*, the epic poems of Homer. Virgil's contemporary, the poet Horace, could think of no better achievement than his adapting of Greek verse-forms to the requirements of Latin lyric. The modern concept of originality would have been meaningless to these Latin writers. They had a strong sense of form and a liking for Greek models, and the success of their work depended upon the use they made of what they annexed. The *Aeneid* has echoes of Greece on every page, yet remains a triumph of Italian creativity and the Latin language.

1. At the beginning of the 2nd century BC, with Carthage no longer a threat, Rome's empire-builders were tempted eastwards to Greece, which at this time was under Macedonian control.

pacem Punicam bellum Macedonicum excepit.

(Livy XXXI,1,vi)

pacem [acc.] *peace*	**Macedonicus-a-um** *Macedonian*
Punicus-a-um *Carthaginian*	**excepit** *took the place of*
bellum [nom./acc.] *war*	

2. After the defeat of the Macedonians, Rome was hailed as a liberator. A Roman victory over the Macedonians was reported to the Greeks at the Isthmian Games in 196 BC.

audita voce praeconis gaudium fuit.

(Livy XXXIII,32,vi)

audita voce *the voice having been heard*
praeconis [gen.] *herald*

gaudium [nom./acc.] *joy*
fuit *there was*

3. Many Romans were genuinely attracted to Greek culture and lifestyle, though for some people this interest was just another exercise in public relations. Rome had to control Greece if she was to counter the eastern threat from Syria – where Hannibal had taken refuge.

Hannibal patria profugus pervenerat ad Antiochum.

(Livy XXXIV,60,ii)

patria [nom./abl.] *country*
profugus [nom.] *fugitive*

pervenerat *had come*
Antiochum [acc.] *Antiochus, king of Syria*

4. When the Romans first encountered Greek culture, they cast themselves as poor country cousins.

Graecia capta ferum victorem cepit et artis
intulit agresti Latio.

(Horace, *Epistles* II,1,156-7)

Graecia capta [nom.] *Greece, when captured*
ferus-a-um *wild*
victorem [acc.] *conqueror*
cepit *captivated*

artis [acc. pl.] *art*
intulit *brought*
agresti [dat./abl.] *rustic*
Latio [dat./abl.] *Latium*

5. Some people, according to Pliny, believed that civilization, literature, and even the cultivation of crops originated in Greece.

in Graecia primum humanitas, litterae, etiam fruges inventae
esse creduntur.

(Pliny, *Letters* VIII,24,2)

primum *first of all*	**fruges** [nom. pl./acc. pl.] *crops*
humanitas [nom.] *civilization*	**inventae esse** *to have been discovered*
litterae [nom. pl.] *literature*	**creduntur** *are believed*
etiam *even*	

6. There were Romans who felt that such refinements as Greece had to offer were out of keeping with their own traditional values. These people wanted to retain a simple and uncomplicated lifestyle, and, like Cato below, complained about those who grew too fond of Greece.

> **iam nimis multos audio Corinthi et Athenarum ornamenta laudantes mirantesque.**

(Livy XXXIV,4,iv)

iam *now*	**Athenarum** [gen.] *Athens*
nimis *excessively*	**ornamenta** [nom. pl./acc. pl.] *ornaments*
multos (multus-a-um) *many (people)*	**laudantes** [nom. pl./acc. pl.] *praising*
audio *I (Cato) hear*	**mirantes** [nom. pl./acc. pl.] *admiring*
Corinthi [gen.] *Corinth*	

7. This resistance was not successful, but a hundred years later we find Cato's attitude echoed by the historian Sallust.

> **at populo Romano numquam scriptorum copia fuit,**
> **quia optimus quisque facere quam dicere malebat.**

(Sallust, *Bellum Catilinae* 8,5)

at *but*	**quia** *because*
populo [dat./abl.] *people*	**optimus quisque** [nom.] *all the best people*
Romano [dat./abl.] *Roman*	**facere** *to do*
numquam *never*	**quam** *than*
scriptorum [gen. pl.] *writer*	**dicere** *to talk*
fuit [+ dat. to show possession] *there was*	**malebat** *preferred*
copia [nom./abl.] *abundance*	

8. Virgil recognized Greek mastery of the arts.

> **excudent alii spirantia mollius aera**
> **(credo equidem), vivos ducent de marmore vultus.**

(Virgil, *Aeneid* VI,847-8)

excudent *will mould*

alii [nom. pl.] *others*

spirantia [nom. pl./acc. pl.] *breathing*

mollius *more delicately*

aera [nom. pl./acc. pl.] *bronze statue*

credo equidem *indeed I believe it*

vivos vultus [acc. pl.] *living faces*

ducent *they will bring*

de [+ abl.] *from*

marmore [abl.] *marble*

9. Yet Romans had qualities of their own.

> **tu regere imperio populos, Romane, memento**
> **(hae tibi erunt artes), pacique imponere morem,**
> **parcere subiectis et debellare superbos.**

(Virgil, *Aeneid* VI,851-3)

tu [nom.] *you* (sing.)

regere *to rule, guide*

imperio [dat./abl.] *power, empire*

populos [acc. pl.] *people*

Romane *Roman(s)* (being addressed)

memento *remember!*

hae artes [nom.] *these skills, qualities*

tibi [dat.] *to you, your*

erunt *will be*

paci [dat.] *peace*

imponere *to impose*

morem [acc.] *habit, custom*

parcere [+ dat.] *to spare*

subiectis [dat. pl./abl. pl.] *the conquered*

debellare *to subdue*

superbos [acc. pl.] *the proud*

10. Cicero had only praise for the culture of Greece. But he was less sure about the Greeks themselves. He once claimed that evidence given in court by Greek witnesses could not be relied upon.

> **sed sunt in illo numero multi boni, docti, pudentes et etiam**
> **impudentes, illiterati, leves. verum tamen hoc dico de toto**
> **genere Graecorum: tribuo illis litteras, do multarum artium**
> **disciplinam. testimoniorum religionem et fidem numquam**
> **ista natio coluit.**

(Cicero, *Pro Flacco* IV,9)

sed *but*

illo [abl.] *that*

numero [dat./abl.] *number*

multi (multus-a-um) *many (people)*

docti (doctus-a-um) *learned*

pudentes [nom. pl./acc. pl.] *modest*

etiam *also*

leves [nom. pl./acc. pl.] *frivolous*

dico hoc verum *but I make this point*

tamen *however*

de [+ abl.] *concerning*

toto genere [abl.] *whole race*

Graecorum [gen. pl.] *Greek*

tribuo *I concede*

illis [dat. pl./abl. pl.] *them*

litteras [acc. pl.] *literature*

29

do *I give, grant*
multarum [gen. pl.] *much, many*
artium [gen. pl.] *art*
disciplinam [acc.] *knowledge*
testimoniorum [gen. pl.] *evidence, testimony*

religionem [acc.] *awe, sacredness*
fidem [acc.] *reliability*
numquam *never*
ista natio [nom.] *that nation*
coluit *has cultivated*

11. Before Aeneas escaped from Troy, a few Greeks had entered the city concealed in the famous Wooden Horse. They opened the gates to the invading army, which then sacked the city. Virgil's story of Laocoon urging the Trojans not to trust the Greeks must have struck a contemporary note.

> **Laocoon ardens summa decurrit ab arce,**
> **et procul 'o miseri, quae tanta insania, cives?**
> **quidquid id est, timeo Danaos et dona ferentis.'**

(Virgil, *Aeneid* II,41-2;49)

ardens [nom.] *raging, burning*
summa arce [abl.] *from the topmost citadel*
decurrit *runs down*
procul *from afar*
quae tanta *why such*
insania [nom.] *madness*
o miseri cives *o wretched citizens*

quidquid [nom./acc.] *whatever*
id [nom./acc.] *that (i.e. the Wooden Horse)*
timeo *I fear*
Danaos [acc. pl.] *Greek*
et *even*
dona [nom. pl./acc. pl.] *gift*
ferentis [acc. pl.] *bearing*

12. The art and literature of the Greeks were not the only examples of their creativity to influence Roman society. Professional skills outside soldiery and law were not very highly thought of, and Roman aristocrats tended to employ Greeks as their doctors, accountants, architects, artists and teachers. Actors were often Greek, and so too were singers, athletes and performers of various kinds. There was a mixture of snobbery and resentment towards Greeks, because the Romans' military and administrative power was combined with a sense of cultural inferiority; and because Greeks were displacing less gifted Italians in profitable occupations. The complaining persona adopted by the poet Juvenal, who was writing around AD 120, has something in common with an Alf Garnet or Basil Fawlty.

> **grammaticus, rhetor, geometres, pictor, aliptes,**
> **augur, schoenobates, medicus, magus – omnia novit**
> **Graeculus esuriens.**

(Juvenal, *Satire* III,76-8)

grammaticus [nom.] *teacher*
rhetor [nom.] *professor*
geometres [nom.] *surveyor*
pictor [nom.] *painter*
aliptes [nom.] *masseur*
augur [nom.] *soothsayer*

schoenobates [nom.] *tight-rope artist*
medicus [nom.] *doctor*
magus [nom.] *sorcerer*
omnia novit *is a proper know-all*
Graeculus *Greek chappie*
esuriens [nom.] *hungry*

13. Juvenal is not impressed by Greek acting skills.

> **natio comoeda est. rides, maiore cachinno**
> **concutitur; flet, si lacrimas conspexit amici,**
> **nec dolet.../...si dixeris 'aestuo', sudat.**

(Juvenal, *Satire* III,100-2;103)

natio [nom.] *country (i.e. Greece)*
comoedus-a-um *given to acting*
rides *you smile*
maiore cachinno [abl.] *louder laughter*
concutitur *he is shaken*
flet *he weeps*
si *if*
lacrimas [acc. pl.] *tear*

conspexit *he has seen*
amici [gen./nom. pl.] *friend*
nec *but...not*
dolet *he grieves*
dixeris *you say*
aestuo *I am hot*
sudat *he sweats*

Vocabulary

Text

pacem [nom.: pax]	*peace*	tu	*you (singular)*
patria	*country*	tibi	*to you (singular)*
donum	*gift*	id	*that*
cives	*citizens*	alii	*some, others*
amici	*friends*	sed	*but*
fuit	*was*	etiam	*also, even*
erunt	*will be*	numquam	*never*
timeo	*I fear*	nec	*and not*

cepit	captured, took	quam	than
de [+ abl.]	from, about	si	if

Adjectives

bonus-a-um	good	formosus-a-um	beautiful
malus-a-um	bad	Ignavus-a-um	cowardly
magnus-a-um	great, large	laetus-a-um	happy
parvus-a-um	small	gratus-a-um	pleasing
multus-a-um	much, many	plus-a-um	dutiful
avarus-a-um	greedy	Iratus-a-um	angry

Exercises

1. Identify the case, gender and number of each underlined word and translate:
   a) vinum gratum est.
   b) poeta feminam formosam videt.
   c) servus filium ignavum domini non amat.
   d) agricola cum servis ambulat.
   e) multi viri in villa sunt.

2. Change the underlined words into the plural. You should also alter the endings of other words as necessary. Translate the new version into English:
   a) femina donum filio dat.
   b) nauta laetus amicum videt.
   c) puella equum habet.
   d) vir aquam cum servo bibit.
   e) taurus in villam agricolam fugat.
   f) Augustus filium pium audit.

3. Translate into Latin:
   a) Marcus is a dutiful son.
   b) Julia hears the pleasing poet.

c)   Many slaves are walking in the forum.
d)   Augustus has many gifts (*say:* many gifts are to Augustus).
e)   Masters do not praise cowardly slaves.
f)   The farmer does not chase an angry bull.

4. Optimum and **maximum** were once Latin adjectives in the neuter singular. How would you account for the endings of **errata, media** and **et cetera** ?

5. From which famous conqueror of the east is the name *Sikhander* derived?

6. Can you think of an English word which is a cognate of **ignavus** (i.e. not derived but sharing a common ancestor)? Try replacing **ig-** with a single consonant.

7. Identify derivatives of **magnus, multus** and **avarus.**

O TEMPORA O MORES! 4

Grammar

Verbs: subjects and pronouns

The ending of a verb is **-t** (singular subject) and **-nt** (plural subject). The subject may be a noun, or the subject may be implied in the verb, which we would translate with a pronoun:

e.g. **Marcus taurum videt** *Marcus sees the bull*
taurum videt *he sees the bull*

Verbs also have endings for the subject pronouns *I*, *you* and *we*:

SINGULAR	1st person	*I*
	2nd person (singular)	*you*
	3rd person	*he, she, it*
PLURAL	1st person	*we*
	2nd person (plural)	*you*
	3rd person	*they*

The ending of the verb helps you identify the subject. It also indicates the <u>tense</u> of the verb.

The tenses

Present	*I see, I am seeing*
Future	*I shall see, I am going to see*
Imperfect	*I saw (frequently/continuously), I was seeing*
Perfect	*I saw (momentarily/briefly), I have seen*
Future Perfect	*I shall have seen*
Pluperfect	*I had seen*

The verb-ending also indicates the kind of action being described:

e.g. *I see you*   (ordinary action)
I may see you   (potential action)

and whether the verb is active or passive:

e.g. *I see you*   (active)
I am seen by you   (passive)

Personal pronouns

CASE	*I/me*	*you* (s.)	*we/us*	*you* (pl.)
nom.	**ego**	**tu**	**nos**	**vos**
acc.	**me**	**te**	**nos**	**vos**
gen.	**mei**	**tui**	**nostrum**	**vestrum**
dat.	**mihi**	**tibi**	**nobis**	**vobis**
abl.	**me**	**te**	**nobis**	**vobis**

Pronouns are used in place of nouns (the Latin word **pro** means *in place of*). A personal pronoun is sometimes included as a subject, even though it may already be implied in the verb's ending. This use of a pronoun is for greater emphasis:

e.g. **Ciceronem vidisti**   *you have seen Cicero*
tu Ciceronem vidisti   *you have seen Cicero*

The Latin words for *he, she, they, him, her* and *them* will be seen later.

esse *to be*

esse *to be*	present	future	imperfect	perfect
I	**sum**	**ero**	**eram**	**fui**
you (s.)	**es**	**eris**	**eras**	**fuisti**
he, she, it	**est**	**erit**	**erat**	**fuit**
we	**sumus**	**erimus**	**eramus**	**fuimus**
you (pl.)	**estis**	**eritis**	**eratis**	**fuistis**
they	**sunt**	**erunt**	**erant**	**fuerunt**

See p. 24 for notes on uses of **esse**.

Practice

Fill in each gap (in the illustration) with one of the following: **mihi**, **te**, **vos**, **nostrum**

1. Iulia equos non videt.

2. poeta feminam amat.

3. faenum est tauro.

4. servus amicorum vinum bibit!

36

The fall of the republic

In the 2nd and 1st centuries BC, Rome annexed Sicily, Spain, North Africa, Greece, Asia Minor, Gaul and Egypt. Former consuls were appointed provincial governors, and Rome's character changed from dominant city-state to the capital of the known world.

This growth of empire played a part in the downfall of the republic, for government by annually elected consuls was better suited to acquiring territory than managing it. As generals, the consuls would compete with each other for power and prestige. As administrators, there was little personal gain in careful long-term planning: after twelve months, they were out of office. So the provinces began to suffer from inconsistent and short-lived directives from Rome.

Another problem was the increase in wealth. The virtues of austerity and simplicity once cherished by the aristocracy were now barely being paid even lip service. As new resources poured in from Spain, Africa and the east, there developed a taste for decadent consumerism. Bribery and corruption were not only rife; they were acceptable. Much of the new wealth was in the hands of traders, and the conservative senate's refusal to concede power to this growing group of people caused a political tension which was not going to disappear by being ignored.

In the 1st century BC, the senate began to lose control, first and foremost of its armies. These were posted on the fringes of the empire at great distances from the senate and central authority, and were led by powerful and ambitious generals. There was a succession of bitter civil wars: Sulla against Marius, Pompey against Caesar, and Antony against Octavian. From the last conflict, Octavian (later 'Augustus') emerged as the **princeps** of the Roman empire, and the transfer of authority from the senate to one man marked the beginning of imperial rule.

1. Pessimism and nostalgia were widespread during the 1st century BC.

> **primo magis ambitio quam avaritia animos hominum exercebat.**

(Sallust, *Bellum Catilinae* 11,1)

> **primo pecuniae, deinde imperii, cupido crevit.**
> **avaritia fidem, probitatem, ceterasque artes bonas subvortit.**

(Sallust, *Bellum Catilinae* 10,3-4)

> **nec vitia nostrum nec remedia pati possumus.**

(Livy, *Praefatio* ix)

primo *at first*
magis *rather*
ambitio [nom.] *ambition*
quam *than*
avaritia [nom./abl.] *greed*
animos [acc. pl.] *mind*
hominum [gen. pl.] *man*
exercebat *exercised*
pecuniae [gen./dat.] *money*
deinde *then, next*
imperii [gen.] *power*
cupido [nom.] *desire*
crevit *grew*

fidem [acc.] *trust*
probitatem [acc.] *decency*
ceteras (ceterus-a-um) *other*
artes [nom. pl./acc. pl.] *art, quality*
bonas (bonus-a-um) *good*
subvortit *ruined*
nec...nec *neither...nor*
vitia [nom. pl./acc. pl.] *vice, defect*
nostrum *our*
remedia [nom. pl./acc. pl.] *cure*
pati *to suffer*
possumus *we are able*

2. For the poet Catullus, there was no time like the present.

> vivamus, mea Lesbia, atque amemus,
> rumoresque senum severiorum
> omnes unius aestimemus assis!

(Catullus 5,1-3)

vivamus *let us live*
Lesbia i.e. *his girlfriend*
atque *and*
amemus *let us love*
rumores [nom. pl./acc. pl.] *gossip*

senum [gen. pl.] *old man*
severiorum [gen. pl.] *austere, strict*
omnes [nom. pl./acc.pl.] *all*
unius...assis *at a halfpenny*
aestimemus *let us value*

3. In 65 BC, Cicero stood for the consulship. Not an aristocrat, his claims rested on his reputation as an outstanding orator. When Catiline, the candidate for the other consulship, faced charges of misgovernment, Cicero thought he should help him.

> hoc tempore Catilinam, competitorem nostrum, defendere
> cogitamus. iudices habemus quos voluimus, summa
> accusatoris voluntate.

(Cicero, *Ad Atticum* I,2)

hoc tempore [abl.] *this time*
Catilinam [acc.] *Catiline*
competitorem [acc.] *fellow candidate*
defendere *to defend*

cogitamus *we are contemplating*
iudices [nom. pl./acc. pl.] *judges*
habemus *we have*
quos [acc.] *whom*

voluimus *we wanted*
accusatoris [gen.] *prosecutor*

summa voluntate [abl.] *the utmost good will*

4. In fact Cicero did not take the brief. Catiline failed in his attempt to become consul, and so attempted to take power by less legitimate means. He exploited the political tension arising from the sudden growth of a wealthy middle class and the impoverishment of certain aristocrats. He offered to cancel all debts, which won him support from those in difficulties.

> **cuncta plebes, novarum rerum studio, Catilinae incepta probabat.**

> (Sallust, *Bellum Catilinae* 37,1)

cuncta (cunctus-a-um) *all, whole*
plebes [nom.] *people*
novarum rerum [gen.] *revolution*

studio [dat./abl.] *enthusiasm*
incepta [nom. pl./acc. pl.] *initiative*
probabat *approved of*

5. Catiline's initiatives gained some momentum. Cicero, who had been elected consul, stood in his way.

> **neque interea quietus erat, sed omnibus modis insidias parabat Ciceroni.**

> (Sallust, *Bellum Catilinae* 26,1)

neque *and not*
interea *meanwhile*
erat *he was*
omnibus [dat. pl./abl. pl.] *all, every*

modis [dat. pl./abl. pl.] *way, method*
insidias [acc.] *ambush*
parabat *he prepared*
Ciceroni [dat.] *Cicero*

6. Cicero believed in the republic's system of government by the senate, but not all the senators themselves were well-disposed towards him. He was a **novus homo** (a 'new man' was the first member of his family to hold the consulship), while Catiline, an aristocrat, enjoyed good relations with a number of leading men. Catiline and his supporters were confident enough to attend meetings of the senate, but soon found Cicero's eloquence a powerful enemy.

> **o tempora, o mores! senatus haec intellegit, consul videt: hic tamen vivit. vivit? immo vero etiam in senatum venit.**

> (Cicero, *In Catilinam* I,1)

o tempora *what times!*	**hic** *this man*
o mores *what moral standards!*	**tamen** *still*
senatus [nom./gen.] *senate*	**vivit** *lives*
haec [nom./acc.] *these things*	**immo vero** *why*
intellegit *understands*	**etiam** *even*
videt *sees*	**venit** *he comes*

7. Catiline's supporters had dared to enter the senate.

hic, hic sunt in nostro numero, patres conscripti.

(Cicero, *In Catilinam* I,4)

hic *here*	**numero** [dat./abl.] *number, midst*
nostro [dat./abl.] *our*	**patres conscripti** *senators* (being addressed)

8. Cicero rounded on Catiline.

quotiens vero me consulem interficere conatus es!

(Cicero, *In Catilinam* I,6)

quotiens *how many times*	**interficere** *to kill*
vero *indeed*	**conatus es** *you have tried*
consulem [acc.] *consul*	

9. Catiline withdrew from Rome to gather provincial support. Cicero imprisoned and executed five of his agents left in Rome. Catiline's rebellion was crushed in Italy. Cicero then sought to justify his peremptory treatment of the five conspirators.

ego vitam omnium civium, quinque hominum amentium ac perditorum poena, redemi.

(Cicero, *Pro Sulla* XI,33)

vitam [acc.] *life*	**amentium** [gen. pl.] *crazed*
omnium civium [gen. pl.] *all the citizens*	**perditorum** [gen. pl.] *desperate*
quinque *five*	**poena** [nom./abl.] *punishment*
hominum [gen. pl.] *man*	**redemi** *I have saved*

10. Cicero sensed that the survival of the republic would need the support of the influential Pompey, a respected general. Although Pompey appreciated his interest, and recognized the usefulness of his eloquence, the general had ties and obligations to other individuals, like Julius Caesar. He remained lukewarm about Cicero's success against Catiline, and Cicero did not hide his resentment of this.

aliquam in tuis litteris gratulationem exspectavi.

(Cicero, *Ad Familiares* V,7)

aliquam [acc.] *some*
in tuis litteris *in your letter*

gratulationem [acc.] *thanks*
exspectavi *I expected*

11. Pompey may have wished that he himself had been asked to resolve the Catilinarian crisis, although more to the point is the offence he might have caused elsewhere by publicly praising Cicero's success. At any event, Cicero soon made an enemy of another aristocrat, Publius Clodius, a friend and protégé of Julius Caesar. Clodius had caused a scandal by disguising himself as a woman and participating in the women's festival of Bona Dea, held at his patron's house. In the subsequent court-case, Clodius was acquitted after bribing the jurors, but not before Cicero destroyed his alibi. Resentment ran deep, and though Pompey tried to reassure Cicero that Clodius would not seek revenge, Cicero remained doubtful.

Clodius inimicus nobis. Pompeius confirmat eum nihil esse facturum contra me. mihi periculosum est credere, ad resistendum me paro.

(Cicero, *Ad Atticum* II,21)

inimicus-a-um *hostile*
confirmat *assures*
eum...esse facturum *that he will do*
nihil *nothing*
contra [+ acc.] *against*

periculosus-a-um *dangerous*
credere [+ dat.] *to believe*
ad resistendum *for resistance*
me paro *I am preparing myself*

12. Pompey misled Cicero.

Pompeius de Clodio iubet nos esse sine cura.

(Cicero, *Ad Atticum* II,24)

de [+ abl.] *concerning*
iubet *orders*
esse *to be*

sine [+ abl.] *without*
cura [nom./abl.] *care, anxiety*

13. Clodius was elected tribune, and in 58 BC he got his revenge. With Cicero's executions of the Catilinarians in mind, he introduced a law banishing those who put citizens to death without a trial. Cicero sought help from Pompey and other friends and colleagues, but none was forthcoming. Under considerable threats and duress from Clodius, he left Rome, and in exile he revealed his despair to his friend, Atticus.

> **utinam illum diem videam, cum tibi agam gratias quod
> me vivere coegisti!**

(Cicero, Ad Atticum III,3)

utinam *if only*	**agam gratias** [+ dat.] *I might give thanks*
illum diem [acc.] *that day*	**quod** *because*
videam *I might see*	**vivere** *to live*
cum *when*	**coegisti** *you compelled*

14. On his return, Cicero renewed his enmity towards the Clodii. In court he diverted the attention of judges from a client's crime to the involvement of the infamous Clodia (sister of Clodius and probably 'Lesbia' in Catullus' poems).

> **res est omnis in hac causa nobis, iudices, cum Clodia,
> muliere non solum nobili verum etiam nota.**

(Cicero, Pro Caelio 31)

res [nom.] *matter*	**muliere** [abl.] *woman*
est...cum [+ abl.] *rests with, depends on*	**non solum...verum etiam** *not only...but also*
omnis [nom./gen.] *whole*	**nobili** [dat./abl.] *noble, well-born*
hac causa [abl.] *this case*	**notus-a-um** *well-known, notorious*
iudices *gentlemen of the jury*	

15. Caesar tried to elicit Cicero's support. He was a shrewd political tactician as well as a good general, and he recognized the value of Cicero's talent and contacts. He also appeared to have some genuine affection for Cicero (and had become a friend of Cicero's brother). Here Caesar writes to Cicero.

> **in primis a te peto ut te videam.**

(Cicero, Ad Atticum IX,6A)

in primis *first of all*	**ut** *that, so that*
peto *I seek*	**videam** *I may see*

16. During Caesar's dictatorship, Cicero withdrew from public life and concentrated on his studies and writing. Hundreds of his letters have survived, some with public consumption in mind, others more intimate. He confided in Atticus his joy at the murder of Caesar, but confesses it was short-lived when Antony emerged from the dictator's shadow.

> **o mi Attice, vereor ne nobis Idus Martiae nihil**
> **dederint praeter laetitiam.**

(Cicero, *Ad Atticum* XIV,12)

o mi Attice *my dear Atticus*	**nihil** *nothing*
vereor *I fear*	**dederint** *have given*
ne *that*	**praeter** [+ acc.] *except*
Idus Martiae [nom.] *Ides of March*	**laetitiam** [acc.] *joy*

17. Cicero tried to keep on good terms with Antony, as he made clear to his personal secretary, Tiro, in 44 BC.

> **ego tamen Antoni amicitiam retinere sane volo,**
> **scribamque ad eum, sed non antequam te videro.**

(Cicero, *Ad Familiares* XVI,23)

tamen *however*	**volo** *I want*
Antoni [gen.] *Antonius*	**scribam** *I shall write*
amicitia-ae *friendship*	**eum** *him*
retinere *to keep*	**antequam** *before*
sane *certainly*	**videro** *I see*

18. There were some obstacles to co-operation with Antony. In the first place Antony had been adopted by one of the conspirators Cicero had executed some twenty years before. More significant for Cicero was Antony's marriage to Fulvia, formerly the wife of Clodius. In August 44 BC, Cicero delivered the first of his speeches against Antony (*The Philippics*). To begin with, his tone was critical but conciliatory, and ever hopeful of a return to the republic. When Antony showed his contempt, Cicero produced another speech, with all the vigour of old.

> **defendi rem publicam adulescens, non deseram senex;**
> **contempsi Catilinae gladios, non pertimescam tuos.**

(Cicero, *Phil.* II,118)

defendi *I defended*
rem publicam [acc.] *republic*
adulescens [nom.] *a young man*
deseram *I shall abandon*

senex [nom.] *old man*
contempsi *I scorned*
gladios [acc. pl.] *sword*
pertimescam *I shall fear*

19. Caesar's heir (by adoption), Octavian, though still in his teens, became the focus of Cicero's efforts to restore the constitution. The following words are taken from Cicero's letter to Trebonius, who was killed by Antony's men before he had a chance to read it (43 BC).

> **puer egregius est Caesar.**

> (Cicero, *Ad Familiares* X,28,3)

puer [nom.] *boy*

egregius-a-um *outstanding*

20. Brutus, one of Caesar's assassins, did not share Cicero's enthusiasm for Octavian, and he made his reservations clear to Cicero's friend, Atticus, in 43 BC.

> **licet ergo patrem appellet Octavius Ciceronem, referat omnia, laudet, gratias agat, tamen illud apparebit, verba rebus esse contraria.**

> (Cicero, *Ad Brutum* XVII,5)

licet *let*
ergo *so, therefore*
patrem [acc.] *father*
appellet *let (Octavian) call*
referat *let (...) refer*
laudet *let (...) praise*

gratias agat *let (...) give thanks*
tamen *however*
illud *that*
apparebit *will be apparent*
rebus [dat. pl./abl. pl.] *action*
verba...esse *that his words are*

21. Brutus was right. Octavian agreed terms with Antony and divided the world between them. Antony went east to Egypt while Octavian remained in Rome. To gain this strategic advantage, Octavian was forced to make concessions, one of which was Cicero. He died at the hands of Roman troops while half-heartedly attempting flight to Greece. His head and hands (which had written *The Philippics*) are said to have been nailed up in the forum, and Fulvia to have stuck a hair-pin through his tongue. The following was written some sixty years later.

> **omnis posteritas Ciceronis in te** (Antony) **scripta mirabitur,**

**tuum in eum factum exsecrabitur; citiusque e mundo genus
hominum quam Cicero cedet.**

(Velleius Paterculus II, 66)

omnis [nom.] *all*
posteritas [nom.] *posterity*
Ciceronis [gen.] *Cicero*
in te *against you*
scripta [nom. pl./acc. pl.] *writings*
mirabitur *will admire*
eum [acc.] *him*
factum [nom./acc.] *deed*

exsecrabitur *will curse*
citius *more quickly*
mundo [dat./abl.] *world*
genus [nom./acc.] *race*
hominum [gen. pl.] *man*
quam *than*
cedet *will fade away*

Vocabulary

Text

primo	at first	vero	indeed, but
hic	here, this (man)	puer	boy
tamen	however	vita	life
ergo	so, therefore	sine [+ abl.]	without

Nouns and adjectives

cena	dinner	ager	field
fortuna	fortune	vir	man
culina	kitchen	hortus	garden
magister	master, teacher	fatum	fate
saevus-a-um	cruel	primus-a-um	first
acerbus-a-um	bitter	superbus-a-um	proud

Numbers 1-10

unus	one	tres	three
duo	two	quattuor	four

quinque	*five*	octo	*eight*
sex	*six*	novem	*nine*
septem	*seven*	decem	*ten*

Prepositions

inter [+ acc.]	*among*	contra [+ acc.]	*against*
post [+ acc.]	*after*	ante [+ acc.]	*before*

Exercises

1. If the underlined words were translated into Latin, what would be their tense?

Every morning during his tutorial the emperor would lie on the couch and throw fruit at the philosopher. The philosopher stood still and was not troubled by the emperor's poor aim.

One day the door suddenly opened and the emperor's mother swept into the room, only to intercept a rather soft peach. With remarkable dignity the matron of Rome wiped the battered fruit from her neck, removed her cloak and gave it to a slave.

'I was trying to put it in the bucket,' stammered the young autocrat.

'Are you going to give me your attention for a moment?' said his mother, ignoring his apologies.

2. Identify the case of each underlined word and translate:
   a) **Augustus erat princeps primus .**
   b) **Iulius erat mihi pater.**
   c) **nos servi Augusto grati sumus.**
   d) **poeta non me sed formosam feminam amat.**
   e) **Augustus patriae amicus est.**
   f) **servus ignavus vinum tui bibit!**

3. Translate into Latin:
   a) Your teacher does not see you (*s.*).
   b) Augustus does not drink bitter wine.
   c) You (*pl.*) are greedy, and we are angry.
   d) Our proud bull is chasing the cruel man.
   e) I will not have greedy slaves (*use* **erunt** *with the dative*).

46

4. Cicero spent much of his leisure reading Greek literature and philosophy. His own philosophical writings did not contribute many new ideas but were more a synthesis of Greek ones, adapted to a Roman outlook on life. By his reworking of Greek ideas, Cicero made Latin a vehicle for philosophical discussion, and many of the abstract words he used have since passed into English with slight changes of form and meaning:

    e.g. **libertas, humanitas, constantia, moderatio**

Identify English words with abstract meanings whose Latin ancestors appear in this chapter.

5. What do **ante meridiem, post meridiem, inter alia** and **curriculum vitae** mean?

6. *September* is now the ninth month of the year. What were *September*, *October*, *November* and *December* when they were first introduced?

AUGUSTUS 5

Grammar

Verbs

There are four main types (for all the endings see p. 154f.):

1. Verbs like **paro, parare** (e.g. **am_at, ambulant, par_amus**).
2. Verbs like **moneo, monere*** (e.g. **hab_emus, vid_ent, mon_et**).
3. Verbs like **mitto, mittere*** (e.g. **bibit, mittunt**).
4. Verbs like **audio, audire** (e.g. **aud_it, ven_iunt**).

* The penultimate 'e' of **monere** is long, of **mittere** is short.

Principal Parts

A dictionary shows four key parts of a verb, which are called *principal parts*. These are formed from the 1st person of the present tense (**paro** *I prepare*), the infinitive (**parare** *to prepare*), the 1st person of the perfect tense (**paravi** *I prepared*), and the supine, or the neuter form of the past participle, (**paratum** *having been prepared*):

PRESENT	paro	moneo	mitto	audio
INFINITIVE	parare	monere	mittere	audire
PERFECT	paravi	monui	misi	audivi
SUPINE	paratum	monitum	missum	auditum

If a verb has principal parts like **paro-are**, then it belongs to the first group (or *conjugation*), if like **moneo-ere** to the second, if like **mitto-ere** to the third, and if like **audio-ire** to the fourth.

Practice A

With the help of the table on p. 154, translate:

a) **paramus**   e) **audivit**
b) **mittemus**   f) **monuisti**
c) **monetis**   g) **parabatis**
d) **mittit**   h) **audietis**

Nouns

The following nouns belong to the same group as **servus,** with the same endings outside the nominative case:

CASE	SINGULAR			PLURAL		
	boy	*man, husband*	*master, teacher*	*boys*	*men, husbands*	*masters, teachers*
nom.	puer	vir	magister	pueri	viri	magistri
acc.	puerum	virum	magistrum	pueros	viros	magistros
gen.	pueri	viri	magistri	puerorum	virorum	magistrorum
dat.	puero	viro	magistro	pueris	viris	magistris
abl.	puero	viro	magistro	pueris	viris	magistris

Practice B

Identify the correct form of each verb and translate:

1. **pueri magistrum non ....**
   [audio-ire: imperfect].

2. **vir servum in amphitheatrum**
   .... [mitto-ere: perfect].

49

3. **femina virum** ....
    [**mitto-ere:** future].

4. **servus Neronem** ....
    [**moneo-ere:** future].

First among equals

Antony and Octavian were joined by Lepidus in a triangle of power, a triumvirate. As happened to the earlier triumvirate of Pompey, Caesar and Crassus, this became increasingly less secure, until 31 BC when the issue was resolved in Octavian's favour at the sea-battle of Actium off southern Greece. A few years later, Octavian was given the title 'Augustus'.

Augustus turned out to be a shrewd politician and an imaginative administrator. At the moment of Antony's defeat, and after decades of internal conflict, few contemporaries could have anticipated the forty-four years of his political supremacy. He was the best of all leaders – a lucky one, or rather, as the Romans might have put it, **Fortuna** smiled on him. According to Suetonius (whose tempting stories leave a little to be substantiated), he predicted the outcome of a naval engagement from the activity of one small fish. Implausible as it may seem, such sign-reading was an integral part of religious belief.

With the hindsight of history, Augustus' good fortune probably owed more to social and political circumstances than the spasms of a fish. Opposition to his rise to power was wearing thin, and most people were prepared to welcome any leader who could deliver them from the constant insecurity and brutality of civil war, even if this meant changes to the republic's constitution.

But Augustus took care to maintain the constitution, in appearance at least. If the senate lost authority to the princeps, it still retained the functions, privileges and facade of government. Augustus avoided the image of autocrat, preferring the role of first citizen, **primus inter pares**. The senate may have resented this diminution of its authority, but the equestrians (wealthy non-senatorial class) welcomed it. Augustus developed a much-needed administrative system for the empire, and employed people from different backgrounds to manage it. Moreover, he made Italians feel part of Rome and did not neglect the interests of the distant provinces.

A statesman as well as politician, Augustus sensed that his own political fate was wrapped up in the destiny of Rome: he secured his position by being seen as the bringer of peace, security and a new age of optimism. He initiated a series of social, military and religious reforms, and revitalized obsolete traditions: stricter discipline was restored to the army; religious rituals were observed; temples were rebuilt and new ones constructed; divorce penalties and child benefit were introduced in an attempt to increase the senatorial body, which had been depleted during the wars; adoption was discouraged; abandonment (and killing) of unwanted children was checked by a law forbidding it until the child was three; family morality was revitalized; once-fashionable debaucheries and depravity amongst the aristocracy were severely frowned upon – although this message scarcely got through to his own daughter, Julia.

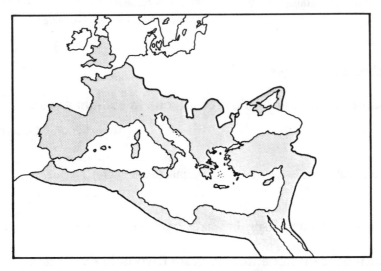

The Roman Empire at its greatest extent (2nd century AD).

He offered support to writers and poets, especially if they had something to say about his revival of Rome. He was not so unsubtle as to insist on obsequiousness, but expected them to share his vision and enthusiasm. Virgil, Horace and Livy were amongst those who thrived on his patronage.

1. Augustus emerged as **princeps** after the failure of the triumvirate.

> **Lepidi atque Antonii arma in Augustum cesserunt, qui cuncta discordiis civilibus fessa nomine principis sub imperium accepit.**

(Tacitus, Annals I,1)

Lepidi [gen.] *Lepidus*	**cuncta...fessa** [nom./acc.] *everything*
Antonii [gen.] *Antony*	*exhausted*
arma [nom. pl./acc. pl.] *weapons*	**nomine** [abl.] *name*
(armed forces)	**principis** [gen.] *'princeps'*
cesserunt (cedo-ere) *yielded*	**sub imperium** *into his control*
qui [nom.] *who*	**accepit (accipio-ere)** *he received*

2. He avoided obvious symbols of power.

> **dictaturam mihi delatam et a populo et a senatu non recepi.**

(Augustus, Res Gestae 5)

dictaturam [acc.] *dictatorship*	**et...et** *both...and*
delatus-a-um *offered*	**recepi (recipio-ere)** *I accepted*

3. He punished his opponents.

> **qui parentem meum trucidaverunt, eos in exilium expuli.**

(Augustus, Res Gestae 2)

qui [nom.] *who*	**eos** [acc.] *them, those men*
trucidaverunt (trucido-are) *murdered*	**expuli (expello-ere)** *I banished*

4. According to Suetonius, Augustus was savagely vindictive.

> **scribunt quidam trecentos ad aram Divo Iulio extructam Idibus Martiis hostiarum more mactatos.**

(Suetonius, Augustus 15)

scribunt (scribo-ere) *they write*
quidam [nom.] *some (people)*
trecentos [acc.] *three hundred men*
aram [acc.] *altar*
divo (divus-a-um) *divine*

Iulio [dat./abl.] *(in honour of)* Julius
extructus-a-um *constructed*
hostiarum [gen. pl.] *sacrificial victim*
more [abl.] *manner, custom*
mactatos *were slaughtered*

5. He renewed former traditions, religious, social and moral.

multa exempla maiorum reduxi.

(Augustus, *Res Gestae* 8)

maiorum [gen. pl.] *ancestor*

reduxi (reduco-ere) *I brought back*

6. Temples were rebuilt.

aedes sacras vetustate conlapsas aut incendio absumptas refecit, easque et ceteras opulentissimis donis adornavit.

(Suetonius, *Augustus* 30)

aedes [nom. pl./acc. pl.] *shrines*
vetustate [abl.] *age*
aut *or*
incendio [dat./abl.] *fire*
absumptus-a-um *consumed*

refecit *he restored*
eas et ceteras [acc.] *these and the rest*
opulentissimus-a-um *most lavish*
donis [dat. pl./abl. pl.] *gifts*
adornavit (adorno-are) *decorated*

7. The new era is to be celebrated.

nunc est bibendum, nunc pede libero
pulsanda tellus.

(Horace, *Odes* I,XXXVII,1-2)

nunc est bibendum *now there is to be drinking*
pede [abl.] *foot*

liber-a-um *free, unfettered*
tellus pulsanda *the earth is to be beaten (danced upon)*

8. Augustus was anxious to restore the numbers, self-respect and morality of his own social class. Suetonius suggests he was not the perfect model....

adulteria quidem exercuisse ne amici quidem negant.

(Suetonius, *Augustus* 69)

adulteria [nom. pl./acc. pl.] *act of adultery*
quidem *indeed*
exercuisse *that he practised*

ne...quidem *not even*
amici [gen./nom. pl.] *friend*
negant (nego-are) *deny*

9. ...but leaders allegedly need some licence.

consilia adversariorum per cuiusque mulieres exquirebat.

(Suetonius, *Augustus* 69)

consilia [nom. pl./acc. pl.] *plans*
adversariorum [gen. pl.] *opponent*
cuiusque [gen.] *each person*

mulieres [nom. pl./acc. pl.] *woman, wife*
exquirebat (exquiro-ere) *he discovered*

10. Augustus worked hard himself....

ipse ius dixit assidue et in noctem nonnumquam.

(Suetonius, *Augustus* 33)

ipse *he himself*
ius [nom./acc.] *justice*
dixit *he said (administered)*

assidue *assiduously*
noctem [acc.] *night*
nonnumquam *sometimes*

11. ...and expected similar standards from others.

cohortes, si quae loco cessissent, decimatas hordeo pavit.

(Suetonius, *Augustus* 24)

cohortes [nom. pl./acc. pl., f.] *troop*
si *if*
quae *any*
loco [dat./abl.] *place, position*
cessissent (cedo-ere) *had withdrawn*
  (in battle)

decimatus-a-um [agrees with cohortes]
  decimated
hordeo [dat./abl.] *barley*
pavit (pasco-ere) *he fed*

12. He reorganized the administration of the empire.

**exiit edictum a Caesare Augusto, ut describeretur
universus orbis.**

(Luke, *New Testament* 2,1) [Trans. Jerome]

exiit (exeo-ire) *went out*
edictum [nom./acc.] *decree*
ut *that*

describeretur *should be registered*
universus orbis *the whole world*

13. People outside the senatorial body, and even former slaves, were given opportunities within the new administration. But corruption and abuse of power by new 'civil servants' was discouraged:

**Augustus, quod Thallus pro epistula prodita denarios
quingentos accepisset, crura ei fregit.**

(Suetonius, *Augustus* 67)

quod *because*
pro [+ abl.] *in return for*
epistula [nom./abl.] *letter*
proditus-a-um *disclosed, 'leaked'*
denarios [acc.] *denarii*

quingentos [acc.] *five hundred*
accepisset (accipio-ere) *he had received*
crura [nom. pl./acc. pl.] *leg*
ei [dat.] *him* (dative of possession)
fregit *(he) broke*

14. Augustus was not fond of comedians.

Hylan pantomimum in atrio domus suae flagellis verberavit.

(Suetonius, *Augustus* 45)

Hylan [acc.] *Hylas*
pantomimum [acc.] *pantomime artist*
atrio [dat./abl.] *hall*
domus [nom./gen.] *house, home*

suae [gen./dat.] *his own*
flagellis [dat. pl./abl. pl.] *whips*
verberavit (verbero-are) *he beat*

15. But he was kinder to poets. They in turn were grateful for his support, and welcomed the widespread relief after decades of civil war. Anchises prophesies the rule of Augustus to his son Aeneas.

**hic vir, hic est, tibi quem promitti saepius audis,
Augustus Caesar, divi genus, aurea condet
saecula.**

(Virgil, *Aeneid* VI,791-3)

quem [acc.] *whom*
promitti *being promised*
saepius *quite often*
audis (audio-ire) *you hear*

Augustus Caesar [nom.] *Augustus Caesar*
divi genus *offspring of a god*
condet (condo-ere) *will found*
aurea saecula [nom./acc.] *golden age*

16. Augustus may have looked for echoes of his own character in that of Virgil's Aeneas, but other characters are also suggested by the poem's hero: Mark Antony's bid for sole power came from the east – where Aeneas' wanderings started, and it was Antony who was enslaved by an 'African' queen.

> **arma virumque cano, Troiae qui primus ab oris**
> **Italiam fato profugus Lavinaque venit**
> **litora.**

> > (Virgil, *Aeneid* I,1-3)

arma [nom. pl./acc.pl.] *weapons*
virum [acc.] *man*
cano (cano-ere) *I sing of*
oris [dat. pl./abl. pl.] *lands, shore*

fato [dat./abl.] *fate*
Lavinus-a-um *Latin*
litora [nom. pl./acc. pl.] *shore*

17. In AD 8, the poet Ovid was banished by Augustus for participating (it seems) in some kind of conspiracy. But the publication of the *Ars Amatoria* some years earlier was also held against him. The princeps was in no mood to tolerate witty erotic poetry only a few months after his own daughter, Julia, had been banished for licentious behaviour. Now in exile, Ovid wistfully recalls his final day.

> **iam prope lux aderat, qua me discedere Caesar**
> **finibus extremae iusserat Ausoniae.**

> > (Ovid, *Tristia* I,3,5-6)

iam *now, already*
prope *almost*
lux [nom.] *day*
aderat (adsum-esse) *was present*
qua [abl.] *which*

discedere (discedo-ere) *to depart*
finibus [dat. pl./abl. pl.] *boundary, limit*
iusserat (iubeo-ere) *ordered*
Ausoniae [gen./dat.] *Ausonia* (old name for Italy)

18. Cicero is said to have had a dream in which the young Octavian appeared as the future ruler of Rome.

> **M. Cicero somnium pristinae noctis familiaribus forte**

narrabat: puer facie liberali demissus e caelo catena aurea ad
fores Capitoli constitit eique Iuppiter flagellum tradidit;
deinde repente Augusto viso, affirmavit ipsum esse.

(Suetonius, *Augustus* 94)

somnium-i *dream*
pristinus-a-um *previous*
familiaribus [dat. pl./abl. pl.] *friend*
forte *by chance*
narrabat (narro-are) *was recounting*
facie [abl.] *face*
liberali [dat./abl.] *noble*
demissus (est) *was sent down*
catena [nom./abl.] *chain*
aureus-a-um *golden*

fores [nom. pl./acc. pl.] *door*
Capitoli [gen.] *the Capitol (temple)*
constitit (consisto-ere) *he stood*
ei [dat.] *him*
tradidit (trado-ere) *he handed over*
deinde *then*
repente *suddenly*
Augusto viso *on seeing Augustus*
affirmavit (affirmo-are) *he declared*
ipsum esse *him to be the one*

Vocabulary

Text

quidem	indeed	consilium	plan, advice
iam	now, already	epistula	letter
nunc	now	gladius	sword
vel	or	ludus	game
aut	or	ne	so that not, lest
eos	them	senatus	senate
qui	who	ut	so that, as

Verbs

	PRESENT	INFINITIVE	PERFECT	SUPINE
prepare	paro	parare	paravi	paratum
chase	fugo	fugare	fugavi	fugatum
work	laboro	laborare	laboravi	laboratum
love	amo	amare	amavi	amatum

beg	oro	orare	oravi	oratum
watch	specto	spectare	spectavi	spectatum
give	do	dare	dedi	datum
sail	navigo	navigare	navigavi	navigatum
blame	culpo	culpare	culpavi	culpatum
praise	laudo	laudare	laudavi	laudatum
warn	moneo	monere	monui	monitum
see	video	videre	vidi	visum
fear	timeo	timere	timui	–
have	habeo	habere	habui	habitum
teach	doceo	docere	docui	doctum
hold	teneo	tenere	tenui	tentum
sit	sedeo	sedere	sedi	sessum
send	mitto	mittere	misi	missum
seek	peto	petere	petivi	petitum
lead	duco	ducere	duxi	ductum
say	dico	dicere	dixi	dictum
rule	rego	regere	rexi	rectum
write	scribo	scribere	scripsi	scriptum
drink	bibo	bibere	bibi	–
hear	audio	audire	audivi	auditum
come	venio	venire	veni	ventum

Exercises

1. Change the underlined words into the plural, alter the ending of the verb (if necessary), and translate your answer:

a) <u>agricola</u> taurum vidit.
b) <u>donum</u> est puellae.
c) fortuna <u>mihi</u> est saeva.
d) Augustum-ne <u>tu</u> audivisti?

e) **filiam Augusti ego laudabam.**
f) **magister pueros in forum ducet.**

2. Change the tense of each verb as directed, and translate your answer:
   a) **servus in culina sedet** (FUTURE).
   b) **pueri ludos in amphitheatro spectant** (IMPERFECT).
   c) **Augustus nobis in foro dicit** (FUTURE).
   d) **femina puellas in horto videt** (PERFECT).
   e) **agricolae consilium Augusti audiunt** (PERFECT).
   f) **poeta Iuliae non gratus est** (IMPERFECT).

3. Translate the underlined words into Latin:
   a) The Romans often watched the games in the amphitheatre.
   b) Antony will lead his forces against Rome.
   c) Iulius saw the incident.
   d) Augustus heard the news from Gaul.
   e) The emperor will warn us all.
   f) The farmer would come to see us every day.

4. Translate into Latin:
   a) We heard the woman's advice.
   b) Augustus came to the amphitheatre.
   c) The master is greedy, the slaves are lazy.
   d) The gods will not drink bitter wine.
   e) The farmer works in the field, the woman works in the garden, but the slave drinks wine in the kitchen.

5. What is a *perambulator* usually called?

6. What does *culture* mean when it forms part of *agriculture* and *horticulture*?

7. What do *culinary* and *puerile* mean?

8. Identify English derivatives from the supine forms of the verbs listed in the vocabulary section of this chapter.

9. What is the original meaning of *decimated*, and how is it used today?

THE FAMILY 6

Grammar

Nouns

Look back at the passages and their vocabulary lists, and identify the following:

1. Nouns like **femina** in the accusative singular, in the genitive or dative singular, in the ablative singular, in the nominative plural, and in the accusative plural.
2. Nouns like **servus** or **vinum** in the accusative singular, the genitive singular, and the dative or ablative singular.
3. Nouns like **servus** in the nominative plural, and in the accusative plural.
4. Any five nouns in the genitive plural.
5. Any five nouns in the dative or ablative plural.
6. Neuter nouns like **vinum** in the nominative or accusative plural.

Nouns like **femina** belong to the first group (or *declension*), **servus** and **vinum** belong to the second declension. There are five declensions in all. You have already met many nouns from the third and fourth declensions, and a few from the fifth:

SINGULAR	*3rd declension*	*4th declension*	*5th declension*
nom.	various endings	-us	-es
acc.	-em (neuter -us)	-um	-em
gen.	-is	-us	-ei
dat.	-i	-ui (-u)	-ei
abl.	-e (-i)	-u	-e
PLURAL			
nom.	-es (neuter -a)	-us	-es
acc.	-es (neuter -a)	-us	-es
gen.	-um	-uum	-erum
dat.	-ibus	-ibus	-ebus
abl.	-ibus	-ibus	-ebus

For the all the declensions, see p. 150. On p. 163 there is a summary of the functions of cases, followed on p. 168 with an index of endings: this index gives all possible functions an ending can imply.

Note that nouns are identified by two of their cases: the nominative and genitive.

e.g. **servus-i, femina-ae, vinum-i,**
pater-tris, civis-is, dux-cis, tempus-oris,
gradus-us, manus-us, res, rei.

The nominative and genitive together tell you which declension a noun belongs to. From that information you can identify other endings.

Practice A

To which declension do these nouns belong?

a) **opus-eris** (*work*)   c) **mater-tris** (*mother*)

b) **exercitus-us** (*army*)   d) **dies, diei** (*day*)

Practice B

Give the genitive singular form of each underlined word:

a) **in loco parentis**   c) **ante meridiem**

b) **o tempora o mores!**   d) **per annum**

Practice C

With help from the nominative and genitive forms shown in brackets, identify the correct endings:

1. **equus est in villa**
.... [pater, patris]

2. **dux** .... [civis, civis]
    ad agros mittit.

3. **puella donum in** ....
    [manus, manus] **pueri vidit.**

4. **cives** ....
    [dux, ducis] **non timent.**

Family ties

The dreadful practice of abandoning unwanted children happened frequently enough for rulers to legislate against it. In some cases the parents were just too poor to afford the cost of bringing up a child. For others, the socialites and the ambitious, children were an extra burden they could do without. If the rudimentary methods of contraception (always female) failed to work, the next step was to induce a miscarriage, sometimes with serious consequences. When that failed, the final rejection by parents of their children was to abandon them. Girls suffered more frequently than boys, who could later earn an income and would not cost parents a dowry. It is no wonder that so many ancient plays used the plot of the abandoned child who is rescued and brought up by others, then sold or otherwise separated from his adoptive parents, and eventually recognized as being free-born. For the ancient audience there was nothing remote or quaint about this kind of comedy of errors.

If the pleasures of family life were lost on some Romans, the instinct for wanting an heir remained. Adoption was the convenient alternative, and was frequently practised. Augustus himself was adopted by his great-uncle Julius Caesar, and he later adopted Tiberius to secure the succession. At least this meant that some degree of choice was exercised in the preferment of imperial power, although such decisions were not always taken dispassionately with the interests of the state primarily in mind.

Like adoption, divorce and remarriage were commonplace. Children would remain with their father, and in some cases did not see their mother again. By the time Cicero's daughter Tullia was in her early thirties, she was separated from her third husband. This was an unfortunate but not unusual marital statistic from the latter half of the 1st century BC. When Augustus rose to power, he identified the reinforcement of the family unit as a remedy for society's ills. Abandonment of children, divorce and adoption were all discouraged, especially amongst the senatorial class whose numbers had dwindled in the civil wars.

The **paterfamilias** (father of the family) was the formal head of the household, while the **matrona** would supervise the day-to-day activities and often the education of the children. A father even had the right to execute his offspring, though this was seldom exercised, and he was also entitled to sell them into slavery, which in extreme cases he might do to avoid his (and their) starvation. The mother had less legal authority over her young, and a widow had to depend on her children for support.

Family in the sense of all the relatives, like a Scottish *clan*, was **gens**. The **familia** included not only the immediate family but the entire household, including the slaves. From early republican days, Roman society encouraged social patronage: a man would have a patron, **patronus**, for whom he would vote, run errands, and perform all kinds of services, depending on the patron's social position. In return a dependant, **cliens**, could expect legal and financial support and various favours. In the period of the empire, many clients were former slaves.

Romans much admired the quality of **pietas**, which was the sense of duty to family, country and gods. **Pietas** included good will and support between patron and client. Today's mafia hoodlum does not have *piety* in the Christian sense, but he does have **pietas**. The word **patronus** has much in common with *patron*, and perhaps even more with the Italian *padrone* (*godfather*). The idea of *family* in Sicily and New York has its roots in the **familia** of ancient Rome.

1. In Terence's play *The Lady from Andros*, a man finds his long lost daughter.

> **propero ad filiam. illam me credo haud nosse.**

(Terence, The Lady from Andros 951-2)

propero *I am hurrying*	**haud** *not*
illam *her*	**illam...nosse** *that she knows*
credo *I believe*	

2. Nero was adopted by his step-father, the emperor Claudius.

> **Nero undecimo aetatis anno a Claudio adoptatus est.**

(Suetonius, Nero 7,1)

undecimus-a-um *eleventh*	**aetas, aetatis** *age, life*

3. Agricola's mother discouraged her son from reading too much philosophy.

> **Agricola prima in iuventa studium philosophiae acrius, ultra quam concessum Romano ac senatori, hausisset, ni prudentia matris incensum ac flagrantem animum coercuisset.**

(Tacitus, Agricola 4)

iuventa-ae [f.] *youth*	**hausisset** *he would have drained*
studium-i *pursuit, study*	**ni** *if not*
philosophia-ae *philosophy*	**prudentia-ae** *good sense*
acrius *too/more keenly*	**incensus-a-um** *inflamed*
ultra quam *more than*	**flagrantem** [acc.] *burning*
concessum *(was) conceded*	**animus-i** [m.] *spirit, temperament*
senator-is *senator*	**coercuisset** *had restrained*

4. The theme of family versus state was popular with historians, for they could point to moral paradigms and focus upon personal suffering: Brutus, the legendary creator of the republic, executed his sons for plotting to bring back the king (see p. 9, no. 8). The conflict of loyalty in the case of Coriolanus was also between family and state, but here the state was not Rome. Coriolanus had sided with the enemy, and members of his own family were Rome's final defence:

> **Veturia, mater Coriolani, et Volumnia, duos parvos ferens filios, in castra hostium ibant. ubi ad castra ventum est, nuntiatumque Coriolano est adesse ingens mulierum agmen, primum multo obstinatior adversus lacrimas muliebres erat. dein familiarium quidam inter ceteras cognoverat Veturiam: 'nisi me frustrantur' inquit, 'oculi, mater tibi coniunxque et liberi adsunt.'**

(Livy II,40)

duos [acc.] *two*
parvus-a-um *small*
ferens *carrying*
castra-orum *camp*
hostes-ium *enemy*
ibant (eo-ire) *they went*
ubi *when*
ventum est *they came* (lit: *it was come*)
nuntiatum est *it was announced*
adesse (adsum-esse) *to be present*
ingens *huge*
mulier-is *woman*
agmen-inis *crowd*
primum *at first*
multo obstinatior *much more stubborn*

adversus [+ acc.] *against*
lacrima-ae *tear*
muliebres [acc. pl., f.] *female*
dein *then*
familiaris-is *attendant*
quidam [nom.] *one*
inter [+ acc.] *among*
ceterus-a-um *other*
cognoverat *had recognized*
nisi *unless*
frustrantur *deceive*
inquit *he said*
oculus-i *eye*
coniunx-gis *spouse*
liberi-orum *children*

5. Horace reminds his contemporaries of the bravery of Regulus, who was captured by the Carthaginians during the Punic wars and sent home to negotiate a ransom for his fellow prisoners. In spite of pleas from his family and friends, he urged the senate to reject all terms, and returned to his captors:

> **atqui sciebat quae sibi barbarus**
> **tortor pararet. non aliter tamen**
>   **dimovit obstantes propinquos**
>   **et populum reditus morantem,**

> quam si clientum longa negotia
> diiudicata lite relinqueret,
>   tendens Venafranos in agros
>   aut Lacedaemonium Tarentum.

(Horace, Odes III,5,49-56)

atqui *and yet*
sciebat (scio-ire) *he (Regulus) knew*
sibi *for him*
tortor-is *torturer*
pararet (paro-are) *was preparing*
non aliter *just the same*
dimovit (dimoveo-ere) *he removed*
obstantes *blocking his path*
propinquus-i *relative*
reditus [acc. pl.] (reditus-us) *return*
morantem *delaying*

quam si *as if*
cliens-tis *client*
negotium-i *affair, business*
diiudicata lite *a case having been decided*
relinqueret *he were leaving*
tendens *hastening*
Venafranus-a-um *Venafran* (suburb of Rome)
Lacedaemonius-a-um *Lacedaemonian (Spartan)*
Tarentum-i *Tarentum* (in southern Italy)

6. After the death of Cicero's daughter (45 BC), Servius Sulpicius wrote to him and criticized his personal grief at a time of political oppression (Caesar's dictatorship).

> quid te commovet tuus dolor intestinus? ea nobis erepta
> sunt, quae hominibus non minus quam liberi cara esse
> debent, patria, honestas, dignitas, honores omnes. at vero
> malum est liberos amittere. malum; nisi peius est, haec
> sufferre et perpeti.

(Cicero, Ad Famm. IV,5,ii,iii)

quid *why*
commovet (commoveo-ere) *disturbs*
intestinus-a-um *private*
dolor-is *grief*
ea *those things*
erepta sunt *have been snatched*
nobis *from us*
quae [nom. pl.] *which*
homo-inis *man*
minus *less*
liberi-orum *children*
carus-a-um *dear*
debent (debeo-ere) *ought*

patria-ae *country*
honestas-tatis *reputation*
dignitas-tatis *prestige*
honor-is *public honour*
at vero *but indeed*
malus-a-um *bad*
amitto-ere *lose*
nisi *except*
peius *worse*
haec *these things*
sufferre *to suffer*
perpeti *to endure*

7. In imperial times it was not the theme of family and state, but the struggles within the same (imperial) family which interested the historians. Tacitus recounted Nero's poisoning of Britannicus (AD 55), Claudius' natural son:

> **ita venenum cunctos eius artus pervasit, ut vox pariter et spiritus raperentur. facinori plerique hominum ignoscebant, antiquas fratrum discordias et insociabile regnum aestimantes.**

(Tacitus, *Annals* XIII,16,17)

ita...ut *in such a way...that*	**raperentur (rapio-ere)** *were taken*
venenum-i *poison*	**facinus-oris** *crime*
cunctus-a-um *all*	**plerique hominum** *most people*
eius *his*	**ignoscebant [+ dat.] (ignosco-ere)** *they*
artus-us [m.] *limb*	*forgave*
pervasit (pervado-ere) *pervaded*	**frater-tris** *brother*
vox-cis *voice*	**insociabile** *impossible to divide*
pariter *at the same time*	**regnum-i** *kingdom*
spiritus-us *breath*	**aestimantes** *putting it down to*

8. Virgil idealizes the role of the mother.

> **(mater) cinerem et sopitos suscitat ignis**
> **noctem addens operi, famulasque ad lumina longo**
> **exercet penso, castum ut servare cubile**
> **coniugis et possit parvos educere natos.**

(Virgil, *Aeneid* VIII,410-13)

cinis-eris *ash*	**exerceo-ere** *put to work*
sopitus-a-um *sleeping*	**pensum-i** *weight (of wool)*
suscito-are *revive*	**castus-a-um** *chaste*
ignis [acc. pl.] *flames*	**ut...possit** *so that she can*
nox-ctis *night*	**servo-are** *keep*
addens *adding*	**cubile-is** [n.] *couch, bed*
opus-eris *work, working hours*	**coniunx-gis** *husband*
famula-ae *maid-servant*	**parvus-a-um** *small*
lumen-inis *light*	**educo-ere** *bring up*
longus-a-um *long*	**natus-i** *son*

9. Pliny advises a father not to be too strict with his son.

castigabat quidam filium suum, quod paulo sumptuosius
equos et canes emeret. huic ego, iuvene digresso, 'heus tu,
numquamne fecisti quod a patre corripi posset? "fecisti",
dico? non interdum facis, quod filius tuus, si repente pater
ille, tu filius, pari gravitate reprehendat?'

(Pliny, *Letters* IX,12)

castigo-are *punish*	**fecisti (facio-ere)** *you have done*
quidam [nom.] *some fellow*	**corripi posset** *could be blamed*
suum *his*	**dico-ere** *say*
quod *because/(that) which*	**interdum** *sometimes*
paulo *a little*	**facis (facio-ere)** *you do*
sumptuosius *too extravagantly*	**tuus-a-um** *your*
emeret *he was buying*	**repente** *suddenly*
huic *to this man*	**ille** *he*
iuvene digresso *after the boy departed*	**pari** [abl.] *equal*
heus *hey!*	**gravitas-tatis** *sternness*
numquam *never*	**reprehendat** *he would scold*

10. The poet Martial complains that his casual manner in the presence of his patron, Caecilianus, has cost him a few coins.

mane salutavi vero te nomine casu
    nec dixi dominum, Caeciliane, meum.
quanti libertas constet mihi tanta, requiris?
    centum quadrantes abstulit illa mihi.

(Martial, *Epigrams* VI,88)

mane *this morning*	**tantus-a-um** *such, so great*
salutavi (saluto-are) *I greeted*	**libertas-tatis** *licence*
verus-a-um *real*	**requiris (requiro-ere)** *you want to know*
nomen-inis *name*	**centum** *hundred*
casu *by chance*	**quadrantes** *farthings*
dixi (dico-ere) *I said*	**abstulit (aufero-erre)** *has taken away*
dominus-i *master*	**illa** [nom.] *that*
quanti...constet *how much...costs*	**mihi** *from me*

11. Clients could be fickle.

nemo te ipsum sequitur, sed aliquid ex te. amicitia olim
petebatur, nunc praeda; mutabunt testamenta destituti

senes, migrabit ad aliud limen salutator.

(Seneca, *Epistulae Morales* 19,4)

nemo *no one*
te ipsum *you yourself*
sequitur *follows*
aliquid *some advantage*
olim *previously*
petebatur (peto-ere) *was sought*
nunc *now*
praeda-ae *loot, plunder*

muto-are-avi-atum *to change*
testamentum-i *will*
destitutus-a-um *lonely*
senex-is *old man*
migro-are *move*
aliud [nom./acc., n.] *other*
limen-inis [n.] *door, threshold*
salutator-oris *visitor*

Vocabulary

Text

postquam	after	nonne	surely
eius	his, her	quod	because, which
quia	because	quidam	a certain (person)
ubi	where, when	igitur	therefore
nisi, ni	unless, if not, except	inter [+ acc.]	among

Nouns

anima-ae	soul, breath	miles-itis	soldier
animus-i	spirit, courage	hostes-ium	enemy
oculus-i	eye	dux-cis	leader
castra-orum	camp	facinus-oris	crime
nomen-inis	name	corpus-oris	body
homo-inis	man	munus-eris	gift
canis-is	dog	exercitus-us	army
mater-tris	mother	gemitus-us	groan
soror-is	sister	senatus-us	senate

frater-tris	*brother*	res, rei	*thing*
senator-is	*senator*	dies, diei	*day*
gladiator-is	*gladiator*	res publica*	*republic*

* Note that **publica** is an adjective agreeing with **res**.

Exercises

1. Choose the correct word for each gap, identify its case, and translate:
   canes, matrem, ducem, hostium, gemitu

   a) **servi** .... **fugant.**
   b) **cives** .... **laudabant.**
   c) **pater** .... **culpat.**
   d) **gladiator ducem** .... **audiebat.**
   e) **dux** .... **ad Africam navigabat.**

2. Identify the case of each underlined word and translate:
   a) **<u>milites</u> pueros ex castris fugabant.**
   b) **<u>facinora</u> servi erant magna.**
   c) **<u>munus</u> Ciceronis servus vidit.**
   d) **Marcus <u>gemitus</u> hostium audiebat.**
   e) **<u>sorores</u> Iulii in Gallia habitant.**

3. Translate into Latin:
   a) The boys walk with the father.
   b) We saw the bodies of the gladiators.
   c) The dogs were watching our dinner.
   d) The brothers will send a letter to the senate.
   e) Great are the gifts of the gods.
   f) You senators used to love the republic!

4. What is the connection between:
   pendulum, pending, pensive and *pension* ?

SOCIETY 7

Grammar

Active and passive verbs

Most of the verbs you have seen so far have been active:

    e.g. **agricola taurum fugat**   *the farmer chases the bull*

When the verb is passive, the object of the active verb becomes the subject:

    e.g. **taurus ab agricola fugatur** *the bull is chased by the farmer*

There is no significant change in meaning, but just in emphasis.

VERB ENDINGS	Active	Passive
3rd person singular (*he, she, it*)	**-t**	**-tur**
3rd person plural (*they*)	**-nt**	**-ntur**

Note how the subject of the active verb (above: **agricola**) has changed in the passive expression to the ablative: **ab agricola** *by the farmer*.

Practice A

Make each verb passive, and change any other words to keep the sense; then translate:

    e.g. **puella equum in agro videt**
        equus a puella in agro videtur
        the horse is seen in the field by the girl

1. **mater pueros monet.**
2. **Augustus canem in villam fugat.**
3. **femina gladiatores laudat.**
4. **cives senatorem audiunt.**

The perfect passive

This is formed from the past participle with **est** (pl.: **sunt**):

    e.g. **agricola a tauro <u>fugatus est</u>**
        the farmer <u>was chased</u> by the bull

The past participle is formed from the supine, with endings identical to
bonus-a-um. It agrees with its subject noun:

> e.g. (above) **agricol<u>a</u>...fugat<u>us</u>** (masculine, singular)

Practice B

Add the correct form of the past participle to complete each sentence, and
translate:

> e.g. **cena a puellis................est** [paro-are, paravi, paratum]
> **cena a puellis <u>parata</u> est**
> *the dinner was prepared by the girls*

1. **hostes a Caesare................sunt** [vinco-ere, vici, victum]
2. **puer a Seneca................est** [doceo-ere, docui, doctum]
3. **epistula a matre................est** [mitto-ere, misi, missum]
4. **vinum Britannico a servo................est** [do-are, dedi, datum]

Past participles

Past participles without **est** or **sunt** agree with their nouns as adjectives do, and
are <u>passive</u>:

> e.g. **serv<u>us</u> a femina vis<u>us</u> e villa venit**
> *the slave, having been seen by the woman, came out of the villa*

> **senator munera fratri dat<u>a</u> vidit**
> *the senator saw the gifts which had been given to his brother*

Practice C

Complete the endings of the participles and translate:

> e.g. **captivi in amphitheatrum..............a gladiatoribus caesi sunt**
>   [duco-ere, duxi, ductum]
> **captivi in amphitheatrum <u>ducti</u> a gladiatoribus caesi sunt**
> *the prisoners were brought into the amphitheatre and were killed*
>   *by the gladiators*

1. **puellae in agros................matrem non viderunt**
                [mitto-ere, misi, missum]
2. **taurus militem in agro................fugavit**
                [video-ere, vidi, visum]
3. **magister puero..............munus dedit**
                [laudo-are, laudavi, laudatum]

Occupations and status

The very poor at least had the freedom to sell themselves into slavery to reduce their debt. Not all those who remained free had voting rights, but only those who were citizens, a status not granted to all provincials until the later years of the empire. This was a cause of discontent, since provincials fought in campaigns, risking their lives and the loss of property in their absence.

There were three classes of citizens: plebeians, equestrians and senators. The vast majority of people were plebeians. Equestrians had to have 400,000 sesterces to qualify, a sum which excluded all but the richest of citizens (an *equestrian* was originally defined as one who could afford his own horse while serving in an army). Senatorial families were limited to aristocratic **gentes** (clans) like the Claudii or Iulii. During the early republican period almost all political power lay in the hands of the senators. They performed duties as magistrates, judges, diplomats, military officers and priests. Senators were not paid for their services, neither did they need to be. Although they held the notion of commerce somewhat in contempt, most of them had business agents who managed their investments in construction, farming and other profitable enterprises.

The equestrians grew in power along with the growth of trading opportunities around the expanding empire. They made up the 'middle class', but were few in number and vastly richer than the average plebeian. In the early republic, plebeians had struggled with patricians (senators) for political rights, and they gained some concessions, including their own council and officers.

These social divisions were formal, and defined by privileges such as preferential seats at a theatre. There was some mobility from one grade to another, although few plebeian businessmen would have amassed the required wealth to join the equestrians. Some talented equestrians broke through into public and senatorial life: Cicero's equestrian family had been involved in local politics in his home-town of Arpinum.

Slavery was the usual destination for prisoners of war, criminals, debtors, and the offspring of slaves. If you were fortunate, you belonged to a master or mistress who wanted to protect their investment and enjoy your loyalty or even affection. If you were not so lucky you could end up in a slave-gang, working on large farms, or in mines where life-expectancy was cheerlessly short.

Another class of person emerged from the process of enslavement: **libertini** (freedmen). From slavery to liberty was the greatest social leap of all, and the talent and ingenuity of freedmen would often earn them the envy and contempt of other citizens. Some achieved positions of considerable importance: Nero's freedmen, Pallas and Narcissus, were highly influential, and they benefited from the distrust between emperor and senate.

1. In the early days of the republic, leading men owned and farmed their own land.

in agris erant tum senatores.

(Cicero, *De Senectute* xvi,56)

2. Cato (2nd century BC) was asked what he believed to be the best occupation.

'bene pascere'; quid secundum 'satis bene pascere'; quid tertium: 'male pascere'; quid quartum 'arare'; et cum ille, qui quaesierat, dixisset 'quid faenerari?' tum Cato 'quid hominem' inquit 'occidere?'

(Cicero, *De Officiis* ii,25)

pasco-ere *raise livestock*	**quid faenerari** *what of money-lending*
bene *well*	**cum...tum** *when...then*
satis *enough*	**quaesierat (quaeso-ere)** *had asked*
tertius-a-um *third*	**dixisset (dico-ere)** *had said*
male *badly*	**quid occidere** *what about murdering*
quartus-a-um *fourth*	**homo-inis** *person*
aro-are *plough*	

3. Roman poets inherited the pastoral tradition from the Greeks, and so farming was perceived to be not only respectable but also a pleasure.

beatus ille qui procul negotiis,
** ut prisca gens mortalium,**
paterna rura bobus exercet suis
** solutus omni faenore,**
libet iacere modo sub antiqua ilice,
** modo in tenaci gramine.**

(Horace, *Epodes* II,1-4,23-4)

beatus-a-um *happy*	**paternus-a-um** *ancestral*
procul [+abl.] *far from*	**rura exerceo-ere** *work the land*
negotium-i *business*	**bobus** [abl. pl. of **bos, bovis**] *ox*
ut *as*	**solutus-a-um** *released*
priscus-a-um *ancient*	**omni** [dat./abl.] *all*
gens-tis [f.] *race*	**faenus-oris** *interest payment*
mortalis-is *mortal*	**libet** *it is pleasing*

laceo-ere *lie*
modo *now*
ilex-icis *oak-tree*

tenaci [dat./abl.] *clinging*
gramen-inis *grass*

4. This fantasy of rural life appealed most to city-dwellers, who had little experience of farming's hardships. Varro had practical advice for serious farmers.

> **neque enim senes neque pueri callium difficultatem ac montium arduitatem atque asperitatem facile ferunt.**

(Varro, Rerum Rusticarum II,10,3)

neque...neque *neither...nor*
enim *for*
senex-is *old man*
callis-is *footpath*
difficultas-tatis *scarcity*

mons-tis *mountain*
arduitas-tatis *steepness*
asperitas-tatis *unevenness*
facile *easily*
ferunt *bear, endure*

5. Making money from commerce was despised by the aristocracy – unless you did so on a large scale.

> **mercatura autem, si tenuis est, sordida putanda est; sin magna et copiosa, non est vituperanda. omnium autem rerum, ex quibus aliquid acquiritur nihil est agri cultura melius, nihil uberius, nihil dulcius, nihil homine libero dignius.**

(Cicero, De Officiis I,42,151)

mercatura-ae *business, profit*
tenuis [nom.] *slender*
putandus-a-um *to be reckoned*
sin *but if*
copiosus-a-um *abundant*
vituperandus-a-um *to be despised*
omnium [gen. pl.] *all*
res, rei *thing*
ex quibus *from which*

aliquid *something*
acquiritur *is acquired*
melius *better*
ager, agri *field*
cultura-ae *tilling*
uberius* *more fruitful*
dulcius* *sweeter*
dignius* [+ abl.] *more worthy*

* look for an ablative for the point of the comparison (**agri cultura**: *than agriculture*)

6. There were many slaves in ancient Rome. Some belonged to the state, but the majority were owned by private citizens. The infrequency of rebellion suggests that the kind of treatment described below did not happen very often.

**hic frangit ferulas, rubet ille flagello,
hic scutica.**

(Juvenal, *Satire* VI,479-80)

hic...ille [nom.] *this (slave)...that (slave)*	**rubeo-ere** *be red*
frango-ere *cause to break*	**flagellum-i** *whip*
ferula-ae *cane*	**scutica-ae** *strap*

7. Vedius Pollio, a friend of Augustus, was especially cruel.

**invenit in hoc animali documenta saevitiae Vedius Pollio
eques Romanus vivariis earum immergens damnata mancipia.**

(Pliny The Elder, *Natural History* IX,39)

invenio-ire-veni-ventum *find*	**vivarium-i** *pond, aquarium*
in hoc animali *in this animal (lamprey)*	**earum** [gen.] *them (the lampreys)*
documentum-i *example*	**immergens** [nom.] *plunging*
saevitia-ae *cruelty*	**damnatus-a-um** *condemned*
eques-itis *knight*	**mancipium-i** *slave*

8. Some domestic slaves were given their freedom. A **libertus**, however, would often stay with the **familia**. If he were talented, loyal, and important to the household, such a 'release' might amount to no more than acknowledgement of his role or a sign of affection. Cicero was fond of his secretary, Tiro, and Pliny showed his concern for the health of his **libertus**, Zosimus.

nihil aeque amorem incitat et accendit quam carendi metus.

(Pliny, *Letters* V,19)

nihil *nothing*	**accendo-ere** *stimulate*
aeque *as much, equally*	**quam** *than, as*
amor-is *love, affection*	**carendi** *of losing*
incito-are *arouse*	**metus-us** *fear*

9. Farm-slaves had a meaner existence than domestic ones, but they could expect some care and protection, for they were after all an investment.

gravia loca utilius est mercenariis colere quam servis.

(Varro, *Rerum Rusticarum* I,17,2)

gravla [neut pl.] *difficult*
locum-l *place*
utilius *more profitable*

mercenarius-l *mercenary, hired hand*
colo-ere *cultivate*
quam *than*

10. Some of the poorer citizens were not much better off than slaves, but their slender hold on liberty made them appreciate it all the more keenly. In this street-level account of life in the 1st century AD, a hired man complains about the weight of the luggage he is carrying.

> '**quid vos**' **inquit 'iumentum me putatis esse aut lapidariam navem? hominis operas locavi, non caballi. nec minus liber sum quam vos, etiam si pauperem pater me reliquit.' nec contentus maledictis tollebat subinde altius pedem et strepitu obsceno simul atque odore viam implebat.**

(Petronius, *Satyricon* 117)

iumentum-l *pack-animal*
puto-are *think*
lapidarius-a-um *stone-carrying*
navis-is *ship*
opera-ae *task*
locavi (loco-are) *I contracted, took on*
caballus-l *horse*
pauper-is *poor man*
reliquit (relinquo-ere) *left*

maledictum-l *abuse*
tollo-ere *raise*
subinde *then*
altius *higher*
pes, pedis *foot*
strepitus-us *noise*
simul *simultaneously*
impleo-ere *fill*

11. At the other end of the social scale were the senators. Below them were ranked the equestrians, who achieved this status by virtue of their wealth. 400,000 sesterces was the requisite sum – part of which Pliny was prepared to lend a fellow-townsman to help him qualify:

> **est autem tibi centum milium census. offero tibi ad implendas equestres facultates trecenta milia nummum.**

(Pliny, *Letters* I,19)

centum milium *of 100,000 sesterces*
census-us *assets*
offero-erre *offer*
equestres facultates *property qualification for the knights*

ad implendas *to be made up*
trecenta milia nummum *300,000 sesterces*

12. Pliny dined with a man who gave guests food and wine according to their social status. Another guest asked him if he approved.

> **animadvertit, qui mihi proximus recumbebat, et, an probarem, interrogavit. negavi. 'tu ergo,' inquit, 'quam consuetudinem sequeris?' 'eadem omnibus pono; ad cenam enim, non ad notam invito cunctisque rebus exaequo, quos mensa et toro aequavi.' 'etiamne libertos?' 'etiam; convictores enim tunc, non libertos puto.' et ille: 'magno tibi constat.' 'minime.' 'qui fieri potest?' 'quia scilicet liberti mei non idem quod ego bibunt, sed idem ego quod liberti.'**

(Pliny, *Letters* II,6)

animadverto-ere *notice*		**mensa-ae** *table*	
proximus-a-um *nearest*		**torus-i** *couch*	
recumbo-ere *recline*		**aequavi (aequo-are)** *I have made equal*	
an *whether*		**etiam** *even*	
probarem (probo-are) *I approved*		**libertus-i** *freedman*	
negavi (nego-are) *I said no*		**convictor-oris** *table companion*	
ergo *therefore*		**tunc** *then*	
consuetudo-inis *custom, habit*		**magno constat** *it costs much*	
sequeris *you follow*		**minime** *not at all*	
eadem [nom./acc.] *the same things*		**qui** *how*	
pono-ere *put*		**fieri** *to be (done)*	
cena-ae *dinner*		**quia** *because*	
nota-ae *social grading*		**scilicet** *of course*	
invito-are *invite*		**libertus-i** *freedman*	
cunctus-a-um *all*		**idem** [nom./acc.] *the same*	
res, rei *thing*		**quod** *which*	
exaequo-are *regard as equal*		**bibo-ere** *drink*	

Vocabulary

Text

bene	*well*	satis	*enough*
quid	*what*	silva-ae	*wood*
tunc	*then*	mons-tis	*mountain*
tum	*then*	senex-is	*old man*

nihil	*nothing*	puto-are, putavi, putatum	*think*
procul	*far from/off*	iaceo-ere, iacui, iacitum	*lie down*
autem	*however*	colo-ere, colui, cultum	*till*
saepe	*often*	relinquo-ere, reliqui, relictum	*leave*

Past participles

actus-a-um	*done*	(ago-ere)
auditus-a-um	*heard*	(audio-ire)
amatus-a-um	*loved*	(amo-are)
captus-a-um	*taken, captured*	(capio-ere)
dictus-a-um	*said*	(dico-ere)
ductus-a-um	*led*	(duco-ere)
factus-a-um	*made, done*	(facio-ere)
latus-a-um	*brought*	(fero, ferre)
laudatus-a-um	*praised*	(laudo-are)
missus-a-um	*sent*	(mitto-ere)
monitus-a-um	*warned, advised*	(moneo-ere)
paratus-a-um	*prepared*	(paro-are)
scriptus-a-um	*written*	(scribo-ere)
victus-a-um	*conquered*	(vinco-ere)
visus-a-um	*seen*	(video-ere)

Exercises

1. Change each word in brackets into the past participle with the correct ending, and translate:

   a) **pueri a magistro** [laudo-are] **sunt.**
   b) **puella a poeta** [amo-are] **est.**
   c) **carmina ab imperatore** [audio-ire] **sunt.**
   d) **gladiatores in amphitheatrum** [duco-ere] **sunt.**
   e) **Caesar a femina** [moneo-ere] **est.**
   f) **vinum a servo** [video-ere] **est.**

2. Change each verb into the passive form, adapt other words as necessary, and translate your answer:
   a) **servus cenam parat.**
   b) **miles in amphitheatrum gladiatores ducit.**
   c) **senator epistulam scribit.**
   d) **femina canes culpat.**
   e) **pueri gladiatorem spectant.**
   f) **Iulius munera matri dat.**

3. Translate into Latin:
   a) The dinner was prepared in the kitchen.
   b) Rome has never been captured.
   c) The enemy were conquered by Caesar.
   d) The girls were praised by the mother.
   e) The letter was written by the senator.
   f) The bull was seen in the garden.

4. The past participles listed in the vocabulary above are simple forms, which can be compounded with certain prefixes:
       e.g. **captus** – acceptus, receptus, susceptus, deceptus, etc.
           ductus – adductus, inductus, productus, conductus, etc.

What English words are related etymologically to compounds of these words:
       dictus   **factus**   **latus**   **missus**
       (e.g. **captus**: *accept, reception, deception*, etc.)

5. Identify derivatives from **relinquo-ere-liqui-lictum** and **puto-are-avi-atum**.

WOMEN 8

Grammar

Pronouns

ille, illa, illud	*he, she, it* or *that* (demonstrative)
hic, haec, hoc	*he, she, it, this* (demonstrative)
is, ea, id	*he, she, it, that*
qui, quae, quod	*who, which*

The above are the nominative forms of the pronouns. For all the endings, see pp. 151-2.

ille and **hic** are demonstrative pronouns, emphasizing *this one here* or *that one there*; **qui** can be either a relative pronoun which defines or describes, as in *the man who knew Caesar*, or an interrogative adjective, which asks a question, e.g. *what man has not heard of Caesar?*; the interrogative pronoun is **quis?** or **quid?** e.g. *who knows Caesar?*

hic, ille and **is** can serve as adjectives as well as pronouns, e.g. **hic equus**, *this horse*.

The subjunctive

The indicative mood of a verb is the one we have seen so far. This describes something which has happened, is happening or will happen:

e.g. **agricola ad villam venit**   *the farmer comes to the villa*

The subjunctive describes potential action:

Expressing a wish:

o agricola ad villam veniat!   *if only the farmer would come to the villa!*

Expressing a command:

agricola ad villam veniat!   *the farmer should come to the villa!*

Expressing a condition which is unlikely to be fulfilled:

si agricola ad villam veniat, eum videam   *if the farmer were to come to the villa, I would see him*

Expressing purpose:

agricola ad villam venit   *the farmer comes to the villa*
ut nos <u>videat</u>   *that he <u>may see</u> us*

Expressing a reported command:

agricola nobis imperat   *the farmer orders us*
ne ad villam <u>veniamus</u>   *not <u>to come</u> to the villa*
(**impero-are** is followed by the dative, not the accusative)

Expressing a reported question:

agricola nos interrogat   *the farmer asks us why we*
cur ad villam <u>veniamus</u>   *<u>are coming</u> to the villa*

Expressing a fear:

timemus ne agricola in   *we fear that the farmer*
villam <u>veniat</u>   *<u>may come</u> into the villa*

Expressing prevention:

miles poetam impedit   *the soldier prevents the poet*
quominus <u>canat</u>   *from <u>singing</u>*

Please note:

i) The subjunctive usually expresses potential action. There are exceptions, however, such as the use of the subjunctive with **cum** (*since, when, although*) to express something that happens, and also with **ut** to express a consequence or result:

e.g. **cum agricola ad villam**   *since the farmer is coming to the*
       <u>veniat</u>, ipse te rogabit   *villa, he will ask you himself*

       agricola ad villam tam   *the farmer comes to the*
       celeriter venit ut nos   *villa so quickly with the*
       <u>videat</u>   *result that he <u>sees</u> us*

ii) The form of the present subjunctive is similar to the indicative, but has an **a** in the ending. The exception is the first conjugation (e.g. **<u>parare</u>**) which already has an **a** in the indicative, and so has an **e** instead. The imperfect form (not used above) has the present infinitive as the stem: e.g. **venire-t** (*he/she might come*). For all the tenses of the subjunctive, see p. 156f.

Practice

Match each sentence with its illustration and translate:

a) **si equus essem, faenum devorarem.**   Illustration no.___

b) **cives ad amphitheatrum veniunt ut ludos spectent.**   Illustration no.___

c) **magister rogat ubi Marcus sit.**   Illustration no.___

d) **servi in agros veniant statim.**   Illustration no.___

1.

2.

3.

4.

possum, volo

The irregular verbs **posse** (*to be able*) and **velle** (*to wish*) are often used with the infinitive of another verb (for the endings of these two verbs, see pp. 158-9):

e.g. **femina poetam <u>audire</u> <u>potest</u>**   *the woman can hear the poet*
    quis poetam <u>audire</u> <u>vult</u>?   *who wants to hear the poet?*

Women in ancient Rome

Classical writers were fond of presenting what they imagined to be the typical woman of the early republican period as a model for contemporaries to emulate: she was hard-working, both in the fields and at home; she attended to the upbringing of her children; and she managed domestic affairs while her husband would be fighting in the army or participating in politics. This image, more often than not, was offered by way of a contrast to the behaviour of contemporary women who were preoccupied with self-amusement and idle recreation. Since, however, we only have records written by men, this evidence probably tells us as much about the men as it does about the women.

Girls were abandoned at birth more often than boys, for they were thought to be less valuable to the state and their parents. Those who escaped this fate grew up under the control of parents who might seek a quick opportunity to marry them off and disengage their own responsibilities. Once married (some as early as thirteen years old), they virtually became the property of their husbands, who even had the right to capital punishment (though not without permission of the in-laws). Such customs and attitudes survived through the classical period, and the glimpses we have of more liberated women, including sports-loving grandmothers and single hostesses, are recorded for their rarity as much as anything else. There was nothing approaching equality of status, in practice or even in theory.

Girls from poor families worked as laundresses, bakers, shop-keepers, nurses, mid-wives and in various other inevitable occupations. Those from wealthier families did not follow careers in business or politics, as the men would, but managed the **familia**, which included slaves and other dependants as well as the immediate family. Education for a girl rarely meant anything beyond primary school, and a career in politics or business was unthinkable.

Some **matronae** grew to be very influential, according to the status of their **familia** or the rank of their husband. Livia, the wife of Augustus, managed many of his responsibilities in his later years; and Agrippina, the mother of Nero, had similar powers when he became emperor. Both women are portrayed by the historian Tacitus in a somewhat sinister light as power-brokers consumed by self-interest to the detriment of the state.

1. During the war with Carthage, women were forbidden to wear gold, multi-coloured clothing, or to ride in carriages except during festivals. When peace and prosperity returned, women asked for the law to be relaxed. The austere

Cato warned his fellow men against concessions (unsuccessfully).

> **volo tamen audire propter quod matronae consternatae
> procucurrerint in publicum ac vix foro se et contione
> abstineant. extemplo, simul pares esse coeperint, superiores
> erunt.**

(Livy XXXIV,3,vi;iii)

volo (velle) *I want*	**se abstineant** *they restrain themselves*
propter quod *for what reason*	**contio-nis** *assembly*
matrona-ae [f.] *lady, matron*	**extemplo** *immediately*
consternatus-a-um *agitated*	**simul** *as soon as*
procucurrerint *have rushed forth*	**pares** *equal*
vix *scarcely*	**coeperint** *they have begun*

2. Equality for women was, Cato argued, desirable – but parity with each other, not with men.

> **vultis hoc certamen uxoribus vestris inicere, Quirites, ut
> divites id habere velint quod nulla alia possit; pauperes, ne
> ob hoc ipsum contemnantur, supra vires se extendant?**

(Livy XXXIV,4,xv)

vultis (volo, velle) *you want*	**nulla alia** *no other (woman)*
certamen-inis [n.] *competition*	**ne** *lest, in case*
uxor-is *wife*	**ob hoc ipsum** *because of this very thing*
inicio-ere *impose*	**contemnantur** *they may be despised*
Quirites *fellow Romans*	**supra** [+ acc.] *beyond*
divites [adj.] *rich*	**vires-ium** *resources*
id...quod *that...which*	**se** *themselves*
velint (volo, velle) *(they) may want*	**extendant** *they may overreach*

3. Lucius Valerius did not agree.

> **matrem familiae tuam purpureum amiculum habere non sines,
> et equus tuus speciosius instratus erit quam uxor vestita.**

(Livy XXXIV,7,iii)

familia-ae *household*	**speciosius** *more lavishly*
amiculum-i *cloak*	**instratus-a-um** *covered*
sino-ere *allow*	**vestitus-a-um** *clothed*

4. Women were perceived to be all but the property of fathers or husbands, particularly during the early years of the republic. The scene below is taken from a comedy (2nd century BC) and shows a wife appealing to her father for help in a marital quarrel. His unlikely response must have amused at least the men in the audience.

MATRONA:	ludibrio, pater, habeor.
SENEX:	unde?
MATRONA:	ab illo quoi me mandavisti, meo viro.
SENEX:	ecce autem litigium! quotiens tandem edixi tibi ut caveres neuter ad me iretis cum querimonia?
MATRONA:	qui ego istuc, mi pater, cavere possum?
SENEX:	men interrogas?
MATRONA:	nisi non vis.
SENEX:	quotiens monstravi tibi viro ut morem geras, quid ille faciat ne id observes, quo eat, quid rerum gerat.
MATRONA:	at enim ille hinc amat meretricem ex proxumo.
SENEX:	sane sapit atque ob istanc industriam etiam faxo amabit amplius.
MATRONA:	atque ibi potat.
SENEX:	tua quidem ille causa potabit minus? quando te auratam et vestitam bene habet, ancillas, penum recte praehibet, melius sanam est, mulier, mentem sumere.

(Plautus, *Menaechmi* 782-92,801-2)

ludibrio habeor *I am an object of scorn*
unde *says who? (from where)*
quoi [cui] *to whom*
mandavisti (mando-are) *you entrusted*
ecce *oh! look!*
autem *however*
litigium-i *dispute*
quotiens *how many times*
tandem *pray, I ask you*
edixi (edico-ere) *I have made clear*
ut *that*
caveres (caveo-ere) *you take care*
neuter *neither of you*
iretis (eo-ire) *you should come*
querimonia-ae *complaint*

qui [old form] *how*
istuc *that*
possum, posse *be able*
men i.e. *me-ne...?*
nisi non vis *if you don't mind*
quotiens *how often*
monstro-are-avi *show*
morem geras [+ dat.] *you should humour*
faciat (facio-ere) *he does*
id *that*
observes (observo-are) *you should observe*
quo *where*
eat (eo-ire) *he goes*
quid rerum gerat *what he gets up to*

hinc *from this house, here*
meretrix-cis *prostitute*
ex proxumo *from next-door*
sane sapit *he has good taste*
ob istanc *because of that*
faxo *I'll warrant*
amplius *more so*
ibi *there*
poto-are *drink*
quidem *indeed*
tua causa *on your account*

minus *less*
quando *since*
auratus-a-um *in gold, jewellery*
ancilla-ae *servant*
penus-i *provisions*
recte *properly*
praehibeo-ere *supply*
melius *better*
mens-tis *mind*
sumo-ere *keep*

5. Friends and relatives would be expected to suggest suitable candidates for arranged marriages.

petis, ut fratris tui filiae prospiciam maritum.

(Pliny, *Letters* I,14)

petis (peto-ere) *you seek, ask*
prospiciam (prospicio-ere) *I watch out for*

maritus-i *husband*

6. Women from poorer backgrounds would seldom have had a moment to themselves. By contrast, upper-class women were barred from professions and careers. Even literary criticism was frowned upon – if Juvenal is to be taken seriously.

illa tamen gravior, quae cum discumbere coepit,
laudat Vergilium.
cedunt grammatici, vincuntur rhetores, omnis
turba tacet.

(Juvenal, *Satire* VI,434-5,438-9)

illa [nom.] *she*
gravior *more troublesome*
quae [f.] *who*
cum *when*
discumbo-ere *recline at table*
coepit *begins*

cedunt (cedo-ere) *they give way*
grammaticus *teacher*
vinco-ere *vanquish*
rhetor-is *professor*
turba-ae *crowd*
taceo-ere *be silent*

7. Pliny, however, praises his wife's good taste in books (his own!).

LATIN *Better Read Than Dead*

meos libellos habet, lectitat, ediscit etiam.

(Pliny, Letters IV,19)

libellus-i *book*
lectito-are *read repeatedly*

edisco-ere *learn by heart*
etiam *even*

8. Many young mothers died in childbirth.

**tristem et acerbum casum Helvidiarum sororum! utraque
a partu, utraque filiam enixa decessit. adficior dolore nec
tamen supra modum doleo; ita mihi luctuosum videtur,
quod puellas honestissimas in flore primo fecunditas
abstulit.**

(Pliny, Letters IV,21)

tristem [acc.] *sad* (see p. 163: Exclamation)
acerbus-a-um *bitter*
casus-us *misfortune*
Helvidiarum sororum *Helvidian sisters.*
utraque *each*
partus-us *birth*
enixus-a-um *having given birth to*
decedo-ere-cessi *withdraw, die*
adficior *I am afflicted*
dolor-is *grief*

supra modum *beyond measure*
doleo-ere *grieve*
ita...quod *in that*
luctuosus-a-um *sorrowful*
videtur *is seen, seems*
honestissimus-a-um *most honourable*
flos-ris [m.] *flower*
fecunditas-tatis *fruitfulness*
abstulit (aufero, auferre) *has taken away*

9. Romans were surprised by the British custom of greater equality between the sexes. Boudicca's speech before leading the British into battle was recorded (and rewritten) by the enemy's historian.

**Boudicca curru filias prae se vehens solitum quidem
Britannis feminarum ductu bellare testabatur;
vincendum illa acie vel cadendum esse; id mulieri
destinatum: viverent viri et servirent.**

(Tacitus, Annals XIV,35,i,ii)

currus-us *chariot*
prae se *before her*
vehens *carrying*
solitum [+ dat.] *(it was) customary for*
ductu (ductus-us) *under the leadership*

bello-are *go to war*
testabatur *declared*
vincendum (esse) *it must be won*
acies-ei *battle*
vel *or*

88

cadendum esse *it must be lost*
mulier-is *woman*
destinatus-a-um *fixed objective*

viverent (vivo-ere) *let (them) live*
vir-i *man*
servirent (servio-ire) *let (them) be slaves*

10. The poet Ovid on the subject of make-up:

> discite, quae faciem commendet cura, puellae:
>   et quo sit vobis forma tuenda modo.
> nec tamen indignum: sit vobis cura placendi,
>   cum comptos habeant saecula nostra viros.

(Ovid, *Medic. Faciei* 1-2,23-4)

discite (disco-ere) *learn*
facies-ei *face*
commendo-are *enhance*
cura-ae *care, attention*
quo...modo *in what way, how*
forma-ae *beauty*
tuendus-a-um *to be preserved*

indignus-a-um *unworthy*
sit *may (it) be*
placendi *of pleasing*
cum *since*
comptus-a-um *well-groomed*
saeculum-i *age, era*

Vocabulary

Text

inde, deinde	then, next
tandem	at last, at length
simul	at the same time
ibi	there
quando	when, at any time, since, seeing that
minus	less
melius	better
ob [+ acc.]	because of
propter [+ acc.]	because of
se	himself, herself, themselves
cura-ae	care, attention
forma-ae	shape, appearance, beauty

uxor-is	*wife*
maritus-i	*husband*
currus-us	*chariot*
nisi	*if not, except, unless*

cum

+ noun in the abl.	*with*
+ subjunctive verb	*when* *since* *although* (occasional)
+ indicative verb	*when*
cum...tum	*both...and*

ut

+ indicative verb	*as* *when* *how* (occasional) *although*
+ subjunctive verb	*so that* (expressing purpose) *that (with the result that)* *to* ('he commanded him *to*...') *if only* (expressing a desire) *how* (occasional)

Please note:

i) **ut** and **cum** are more often used with the subjunctive than the indicative.

ii) **ne** is normally used in place of **ut...non**.

Exercises

1. Change the underlined noun to the correct form of **hic** and translate:
   a) **Fulvia est uxor Antonii.**
   b) **Caesar cum Bruto ambulat.**

    c) **Clodia est soror Clodii.**
    d) **captivi in amphitheatrum ducti sunt.**
    e) **poeta munera feminae dedit.**

2. Change the underlined noun to the correct form of **ille** and translate:
    a) **Caesar in Italiam cum exercitu veniet.**
    b) **Cicero Fulviam non amabat.**
    c) **gladiatores in amphitheatro vidimus.**
    d) **gemitus captivorum audire possumus.**
    e) **vis-ne videre dominum?**

3. Change the underlined noun to the correct form of **is** and translate:
    a) **taurus agricolas fugavit.**
    b) **Plinius libellos feminae dabat.**
    c) **Hannibal a civibus visus est.**
    d) **bellum est saevum.**
    e) **fratrem-ne Ciceronis audivistis?**

4. Complete each sentence with the correct form of **qui** (or **quis**) and translate:
    a) ....**epistulam misit?**
    b) ....**canis est in amphitheatro?**
    c) **a**...............**Romani capti sunt?**
    d) **femina**...............**poeta amabat in hac villa habitabat.**
    e) **puella**...............**poeta dicebat in horto erat.**

5. Translate into English:
    a) **feminae, ut viros viderunt, ridebant.**
    b) **Graeci, ut dicunt, impudentes sunt.**
    c) **non sum tam ignavus ut illud faciam** (**tam**: *so*)
    d) **imperator nobis imperat ut ludos spectemus.**
    e) **venio ut te videam.**
    f) **Caesar cum Romam pervenisset feminam vidit.**
    g) **cum videbis, tum scies.**
    h) **hi, cum servi sint, Romae tamen amici.**

6. Identify Latin words (in this chapter) which are ancestors of *vehicle*, *voluntary* and *simultaneous*.

7. **ille** and **illa** came to mean *the* in medieval Latin. How have these words survived in other European languages?

8. What are the meanings of **id est**, **ad hoc** and **quid pro quo**?

EDUCATION 9

Grammar

More adjectives

As well as adjectives like **bonus-a-um**, there are adjectives like **omnis** (*all*, *every*), and **ingens** (*huge*). The endings of these adjectives are listed on p. 153.

Some adjectives have the same endings as **omnis**, except in the nominative: **acer** (*keen*), **celer** (*swift*), **felix** (*fortunate*), etc.

There are also adjectives like **bonus**, which have the nominative ending **-er**: **pulcher-chra-chrum** (*beautiful*) and **miser-era-erum** (*wretched*).

The comparative form

maior is the comparative form of **magnus** (i.e. *greater*) and other comparative forms have similar endings: **gratus** (*pleasing*), **gratior** (*more pleasing*); **tristis** (*sad*), **tristior** (*sadder*); **celer** (*quick*), **celerior** (*quicker*), etc.

The superlative form

An adjective ending **-issimus, -errimus** or **-illimus** is the superlative form: **gratissimus** (*very/most pleasing*); **tristissimus** (*saddest*); **celerrimus** (*quickest*), etc.

quam

This word can mean a number of different things: it can mean *how*, *whom* (acc. fem. of **qui**), *as* or *than*. With the comparative form of an adjective or adverb, **quam** means *than*:

> e.g. **Caesar est <u>maior quam</u> Pompeius**
> *Caesar is <u>greater than</u> Pompey*

Pompeius is the same case (here, nom.) as the person or object being compared (here, **Caesar**). You will also find a comparison made without **quam**, where the <u>ablative</u> is used to convey the meaning of *than*:

> e.g. **Caesar est <u>maior</u> Pompeio**
> *Caesar is <u>greater than</u> Pompey*

92

Practice A

Identify the <u>comparative</u> form of each adjective:

1. **puella est...............**
   quam puer. [laetus-a-um]

2. **poeta est...............**
   quam miles. [gratus-a-um]

3. **servus est...............**
   senatore. [ignavus-a-um]

Imperatives

In the last chapter you met the subjunctive form which can express a wish or an instruction:

> e.g. **nunc veniat**   *may he come now/he should come now*

The imperative form is more direct and less polite (see p. 161 for the endings):

> e.g. **nunc veni!**   *come now!*

Practice B

Add the missing imperative to each sentence (in the illustration) and translate:

1. [bibo, bibere]

2. [do, dare]

Schools

During the early republic the objectives of an education were kept simple: children would learn literacy and arithmetic, and to speak aloud. Without today's technology, this last subject, oratory, was as indispensable to a lawyer pleading a case as to a greengrocer selling vegetables. Children would also learn how to fight and to farm, to sew and to cook – strictly according to gender.

Schools as centres of education did not appear until the 3rd century BC. Previously, children of wealthy citizens had been taught by tutors, who were usually slaves or freedmen. To set up a school, a freedman would approach several families to send their children to him, and then rent some space in the forum. There was not the same idea of institution as there is with schools today, for you studied with a particular teacher, not at a particular school. Most schools amounted to little more than one class.

In the 2nd century BC, once Rome had discovered Greek culture, the reading of Greek literature became common in schools. The study of rhetoric absorbed the practice of oratory, and young Romans were introduced to Greek thought, debate and scientific analysis. Greek plays and poetry were read, with attention to their didactic and exemplary content.

This development was not solely the result of discovering worthwhile literature; it also reflected the changing needs of the people. No longer were they citizen-farmers belonging to a small state, but controllers of a growing empire with a developing machinery of government, which required a skilled and literate civil service.

There was a certain amount of opposition to these Greek trends. We read of Cato who preferred to educate his son himself rather than entrust the duty to a slave. The subjects he taught were the old-fashioned ones such as oratory, horse-riding, swimming and throwing a javelin.

Though Greek trends prevailed, by no means every child received an education, and the majority had little more than a basic grounding in numeracy and literacy. Some girls went to primary school (7-12 years) with the **litterator**, but only a few remained with the boys for the next stage with the **grammaticus** (12-16 years). A limited number of teenagers would go on to study with a **rhetor**. Athens was popular with the rhetors, so students like Cicero's son stayed in Athens to attend a particular rhetor's course. Athens has been subsequently recognized as the university town of the ancient world. In truth, it resembled more closely the early medieval universities in Europe where a professor, and not the place itself, attracted a following.

The Roman era is celebrated for feats of construction and engineering, though the aristocrats (those who set the curriculum) were not especially interested in these practical sciences. They preferred on the whole to occupy themselves with more abstract or literary studies. If they had not had access to such cheap manpower, perhaps they would have been more curious about applied

95

sciences, and might have developed more advanced forms of mechanisation.

The arts were not highly regarded either. Romans admired and enjoyed the finished products, but thought little of the artists themselves – part perhaps of their inferiority complex towards Greece. Philosophy would be studied with the rhetor, but not before. We have already seen in the case of Agricola's mother how patricians were reluctant to discuss theories of power and their right to wield it.

1. Tacitus criticizes the use of nurses and slaves to look after a baby.

> **at nunc natus infans delegatur Graeculae alicui ancillae, cui adiungitur unus aut alter ex omnibus servis, plerumque vilissimus nec cuiquam serio ministerio adcommodatus. horum fabulis et erroribus teneri statim et rudes animi imbuuntur; nec quisquam in tota domo pensi habet quid coram infante domino aut dicat aut faciat.**

(Tacitus, *Dialogus De Oratoribus* 29)

natus-a-um *born*	**adcommodatus-a-um** *suited*
delegatur (delego-are) *is entrusted*	**horum** [gen.] *these (people)*
Graeculus-a-um *little Greek*	**fabula-ae** *myth*
alicui [dat.] *some*	**tener-a-um** *tender*
ancilla-ae *maid*	**statim** *immediately*
cui *to whom*	**rudis-e** *impressionable*
adiungitur (adiungo-ere) *is attached*	**animus-i** *mind*
alter *other*	**imbuuntur (imbuo-ere)** *are tainted*
plerumque *very often*	**quisquam** [nom.] *anyone*
vilis-e *worthless*	**in tota domo** *in the entire household*
cuiquam [dat.] *any*	**pensi habet** *care a jot*
serius-a-um *serious*	**coram** [+ abl.] *in the presence of*
ministerium-i *service*	**infans dominus** *little master*

2. Quintilian advises competition and encouragement for the young learner.

> **doceatur alius, cui invideat; contendat interim et saepius vincere se putet: praemiis etiam, quae capit illa aetas, evocetur.**

(Quintilian, *Elements of Oratory* I,1,20)

doceatur (doceo-ere) *let...be taught*	**contendat (contendo-ere)** *let him compete*
alius-a-ud *other*	**interim** *sometimes*
invideat [+ dat.] **(invideo-ere)** *he may envy*	**saepius** *more often than not*

96

vincere se *that he wins*
putet (puto-are) *let him think*
praemium-i *reward*
capit (capio-ere) *welcomes*

aetas-tatis [f.] *age, age-group*
evocetur (evoco-are) *let him be encouraged*

3. A school would be small and privately owned, situated in the forum or busy street. The school day started early to take advantage of the peace and quiet – to Martial's dismay:

> **quid tibi nobiscum est, ludi scelerate magister,**
> **invisum pueris virginibusque caput?**
> **nondum cristati rupere silentia galli:**
> **murmure iam saevo verberibusque tonas.**
> **vicini somnum non tota nocte rogamus:**
> **nam vigilare leve est, pervigilare grave est.**
> **discipulos dimitte tuos. vis, garrule, quantum**
> **accipis ut clames, accipere ut taceas?**

(Martial, *Epigrams* IX,68,1-4,9-12)

ludus-i *school*
scelerate magister *wretched teacher*
invisus-a-um *hated*
caput, capitis [n.] *creature*
nondum *not yet*
cristatus-a-um *crested*
rupere (rumpo-ere) *(they) have broken*
silentium-i *silence*
gallus-i *cock*
murmur-is *growling*
verber-is [n.] *whip*
tono-are *thunder*

vicinus-a-um *neighbour*
somnum-i *sleep*
nam *for*
(per)vigilo-are *be awake (all night)*
discipulus-i *student*
dimitte (dimitto-ere) *dismiss!*
vis *do you want (...?)*
garrule *you chatterbox*
quantus-a-um *as much as*
accipis (accipio-ere) *you receive*
clames (clamo-are) *you shout*
taceas (taceo-ere) *you are silent*

4. A character from Petronius's *Satyricon* does not approve of the intellectual nature (Greek-inspired) of schooling.

> **iste, qui te haec docet, est mufrius, non magister. dicebat**
> **enim magister 'sunt vestra salva? recta domum; cave,**
> **circumspicias; cave, maiorem maledicas.'**

(Petronius, *Satyricon* 58)

iste *he*

docet (doceo-ere) *teaches*

mufrius-i *mutton-head*	**cave (caveo-ere)** *take care not to*
magister-tri *teacher*	**circumspicias (circumspicio-ere)**
enim *for*	*look behind you*
vester-tra-trum *your*	**maior-is** *senior*
salvus-a-um *safe*	**cave maledicas** *don't be cheeky to*
recta domum *go straight home*	

5. Juvenal says that a teacher's life is not a happy one. After he has paid his suppliers, landlord and cashier, there are the parents....

> rara tamen merces quae cognitione tribuni
> non egeat. sed vos saevas imponite leges,
> ut praeceptori verborum regula constet,
> ut legat historias, auctores noverit omnes
> tamquam ungues digitosque suos.

(Juvenal, Satire 7,228-32)

rarus-a-um *rare, unusual*	**verbum-i** *word, speech*
merces-edis [f.] *pay*	**regula-ae** *rule, standard*
cognitio-nis *court-order*	**constet** [+ dat.] **(consto-are)**
tribunus-i *tribune*	*should be correct*
egeat [+ abl.] **(egeo-ere)** *needs*	**legat (lego-ere)** *he read*
vos i.e. the parents	**noverit (nosco-ere)** *be acquainted with*
imponite (impono-ere) *impose!*	**tamquam** *as though they were*
lex, legis *law*	**unguis-is** *nail*
praeceptor-is *teacher*	**digitus-i** *finger*

6. And what does the teacher get in return? No more than a sportsman gets in a day.

> 'haec,' inquit, 'cures, et cum se verterit annus, accipe,
> victori populus quod postulat, aurum.'

(Juvenal, Satire 7,242-3)

haec *these matters*	**accipe (accipio-ere)** *take!*
inquit *he/she says*	**victor-is** *winning gladiator/charioteer*
cures (curo-are) *you should attend to*	**postulo-are** *demand*
verterit (verto-ere) *has turned*	**aurum-i** *gold*

7. Whatever little amount teachers were paid, a schooling was only for the children of the rich or of those prepared to make a sacrifice. Horace's father, a **libertinus** (freed slave), refused to send his son to the local school, where he might be teased by the children of local grandees. Instead, Horace went to school in Rome.

> **noluit in Flavi ludum me mittere, magni**
> **quo pueri magnis e centurionibus orti,**
> **sed puerum est ausus Romam portare, docendum**
> **artis.**

(Horace, *Satire* I,6,72-3,76-7)

noluit (nolo, nolle) *he did not want*	**est ausus** *he dared*
Flavius the local schoolmaster	**Romam** *to Rome*
ludus-i *school*	**porto-are** *take*
quo *(to) where (went)*	**docendus-a-um** *to be instructed in*
ortus-a-um *born, descended*	**artis** [acc. pl.] *art*

8. Cicero's son completed his education in Athens, from where he writes to his father's personal secretary, Tiro.

> **praeterea declamitare Graece apud Cassium institui; Latine**
> **autem apud Bruttium exerceri volo.**

(Cicero, *Epistulae ad Familiares* XVI,21,8)

praeterea *moreover*	**apud** [+ acc.] *with*
declamito-are *declaim*	**exerceri (exerceo-ere)** *to be trained in*
institui (instituo-ere) *I have begun*	

9. The young man was anxious to show his father how seriously he was taking his studies; so seriously that he needed help with some of the duties involved.

> **sed peto a te, ut quam celerrime mihi librarius mittatur,**
> **maxime quidem Graecus; multum mihi enim eripietur operae**
> **in exscribendis hypomnematis.**

(Cicero, *Epistulae ad Familiares* XVI,21,8)

quam celerrime *as quickly as possible*	**quidem** *indeed*
librarius *clerk, secretary*	**eripietur (eripio-ere)** *will be taken*
mittatur (mitto-ere) *may be sent*	**opera-ae** *work*
maxime *especially*	**in exscribendis hypomnematis**
enim *for, you see*	*in the taking of notes*

Vocabulary

Text

dum	while, until
forte	by chance
statim	immediately
nam	for
iste-a-ud	that (like **ille**)
quantus-a-um	how much, how great (pl.: how many)
fabula-ae	story
ludus-i	school
praemium-i	reward
aurum-i	gold
lex, legis	law
lego-ere, legi, lectum	read
disco-ere, didici	learn
vinco-ere, vici, victum	conquer, win

Adjectives like **omnis-e**

omnis	every, all	tristis	sad
mollis	soft	fidelis	faithful
gravis	serious, heavy	levis	light
dulcis	sweet	humilis	meek
difficilis	difficult	facilis	easy
utilis	useful	turpis	disgraceful
brevis	short	illustris	famous

Adjectives like **ingens**

sapiens	wise	praesens	present

Comparative forms of adjectives

Regular

cruel	saevus	saevior	saevissimus
sad	tristis	tristior	tristissimus
easy	facilis	facilior	facillimus
wise	sapiens	sapientior	sapientissimus

Irregular

good	bonus	melior	optimus
bad	malus	peior	pessimus
much, many	multus	plus*	plurimus

* **plus** in the singular is used as a neuter noun.

Exercises

1. Identify all possible cases of each of the following (and indicate the gender[s] and whether singular or plural):

a) **tristi**   e) **facilium**
b) **magni**   f) **mollis**
c) **multa**   g) **saevis**
d) **breve**   h) **avidum**

2. Find the correct endings of the words in brackets:

a) [vinum-i] [acerbus-a-um] **erat**
   the wine was bitter

b) [gravis-e] [res-ei] **est fortuna**
   fortune is a serious matter

c) **femina** [dignus-a-um] **meliore viro erat**
   the woman was worthy of a better husband

d) [opus-eris] [difficilis-e] **perfecit**
   he finished the difficult task

e) [praemium-i] [humilis-e], **non** [superbus-a-um], **dentur**

> *rewards should be given to the meek, not to the proud*

f) [imperator-is] **sunt numquam** [laetus-a-um]
    emperors are never cheerful

g) [vultus-us] [tristis-e] **dixit**
    she spoke with a sad face

h) **carmina** [gratus-a-um] **sed non** [utilis-e] **sunt**
    songs are pleasing but not useful

3. Translate into Latin:
   a) The farmer is larger than the slave.
   b) Cicero was wiser than Catiline.
   c) Are girls more faithful than boys?
   d) I want to marry (**nubo-ere** + *dat.*) a better man than Tiberius.
   e) The poet is very pleasing, but lazier than all the slaves.

4. The word *tandem*, a bicycle for two people, was coined directly from the Latin **tandem** meaning *at last, at length*. The word *omnibus* has a less lateral derivation: how would you account for its ending?

5. What English words are at least partly derived from **ancilla, natus** and **optimus**?

6. Find Latin ancestors (in this chapter) of *digit* and *reverberate*.

LEISURE 10

Grammar

Present, past and future participles

Compare these sentences:

1. *Jumping on the horse, he disappeared from view.*

2. *He disappeared from view jumping on the horse.*

In the first sentence, the man has jumped (participle) on the horse before he disappears (main verb); in the second, the jumping and disappearing are both happening at the same time. In Latin, a past participle generally describes an action which happens <u>before</u> that of the main verb (as in the first example above), while a present participle describes something happening <u>at the same time</u> as the action of the main verb (see the second example). The future participle describes something which is <u>yet to happen</u>, e.g. *about to disappear, he jumped on the horse.*

The form of participles

The past participle is formed like the supine (the fourth principal part), has the same endings as **bonus-a-um,** and is usually passive:

    e.g. **vinum captum**   *the wine having been taken*

The present participle is active and has endings like **ingens:**

    e.g. **ille capiens vinum**   *he, (while) taking the wine*

The future participle is also active and has endings like **bonus-a-um:**

    e.g. **ille capturus vinum**   *he, about to take the wine*

Remember that participles, though formed from verbs, are <u>adjectives</u>. For a full list, see p. 162.

Ablative Absolute

The participle is an adjective, and agrees with a noun (or pronoun). So the ending of the participle is determined by the noun's function in the sentence (subject, object, etc.):

    e.g. **<u>ille</u>, capiens vinum, senatori dicebat**
       he, (while) taking the wine, spoke to the senator

However, when the noun and participle have no grammatical relation to the main verb, together they form an independent clause in the <u>ablative</u>:

    e.g. **<u>ille</u>, <u>capto vino</u>, senatori dicebat**
       he, with the wine having been taken, spoke to the senator

       <u>domino interfecto</u> servus effugit
       with the master having been killed, the slave fled away

       <u>magistro intrante</u> pueri tacuerunt
       with the master entering, the boys hushed

Translating participles

             'Galli <u>capti</u> flebant.'

Adjective:	*The captured Gauls wept.*
Co-ordinative:	*The Gauls were captured and began to weep.*
Subordinative:	*The Gauls wept because (when, after, etc.) they had been captured. The Gauls who were captured wept.*
Abstract noun:	*The Gauls wept on their capture.*

'imperator senatores egredientes conspexit.'

Adjective: *The emperor saw the departing senators.*

Subordinative: *The emperor saw the senators as they departed.*
                            The emperor saw the senators while...
                            The emperor saw the senators who were...

Abstract noun: *The emperor saw the senators' departure.*

'attonitae ridebant.'

Noun: *The astonished (women) laughed.*

'manentes tacebant.'

Noun: *The remaining (people) were silent.*

Practice

Identify the case, gender and number of each participle and translate:

1. **dominus servum vinum bibentem vidit.**

2. **dominus servum vino capto dormientem vidit.**
   [dormio-ire: *sleep*]

3. **dominus servum vinum
   capturum vidit.**

Bread and circuses

Drama and other forms of Greek entertainment became popular in Italy, but the experience of Athenian theatre of the 5th century BC was never repeated. During this period, the Athenian dramatists, Aeschylus, Sophocles and Euripides produced tragedies which were intellectually and emotionally engaging, but not exclusive to an educated elite. People from all parts of the community attended these plays, and did not have to be tempted by gimmicks of the kind which have proved popular in Rome and elsewhere.

By the time Italy absorbed Greece's theatrical tradition, the plays of the 5th century had become distant classics, and their appeal in their original form was confined to a small literary class. In the 1st century BC there was an audience for versions of Greek tragedy, but it was mainly mimes, farces, pantomimes and comedies which filled Italian theatres. Terence, whose adaptations of Greek comedies pleased the literati of his day and later generations of scholars, was not especially popular in his lifetime.

Serious works were recited rather than performed, and this had an effect on the style of composition. *Oedipus Rex*, Seneca's adaptation of Sophocles' play, has a richness of language and description that makes the staging of the play almost superfluous. Instead, listeners would lie back on their couches after dinner, and hear in gruesome detail how Oedipus put out his own eyes. It appears that upper-class taste was as bloodthirsty as any other, but such was their 'civilization' that they preferred to indulge themselves at recitals, not performances. Violence in some form or other appears in many works of the time, by writers such as Tacitus, Seneca and Suetonius, all of whom knew well enough what their educated readers wanted.

The taste for the amphitheatre is perhaps the most unpleasant aspect of Roman society. Similar things may still happen today, but that is no defence for these barbaric atrocities served up in the name of entertainment. Derived from funeral rites, the shows presented displays of beasts eating humans, animals being slaughtered in 'hunts', the execution of criminals, duelling gladiators and even sea-battles in flooded arenas. Vast numbers of lions, bears, bulls, elephants and other animals were rounded up from all corners of the empire and brought to Rome. Some combats would involve only animals, such as bulls pitted against bears.

Athletic contests, another import from Greece, were also popular; so too was the racing of chariots and horses: the different teams were fiercely supported, and professional drivers achieved a status on a par with today's footballing stars from Juventus or Lazio. Racing was arguably the most popular of all forms of Roman entertainment: the Colosseum, the major amphitheatre in Rome, could house a maximum of 50,000 spectators; the Circus Maximus, where the horses were raced, might entertain 250,000.

In the republican period, a politician or wealthy citizen would stage a show to encourage support in a forthcoming election or, if successful, as a gratuity after it. The emperors, though not concerned with votes, were sensitive to popular opinion, and such munificence might distract people's attention from serious problems such as shortage of food (just as a win against the West Indies might push the gloomy balance of trade figures out of English minds).

The inhumanity of the amphitheatre seemed largely lost on the moralists of the time. Many thought that such spectacles were distasteful, but there was little sympathy for the victims. One reason for this insensitivity was the long-standing criterion of dramatic criticism, which measured the quality of a performance in terms of its impact upon the audience. The question had been central to Aristotle's criticism of drama, and remained influential long after him, with a wider application to shows and spectacles of all kinds.

1. Catullus invited his friend Fabullus to dinner, but there were strings attached.

> **cenabis bene, mi Fabulle, apud me**
> **paucis, si tibi di favent, diebus,**
> **si tecum attuleris bonam atque magnam**
> **cenam, non sine candida puella**
> **et vino et sale et omnibus cachinnis.**
> **haec si, inquam, attuleris, venuste noster,**
> **cenabis bene: nam tui Catulli**
> **plenus sacculus est aranearum.**

(Catullus XIII, 1-8)

ceno-are *dine*	**cena-ae** *dinner*
apud me *at my place*	**sine** [+ abl.] *without*
pauci-ae-a *few*	**candidus-a-um** *fair, pretty*
faveo-ere [+ dat.] *be kind*	**sal-is** *salt, wit*
dies-iei *day*	**cachinnus-i** *laugh*
attuleris (affero-erre) *you will have brought,*	**inquam** *I say*
bring	**venuste noster** *my charming friend*

107

plenus-a-um *full*   aranea-ae *cobweb*
sacculus-i [m.] *purse*

2. Few guests would have brought their dinner! One or two, however, might have tried to take home what they did not eat.

> quidquid ponitur hinc et inde verris.
> haec cum condita sunt madente mappa,
> traduntur puero domum ferenda:
> nos accumbimus otiosa turba.
> ullus si pudor est, repone cenam.

(Martial, *Epigrams* 2,XXXVII,1,7-10)

quidquid *whatever*   puer-i *boy, slave*
ponitur (pono-ere) *is placed*   ferendus-a-um *to be carried*
hinc et inde *here and there*   accumbo-ere *recline*
verro-ere *sweep away*   otiosus-a-um *inactive*
condita sunt (condo-ere) *have been hidden*   turba-ae *crowd*
madente (madeo-ere) *dripping*   ullus *any*
mappa-ae *napkin*   pudor-is *shame*
traduntur (trado-ere) *are handed over*   repone (repono-ere) *put back!*

3. In 160 BC, the playwright Terence experienced a miserable first night for his play *The Mother-in-law*. He produced it again five years later, adding a new prologue:

> Hecyram ad vos refero, quam mihi per silentium
> numquam agere licitumst: ita eam oppressit calamitas.
> eam calamitatem vostra intellegentia
> sedabit, si erit adiutrix nostrae industriae.

(Terence, *Hecyra*, 2nd Prologue)

hecyra-ae *mother-in-law*   ita *in such a way*
refero-erre *bring back*   sedo-are *calm, stop*
ago-ere *produce, stage*   adiutrix-cis *assistant*
licitum [e]st *it was allowed*

4. The theatre was not much liked by patricians, who considered it vulgar. They preferred to entertain their friends at home, after dinner, with recitals.

quid enim delectationis habent sescenti muli in Clytaemnestra? aut in Equo Troiano craterarum tria milia?

(Cicero, *Epistulae Ad Familiares* VII,1)

delectatio-onis *pleasure*
sescenti *six hundred*
mulus-i *mule*

Clytaemnestra i.e. a play
cratera-ae *bowl*
tria milia *three thousand*

5. The story of Oedipus, who unwittingly murdered his father and married his mother, is dramatized by the Greek playwright Sophocles, and again by Seneca. Once Oedipus discovers the dreadfulness of his predicament, he puts out his eyes, which in the Latin version is more gruesome than symbolic.

rigat ora foedus imber et lacerum caput largum revulsis sanguinem venis vomit.

(Seneca, *Oedipus* 978-9)

rigat (rigo-are) *drench*
os, oris [n.] *facial feature*
foedus-a-um *foul*
imber-bris *shower*

lacer-era-erum *mutilated*
largus-a-um *abundant*
revulsis...venis *from the torn veins*
vomit (vomo-ere) *spurts*

6. Like the theatre, the amphitheatre was thought to be distasteful. Moralists wondered what good could come from watching all this brutality – though concern for the victims was seldom an issue.

sed quae potest homini esse polito delectatio, cum aut homo imbecillus a valentissima bestia laniatur, aut praeclara bestia venabulo transverberatur?

(Cicero, *Epistulae Ad Familiares* VII,1)

homo-inis *man*
politus-a-um *refined*
imbecillus-a-um *weak*
valens *powerful*
bestia-ae *beast*

laniatur (lanio-are) *is torn*
praeclarus-a-um *magnificent*
venabulum-i *hunting-spear*
transverberatur (transverbero-are) *is transfixed*

7. Little had changed by the middle of the 1st century AD.

nihil vero tam damnosum bonis moribus quam in aliquo

spectaculo desidere. tunc enim per voluptatem facilius vitia
subrepunt.

(Seneca, Epistulae Morales VII,2)

vero *indeed*	**voluptas-tatis** *thrills*
tam *so*	**facilius** *more easily*
damnosus-a-um *harmful*	**vitium-i** *vice*
desideo-ere *sit idly*	**subrepo-ere** *advance slowly*
tunc *then*	

8. There was no end to the slaughter.

victorem in aliam detinent caedem. exitus pugnantium mors
est; ferro et igne res geritur. haec fiunt, dum vacat harena.
'sed latrocinium fecit aliquis, occidit hominem.' quid ergo?
quia occidit ille, meruit ut hoc pateretur; tu quid meruisti
miser, ut hoc spectes? 'occide, verbera, ure! quare tam
timide incurrit in ferrum? quare parum audacter occidit?
quare parum libenter moritur?' intermissum est spectaculum:
'interim iugulentur homines, ne nihil agatur.'

(Seneca, Epistulae Morales VII,4-5)

victor-is *winner, survivor*	**spectes (specto-are)** *you should watch*
detineo-ere *keep*	**occide (occido-ere)** *kill!*
caedes-is *killing*	**verbera (verbero-are)** *whip!*
pugno-are *fight*	**ure (uro-ere)** *burn!*
exitus-us *end*	**quare** *why*
pugnantium *of those fighting*	**tam** *so*
mors-tis *death*	**timide** *timidly*
ferrum-i *steel*	**incurro-ere** *run*
ignis-is *fire*	**parum** *not enough*
gero-ere *accomplish*	**audacter** *boldly*
fio-fieri *happen*	**libenter** *willingly*
harena-ae *sand*	**moritur** *he dies*
latrocinium-i *robbery*	**intermissum est** *has an interval*
facio-ere, feci, factum *do, make*	**interim** *meanwhile*
occido-ere-cidi-cisum *kill*	**iugulentur (iugulo-are)** *let...have*
quid ergo? *what then?*	*throats cut*
mereo-ere-ui-itum *deserve*	**ne nihil** *that something*
pateretur *he should suffer*	**agatur (ago-ere)** *is being performed*
miser-a-um *wretched*	

9. The more popular view is expressed by a character in Petronius' *Satyricon*. He complains about the poor quality of a show:

> **quid ille nobis boni fecit? dedit gladiatores sestertiarios iam decrepitos, quos si sufflasses, cecidissent; iam meliores bestiarios vidi. ad summam, omnes postea secti sunt.**

(Petronius, Satyricon 45)

quid boni *what good*
ille i.e. the producer
sestertiarius-a-um *worth twopence*
iam *now, already*
decrepitus-a-um *decrepit*
sufflasses (sufflo-are) *you had blown upon*

cecidissent (cado-ere) *would have fallen over*
bestiarius-i *animal-fighter*
ad summam *in fact*
postea *afterwards*
seco-are-ui, sectum *cut, lash*

10. The emperor Nero staged these entertainments, and 'encouraged' senators and their wives to participate in performances (to their horror).

> **spectaculorum plurima et varia genera edidit: iuvenales, circenses, scaenicos ludos, gladiatorium munus.**

(Suetonius, Nero 11,1)

spectaculum-i *show*
plurimus-a-um *very many*
genus-eris *type*

edo-ere-didi-ditum *put on*
Iuvenales *coming-of-age parties*
munus-eris *display*

Vocabulary

Text

tam	*so*
ne...quidem	*not even*
plane	*clearly*
postea	*afterwards*
sine [+ abl.]	*without*
plenus-a-um	*full*
turba-ae	*crowd*

mors-tis	*death*
pudor-is	*shame*
ignis-is	*fire*
genus-eris	*race, origin, class, character*
ago-ere, egi, actum	*do, manage, produce*

Words commonly confused

anima-ae	*spirit, soul, life-breath*
animus-i	*courage, mind, intention*
cado, cadere, cecidi, casum	*fall, die*
caedo, caedere, cecidi, caesum	*strike, kill*
concilium-i	*council*
consilium-i	*plan, policy*
fugio, fugere, fugi, fugitum	*flee, run away*
fugo, fugare, fugavi, fugatum	*put to flight, rout*
genus, generis	*race, type, kind*
gens, gentis	*family, tribe*
liber-a-um	*free*
liber, libri	*book*
liberi, liberorum	*children*
paro, parare, paravi, paratum	*prepare*
pareo, parere, parui, paritum	*obey*
quidam, quaedam, quoddam	*a certain* (adj.), *someone* (pron.)
quondam	*formerly*
quidem	*even, indeed*
servo, servare, servavi, servatum	*save*

servio, servire, servii, servitum	*serve*
volo, volare, volavi, volatum	*fly*
volo, velle, volui	*want*

Exercises

1. Identify the case of each participle and translate:
   a) **spectatores Augustum in amphitheatrum venturum viderunt.**
   b) **senatores praefecto audito Neronem laudaverunt.**
   c) **ego poetam epistulam scribentem vidi.**
   d) **Caesar Gallos captos Romam duxit.**
   e) **hostes urbem captam incenderunt.**

2. Choose the correct participle and translate:
   a) **senatores consilio Caesaris** [auditi/audito] **tristes erant.**
   b) **Hannibal militem epistulam ex Romanorum castris** [ferens/ferentem] **vidit.**
   c) **servus** [fugitus/fugiturus] **feminam audivit.**

3. Translate into Latin:
   a) After Antonius was killed, Augustus was made princeps.
   b) We were in the amphitheatre, about to see the gladiators.
   c) After saying this (this: *use neuter plural of* **hic**) Caesar was quiet (**taceo-ere-ui-itum**).
   d) Intending to prepare the dinner (*say* have in mind *or use the future participle*), the slave came into the villa.
   e) The man saw his wife working in the fields.

4. Translate: **te morituri salutamus.**

5. Identify Latin words in this chapter which are ancestors of *ferrous*, *bestial*, *disturb* and *polite*.

6. What is a **sine qua non** ?

7. What are the Latin ancestors of *voluntary* and *volatile*?

113

Grammar

Gerundives

A gerundive is an adjective formed from a verb:

e.g.	**paro-are**	*to prepare*
	parandus-a-um	*to-be-prepared*
	cena <u>paranda</u> est	*the dinner is <u>to-be-prepared</u>*

The gerundive often carries a sense of obligation:

e.g.	**cena <u>paranda</u> est**	*the dinner <u>must be prepared</u>*

The gerundive is passive, but is normally translated into English with an active expression:

e.g.	**vino <u>bibendo</u>**	*by <u>drinking</u> wine* (lit. *by wine <u>to-be-drunk</u>*)
	mater ad filium	*the mother came <u>to find</u> her son*
	<u>inveniendum</u> venit	(lit. *for the son <u>to-be-found</u>*)

Practice

Match each sentence with its illustration and translate:

a) **liberi videndi non audiendi sunt.**   Illustration no. .....
b) **vinum domini non bibendum est!**   Illustration no. .....
c) **poeta militibus non laudandus est.**   Illustration no. .....
d) **ludus in amphitheatro videndus est.**   Illustration no. .....

1.

2.

The agent

With other passive forms, the agent is expressed by **a** (**ab** before a vowel) with the ablative:

    e.g   **Cicero <u>a te</u> videtur**   *Cicero is seen by you*

The agent of a gerundive is usually expressed by the dative:

    e.g. **Cicero <u>tibi</u> videndus est**   *Cicero must be seen by you*

The gerundive often carries a sense of obligation, but not always: the context will make it clear.

Deponent verbs

Deponent verbs are <u>passive</u> in form but have an <u>active</u> meaning:

    e.g. **conor-ari, conatus sum**   *try*

Past participles in Latin are all passive with the exception of deponent verbs:

    e.g. **conatus**   *having tried*
         (but **missus**   *having <u>been</u> sent*)

There is a full list of passive endings on pp. 155-6. For other deponent verbs, see the vocabulary section of this chapter.

Conquest and civilization

The Roman invasion of Britain was the first documented occupation of this island. Before the Romans came, Britain was inhabited by different tribes with no national unity; but it was not a happy picture of devolution. Some tribes attempted to join together to resist the invasion, but with little co-ordination or common will. Other tribes were opposed to resistance, and wanted a Roman presence, for the issue was not always liberty or provincialism but a choice of masters: intertribal hostilities had been intensified by the arrival of warlike people from the continent, many of whom had emigrated to escape the authority of Rome.

Caesar had several reasons for his invasions of Britain in 55 and 54 BC: curiosity to see what was over the sea from Gaul; ambition to increase the empire's land and resources (and his own prestige); and concern that those Gauls who were still hostile were supported and sheltered by the Britons.

Caesar's invasions did not give Rome control of the island, for his attention was diverted back to the capital where political rivalries were fast evolving into civil war. Some decades later, when peace had been restored, Augustus expressed an interest in annexing Britain; but it was left to Claudius to accomplish the task. The south of Britain was finally in Roman hands in AD 48, more than a hundred years after Caesar first arrived. The north of the island was under Roman control some thirty years later, though some of Scotland remained outside the province.

Roman Britain.

Many provincials lived contentedly and enjoyed the protection, the scope for commerce and various cultural attractions which Rome offered. From time to time, however, this power was abused and rebellions occurred. The most famous in Britain was that of Boudicca (also known as Boadicea) in AD 61, which took place after the death of Prasutagus, her husband and chieftain of the Iceni. He had left half of his inheritance to Rome, and the rest to his wife. The Romans decided to help themselves to all of it, and Boudicca found herself at the head of a large number of resentful Britons, many displaced by Roman settlers. Colchester and London were stormed and sacked, but the Britons came to grief at some point close to the modern A5 between London and Birmingham (the site is still unknown). Here they encountered the military commander, Suetonius, who was hastily returning from a successful campaign against the druids on the island of Anglesey. Overconfident and undisciplined, the Britons were annihilated by Suetonius' much smaller army, and Boudicca took her own life. Thereafter, the Romans took care not to be so provocative.

Traders were quick to realize the commercial potential of the new province. There were metals to be mined, especially tin; and the plentiful supply of cattle provided hides as well as meat. During the period of conquest, the country was rich in 'human resources', and the flow of captives filled the slave markets.

The local people absorbed Roman ideas, from town-planning and houses with central-heating to politics and religion. Conversely, it was perhaps the most enduring feature of Rome's empire-building that Roman practices, habits and culture could be merged with what was already there. The success of this absorption and co-existence is amply illustrated by the length of time Rome's authority prevailed: over four hundred years – or a fifth of the period of this island's documented history.

1. Caesar describes the people he finds in Britain.

> **ex his omnibus longe sunt humanissimi qui Cantium incolunt, quae regio est maritima omnis, neque multum a Gallica differunt consuetudine. interiores plerique frumenta non serunt, sed lacte et carne vivunt pellibusque sunt vestiti. omnes vero se Britanni vitro inficiunt, quod caeruleum efficit colorem, atque hoc horridiores sunt in pugna aspectu; capilloque sunt promisso atque omni parte corporis rasa praeter caput et labrum superius. uxores habent deni duodenique inter se communes et maxime fratres cum fratribus parentesque cum liberis; sed qui sunt ex his nati, eorum habentur liberi, quo primum virgo quaeque deducta est.**

(Caesar, *De Bello Gallico* V,14)

longe *far*
humanus-a-um *civilized*
Cantium-i *Kent*
incolo-ere *inhabit*
regio-onis *region*
maritimus-a-um *by the sea*
consuetudo-inis *custom*
plerique *for the most part*
frumentum-i *corn*
sero-ere *sow*
lac, lactis *milk*
caro, carnis *meat*
pellis-is *skin*
vitrum-i *woad*
inficio-ere *stain*
caeruleus-a-um *sky-blue*

efficio-ere *produce*
aspectus-us [m.] *appearance*
capillus-i *hair*
promissus-a-um *grown*
pars-tis [f.] *part*
corpus-oris *body*
rasus-a-um *shaved*
praeter [+ acc.] *except*
caput, capitis [n.] *head*
labrum-i *lip*
superior-ius *upper*
deni *in tens*
duodeni *in twelves*
deducta est (deduco-ere) *was escorted,*
  married

2. Cicero, whose brother was on Caesar's staff, passes on information to his friend Atticus.

neque argenti scripulum est ullum in illa insula neque ulla spes praedae nisi ex mancipiis.

(Cicero, *Ad Atticum* IV,17)

argentum-i *silver*
scripulum-i *a small weight*
ullus-a-um *any*
insula-ae [f.] *island*

spes-ei [f.] *hope*
praeda-ae *plunder, resources*
mancipium-i *slave*

3. The Britons were proverbially unfriendly.

visam Britannos hospitibus feros.

(Horace, *Odes* III,4,33)

viso-ere *visit*
hospes-itis *guest*

ferus-a-um *savage*

4. Horace predicts a successful conquest of Britain by Augustus.

praesens divus habebitur

118

Augustus adiectis Britannis
    imperio gravibusque Persis.

(Horace, *Odes* III,5,2-4)

praesens *here and now*
divus-i *a god*
gravis-e *threatening*

habebitur (habeo-ere) *will be regarded*
adiectus-a-um (adicio-ere) *added*

5. In fact, Britain was ignored for many years after Caesar's exploratory visits.

primus omnium Romanorum divus Iulius cum exercitu
Britanniam ingressus, quamquam prospera pugna
terruerit incolas ac litore potitus sit, potest videri
ostendisse posteris, non tradidisse; mox bella civilia et in
rem publicam versa principum arma, ac longa oblivio
Britanniae etiam in pace: consilium id divus Augustus
vocabat, Tiberius praeceptum.

(Tacitus, *Agricola* 13)

exercitus-us *army*
ingredior-i-gressus *invade*
quamquam *although*
pugna-ae *battle*
terruerit (terreo-ere) *he intimidated*
incola-ae *inhabitant*
litus-oris *shore*
oblivio-onis [f.] *neglect*
consilium-i *plan, policy*

potior-iri-itus [+ abl.] *take possession of*
videri (video-ere) *to be seen*
ostendisse (ostendo-ere) *to have
    revealed*
posteri-ae-a *those after* (i.e. *posterity*)
tradidisse (trado-ere) *to have passed on*
mox *soon*
princeps-ipis *leader*
praeceptum-i *doctrine, precept*

6. Britain was finally annexed during the reign of Claudius, but not without resistance. The chieftain Caratacus was captured only after the treachery of Cartimandua, the queen of another tribe. Caratacus was taken to Rome, where he impressed his captors.

habui equos, viros, arma, opes: quid mirum, si haec invitus
amisi? nam si vos omnibus imperitare vultis, sequitur ut
omnes servitutem accipiant?

(Tacitus, *Annals* XII,37)

habeo-ere-ui *have*

ops, opis *wealth*

quid *what*	**imperito-are** [+ dat.] *rule over*
mirus-a-um *extraordinary*	**vultis (volo, velle)** *you want*
invitus-a-um *unwilling*	**sequor, sequi** *follow*
amitto-ere, amisi *let go, lose*	**servitus-tutis** *slavery*
nam *for*	**accipio-ere** *welcome*

7. Boudicca led a revolt against Rome.

> **femina duce (neque enim sexum in imperiis discernunt) sumpsere universi bellum.**

(Tacitus, *Agricola* 16)

femina duce *under a woman's leadership*
sumpsere (sumo, sumere) *they took up*
universus-a-um *all*

8. Britons were similar to their Gallic neighbours.

> **Gallos vicinam insulam occupasse credibile est. sermo haud multum diversus, in deposcendis periculis eadem audacia et, ubi advenere, in detrectandis eadem formido. plus tamen ferociae Britanni praeferunt, ut quos nondum longa pax emollierit. nam Gallos quoque in bellis floruisse accepimus; mox segnitia cum otio intravit, amissa virtute pariter ac libertate. quod Britannorum olim victis evenit: ceteri manent quales Galli fuerunt.**

(Tacitus, *Agricola* 11)

vicinus-a-um *neighbouring*	**nondum** *not yet*
occupasse (occupo-are) *to have occupied*	**emollierit (emollio-ire)** *softened*
sermo-onis [m.] *speech*	**floruisse** *that...were successful*
haud *not*	**accepimus (accipio-ere)** *we heard*
multum [adverb] *much*	**floruisse (floreo-ere)** *flourish*
diversus-a-um *different*	**segnitia-ae** *sluggishness*
in deposcendis *in...to be challenged*	**otium-i** *peace*
audacia-ae [f.] *boldness*	**amissus-a-um (amitto-ere)** *lost*
ubi *when*	**virtus-tutis** [f.] *courage*
advenere *(the dangers) arrived*	**pariter** *equally*
in detrectandis *in...to be refused*	**olim** *some time ago*
isdem, eadem, idem *the same*	**evenit** *(it) happened*
formido-inis *fear*	**quales** *just as*
praefero-ferre *display*	**maneo-ere** *remain*
ut quos *because...them*	**fuerunt (sum, esse)** *were*

120

9. Our weather has not changed much over the last two thousand years.

> **caelum crebris imbribus ac nebulis foedum; asperitas frigorum abest.**

(Tacitus, Agricola 12)

caelum-i *sky*	**foedus-a-um** *dirty*
creber-a-um *frequent*	**asperitas-tatis** *harshness*
imber-bris *rain-cloud*	**frigus-oris** *cold*
nebula-ae *mist*	**absum, abesse** *be absent*

10. British people readily absorbed Roman culture, and learned to speak Latin – a sign of their moral collapse, says Tacitus.

> **qui modo linguam Romanam abnuebant, eloquentiam concupiscebant. paulatimque descensum ad delenimenta vitiorum, porticus et balinea et conviviorum elegantiam. idque apud imperitos humanitas vocabatur, cum pars servitutis esset.**

(Tacitus, Agricola 21)

modo *recently*	**porticus-us** *colonnade*
lingua-ae *language*	**balineum-i** *bath*
abnuo-ere *reject*	**convivium-i** *dinner-party*
concupisco-ere *desire, aspire to*	**apud** [+ acc.] *among*
paulatim *little by little*	**imperitus-a-um** *ignorant*
delenimentum-i *allurement*	**humanitas-tatis** *civilization*
vitium-i *vice*	**cum** *although*

Vocabulary

Text

insula-ae	*island*	**exercitus-us**	*army*
pugna-ae	*battle*	**incolo-ere**	*inhabit*
lingua-ae	*tongue, language*	**pareo-ere** [+ dat.]	*obey*
periculum-i	*danger*	**pugno-are**	*fight*

caelum-i	*sky, heaven*	**olim**	*once upon a time*
ars, artis	*art, skill*	**quamquam**	*although*
hospes-itis	*guest, host*	**mox**	*soon*
litus-oris	*shore*	**apud** [+ acc.]	*in the presence of*
caput-itis	*head*	**praeter** [+ acc.]	*except, besides*

Deponent verbs

confiteor, confiteri, confessus sum	*admit*
conor, conari, conatus sum	*try*
fateor, fateri, fassus sum	*speak*
hortor, hortari, hortatus sum	*encourage*
ingredior, ingredi, ingressus sum	*go in, attack*
loquor, loqui, locutus sum	*speak*
minor, minari, minatus sum	*threaten*
miror, mirari, miratus sum	*admire*
morior, mori, mortuus sum	*die*
moror, morari, moratus sum	*delay*
patior, pati, passus sum	*suffer, allow*
proficiscor, proficisci, profectus sum	*set out, depart*
progredior, progredi, progressus sum	*advance*
reor, reri, ratus sum	*think*
sequor, sequi, secutus sum	*follow*
utor, uti, usus sum [+ abl.]	*use*

Exercises

1. Identify the ending of each gerundive and translate:

    a) **Cicero** [laudandus-a-um] **est.**

    b) **carmina post cenam** [audiendus-a-um] **sunt.**

   c)   **Caesar in templum ad deos** [laudandus-a-um] **venit.**
   d)   **vinum servis non** [bibendus-a-um] **est.**

2. Replace each infinitive with the gerundive and translate:
   e.g.   **nunc est** [bibere]
   answer: **nunc est bibendum**   *now it is to be drunk*
                                             (now is the time for drinking)

   a)   **nunc est** [laborare]
   b)   **nunc est** [vivere]
   c)   **nunc est** [dormire]
   d)   **nunc est** [agere]

3. Translate into Latin:
   a)   I tried to encourage the soldiers.
   b)   We set out before midday.
   c)   The dinner must be prepared by the slaves.
   d)   Caesar encouraged the Gauls.
   e)   We set out from the city to Cicero's villa.

4. What is the etymology of

   Amanda, Miranda, memorandum, referendum, addendum and *agenda?*

5. Mutatis mutandis is an ablative absolute comprising the gerundive and past participle of the verb **muto-are** (*to change*). What is the literal meaning?

6. What is the meaning of **quod erat demonstrandum**?

RELIGION 12

Grammar

Infinitives

	PRESENT	FUTURE	PERFECT
ACTIVE	parare *to prepare*	paraturus esse* *to be about to prepare*	paravisse *to have prepared*
PASSIVE	parari *to be prepared*	paratum iri *to be about to be prepared*	paratus esse* *to have been prepared*

*The forms **paraturus** and **paratus** are like **bonus-a-um** and agree with the infinitive's subject.

The infinitive is used with verbs like **volo** (*I want*) and **possum** (*I am able*):

e.g. **Ciceronem <u>videre</u> volo**   *I want <u>to see</u> Cicero*
     poetam <u>audire</u> non poteramus   *we were unable <u>to hear</u>
                                                  the poet*

The Accusative and Infinitive

The infinitive is also used to express a reported statement or thought:

e.g. **Ciceronem in urbe**   *he said Cicero <u>to be</u> in the city*
     <u>esse</u> dixit   (*he said that Cicero was in the city*)

In this expression, the infinitive is used with an accusative (here: **Ciceronem**). This was what was actually said (the direct statement):

Cicero in urbe est   *Cicero is in the city*

The tense of the infinitive in the indirect statement (**esse**) is in the same tense as the verb of the direct statement (**est**), i.e. present. Consider these different tenses:

124

DIRECT	INDIRECT
Cicero in urbe fuit *Cicero was in the city*	**Ciceronem in urbe fuisse dixit** *he said that Cicero had been in the city*
Cicero in urbe erit *Cicero will be in the city*	**Ciceronem in urbe futurum esse dixit** *he said that Cicero would be in the city*

In the last example, **futurum esse** agrees with its subject **Ciceronem** (see *
above).

The Accusative and Infinitive construction is used to express an indirect thought
as well as statement:

DIRECT	INDIRECT
Cicero in urbe est *Cicero is in the city*	**Ciceronem in urbe esse putat** *he thinks that Cicero is in the city*
Cicero in urbe est *Cicero is in the city*	**Ciceronem in urbe esse credit** *he believes that Cicero is in the city*

The reflexive pronoun **se** (*him, her, them*) is used when the person referred to is
the same as the subject of the verb of speaking or thinking.

e.g. **puellae dixerunt se in agris ambulare**
the girls said that they were walking in the fields

Hannibal credidit se Romam victurum esse
Hannibal believed that he would conquer Rome

Practice

Complete each indirect statement:

	DIRECT	INDIRECT
e.g.	**Cicero est in urbe**	**dixit** *Ciceronem in urbe esse*
1.	**Brutus Ciceronem vidit**	dixit..................................
2.	**servi cenam parabunt**	dixit..................................
3.	**Marcus est civis Romanus**	**Marcus dixit**........................

125

Beliefs and attitudes

At first sight it is tempting to assume that religion in ancient Rome was not taken very seriously. We read of gods behaving wantonly or trivially; there was no singular coherent religion; the empire embraced a variety of different cults and beliefs; and there were countless gods and spirits. Roman gods were often perceived as frivolous and fancy-free, but this has an underlying menace which subsequent Christian thinking has sometimes obscured.

Roman religion had its roots in animism. Spirits were identified in all things which could influence human life, and people prayed and sacrificed to these spirits in the hope that the activity or condition each spirit represented would turn out to their advantage. Belief in predestination was widespread, and the idea of fate or destiny appears throughout Roman literature. The relationship between fate and the gods is often vague, for sometimes the gods conform to fate, while elsewhere they shape it. The apparent paradox can be partly explained by the strong sense of self-will many Romans seem to have had. This ran side by side with their belief in predestination, creating uncertainties which we can still see in their poetry.

Romans were superstitious, and would look for signs and portents which might reveal future events. The future could be predicted, they believed, by the study of animals' entrails, the flight of birds, the weather and dreams. Sacrifices were observed to encourage divine favour and celebrate particular festivals. Such rituals of killing may now be beyond our comprehension, but then they were part of a variety of commonplace routines. If you imagine a cathedral being used as an abattoir, you begin to appreciate the awesomeness of such an occasion.

In the 2nd and 3rd centuries BC, Romans had their first taste of Greek literature, and of the stories and traditions of their gods. Until this point, Roman gods had no personality or physical shape for writers and artists to exploit. Now Roman deities became identified with Greek Olympians, and absorbed their properties and functions (e.g. Jupiter and Zeus, Juno and Hera, Minerva and Athene, Diana and Artemis, Mars and Ares, Venus and Aphrodite, Vulcan and Hephaestus, Mercury and Hermes, Neptune and Poseidon).

State religion grew out of family religion. Religious rituals practised by the state were similar to domestic rituals, but on a larger scale. Protection, food, happiness and other things which contributed to the quality of life became the object of public prayers as well as private ones. Vesta, the hearth goddess, was worshipped in the home and at public functions. Jupiter and Juno were the divine **paterfamilias** and **matrona** of Rome.

Greek philosophy was studied and respected, though with some reservation. The Greeks enjoyed the intellectual and sociable aspects of philosophy, where the activity of discussion and reasoning was an end in itself. Romans were more interested in an argument's conclusion than the rhetoric leading up to it, and discussions of ethical questions rarely lost sight of their practical value. Two

Greek schools of philosophy had lasting influence in Rome: the Stoics and the Epicureans. The Stoics taught people to confront all life's dangers and losses, including death, with equanimity. This 'chin up' attitude proved popular with military disciplinarians and with senators who suffered under bullying emperors. The Epicureans, on the other hand, encouraged people to avoid life's troubles: they cherished the Greek concept of *ataraxia* (*freedom from stress*), which in its extreme form meant no ambition, career, marriage, family or anything else that might upset the peace.

As Rome annexed lands in the east, new cults were discovered, and these found their way back to the capital. At the time of Augustus' rise to power, there were many different cults being practised in Rome. He did not persecute them, but nevertheless encouraged traditional ones. He even introduced a new god to counter the wide variety of religious cults in the empire: himself. The cult of Divus Augustus was publicized to promote loyalty to the empire and his leadership. This was not meant to supplant existing cults, but to give greater coherence. The authorities were on the whole very tolerant of all the different cults and practices. They even allowed their own cults and spirits to be merged with provincial ones – for diplomatic gains. However, not all religions welcomed such conciliation: no doctrine could embrace both the Roman pantheon and Christianity.

1. Saint Augustine ridiculed the pagan belief in so many gods. Even a doorway had to have three spirits.

> **unum quisque domui suae ponit ostiarium, et quia homo est, omnino sufficit: tres deos isti posuerunt, Forculum foribus, Cardeam cardini, Limentinum limini. ita non poterat Forculus simul et cardinem limenque servare.**

(Augustine, De Civitate Dei IV,8)

quisque [nom.] *each man*
domus-us [f.] *house*
pono-ere, posui *place*
ostiarius-i *door-keeper*
quia *because*
homo-inis *man, human being*
omnino *altogether*
sufficio-ere *be enough*
isti (like **ille** in form and meaning)
  those people (pagans)

Forculus-i *spirit (of the door)*
fores-um *gate*
Cardea-ae *spirit (of the hinge)*
cardo-inis *hinge*
Limentinus-i *spirit (of the threshold)*
limen-inis *threshold*
ita *thus*
simul *at the same time*
servo-are *look after*

2. On his visit to the underworld, Aeneas passed the home of some spirits.

> **vestibulum ante ipsum primis in faucibus Orci**
> **Luctus et ultrices posuere cubilia Curae;**
> **pallentes habitant Morbi tristisque Senectus,**
> **et Metus et malesuada Fames ac turpis Egestas,**
> **terribiles visu formae, Letumque Labosque.**

(Virgil, *Aeneid* VI,273-7)

vestibulum-i *hall*	**senectus-us** *old age*
ipsum [acc.] *itself*	**metus-us** *fear*
faux-faucis *jaw*	**malesuadus-a-um** *evil-counselling*
Orcus-i *Hades*	**fames-is** [f.] *hunger*
luctus-us *grief*	**turpis-e** *disgraceful*
ultrix-icis *avenging*	**egestas-atis** *need, poverty*
posuere (pono-ere) *have placed*	**terribilis-e** *terrible*
cubile-is [n.] *couch*	**visu** *to see*
cura-ae *care, anxiety*	**forma-ae** *shape*
pallens *pallid-making*	**letum-i** *death*
morbus-i *disease*	**labos-oris** *toil*

3. Deities were responsible for stirring up Horace's amorous feelings.

> **mater saeva Cupidinum**
> **Thebanaeque iubet me Semelae puer**
> **et lasciva Licentia**
> **finitis animum reddere amoribus.**

(Horace, *Odes* I,XIX,1-4)

mater Cupidinum *mother of the Cupids* (Venus)	**lascivus-a-um** *playful*
	licentia *wantonness*
Thebanus-a-um *Theban*	**finitus-a-um** *ended*
iubeo-ere *command*	**animus-i** *mind, heart*
Semela-ae i.e. Bacchus' mother	**reddo-ere** *restore, give again*
puer-i *boy, son*	**amor-is** *passion* (pl. for sing.)

4. Fortuna was the spirit of fate, and her favours were much courted (she was worshipped all over the empire).

> **Fortuna saevo laeta negotio et**
> **ludum insolentem ludere pertinax**

**transmutat incertos honores,
nunc mihi, nunc alii benigna.**

(Horace, *Odes* III,XXIX,49-52)

negotium-i *business, work*

ludus-i *game*

insolens-tis *wanton*

ludo-ere *play*

pertinax-acis *persistent*

transmuto-are *transfer, switch*

incertus-a-um *uncertain, fickle*

honor-is [m.] *honour, favour*

alii [dat.] *other*

benignus-a-um *kind*

5. Followers of the Epicurean school of philosophy believed that although the gods existed, they had no relevance to people.

**nos te,
nos facimus, Fortuna, deam caeloque locamus.**

(Juvenal, *Satire* 10,365-6)

6. The Stoics, on the other hand, did believe in Fortuna, and sought to endure whatever she brought to them.

**tolerabimus damna et dolores, ignominias, locorum
commutationes, orbitates, discidia, quae sapientem,
etiam si universa circumveniant, non mergunt.**

(Seneca, *De Constantia* 8,3)

tolero-are *endure*

damnum-i *loss*

dolor-is *grief*

ignominia-ae *disgrace*

commutatio-nis *change*

orbitas-tatis *bereavement*

discidium-i *divorce*

sapiens-tis *wise person*

universus-a-um *all together*

mergo-ere *overwhelm*

7. The Greeks had enjoyed the intellectual arguments of philosophy. The Romans preferred practical benefits, and ridiculed Greek-inspired games with logic.

**mus syllaba est. mus autem caseum rodit; syllaba ergo
caseum rodit. verendum est ne, si neglegentior fuero,
caseum liber comedat.**

(Seneca, *Epistulae Morales* 48,6)

mus, muris *mouse*	**ne** *lest*
syllaba-ae *syllable*	**neglegentior** *too careless*
caseus-i *cheese*	**fuero** *I shall have been, am*
rodo-ere *gnaw*	**liber, libri** *book*
verendum est *it is to be feared*	**comedo-ere** *gobble up*

---

8. Horace, like many others of his day, was an eclectic. Echoes of both Stoicism and Epicureanism appear in his poems. Below, his (imaginary?) girlfriend, Leuconoe, is advised not to worry about her future:

> **tu ne quaesieris – scire nefas – quem mihi, quem tibi**
> **finem di dederint, Leuconoe, nec Babylonios**
> **temptaris numeros.../...sapias, vina liques, et spatio brevi**
> **spem longam reseces. dum loquimur, fugerit invida**
> **aetas: carpe diem, quam minimum credula postero.**

(Horace, *Odes* I,XI,1-3,6-8)

quaesieris (quaero-ere) *you should inquire*	**spatium-i** *space*
scire nefas *not ours to know*	**reseces (reseco-are)** *cut back!*
finis-is *end, death*	**loquimur (loquor-i)** *we speak*
deus-i (di: nom. pl.) *god*	**invidus-a-um** *hateful*
dederint (do-dare) *have given*	**aetas-tatis** *time*
temptaris (tempto-are) *you should try*	**carpe** *pluck! enjoy!*
numerus-i *number (astrologer's)*	**quam minimum** *as little as possible*
sapias (sapio-ere) *be wise!*	**credulus-a-um** [+ dat.] *trusting*
liques (liquo-are) *strain!*	**postero (diei)** *tomorrow*

9. Horace commemorates a sacrifice to the fountain of Bandusia, but his attention is drawn to the victim.

> **o Fons Bandusiae, splendidior vitro,**
> **dulci digne mero non sine floribus,**
> **cras donaberis haedo,**
> **cui frons turgida cornibus**
>
> **primis et venerem et proelia destinat.**
> **frustra: nam gelidos inficiet tibi**
> **rubro sanguine rivos**
> **lascivi suboles gregis.**

(Horace, *Odes* III,XIII,1-8)

splendidus-a-um *bright*
vitrum-i *glass*
dulcis-e *sweet*
digne* [+ abl.] *deserving*
merum-i *wine*
cras *tomorrow*
donaberis (dono-are) *you'll be presented*
haedus-i *young goat, kid*
cui *whose*
frons-tis [f.] *forehead*
turgidus-a-um *swollen*
cornu-us *horn*
grex-gis *flock*

* agrees with **Fons**

venus-eris *love, mating*
proelium-i *battle, joust*
destinat (destino-are) *foretells*
frustra *in vain, not to be*
gelidus-a-um *cool*
inficio-ere *stain*
tibi *your* (i.e. the fountain's)
ruber-bra-brum *red*
sanguis-inis *blood*
rivus-i *stream*
lascivus-a-um *playful*
suboles-is *offspring*

10. Sacrifices were commonplace. Virgil described one which went awry as a simile for the death of Laocoon (see p. 30, no. 11). The story of Neptune sending a pair of serpents to kill him tells us something about the ancients' perception of divine justice. Poor Laocoon accurately foresaw the dangers of the Wooden Horse, but the grander scheme of things would not permit his comrades to believe him.

> ille simul manibus tendit divellere nodos
> perfusus sanie vittas atroque veneno,
> clamoresque simul horrendos ad sidera tollit:
> qualis mugitus, fugit cum saucius aram
> taurus et incertam excussit cervice securim.

(Virgil, *Aeneid* II,220-4)

ille [nom.] *he*
simul *at the same time*
manus-us *hand*
tendo-ere *struggle*
divello-ere *tear apart*
nodus-i *knot*
perfusus vittas *his headband spattered*
sanies-ei *slaver*
ater-tra-trum *black*
venenum-i *poison*
clamor-is *shout, cry*

sidus-eris *star*
tollo-ere *raise*
qualis *just like*
mugitus-us *bellowing*
fugio-ere *escape*
saucius-a-um *wounded*
ara-ae *altar*
incertus-a-um *ill-aimed*
excussit (excutio-ere) *has shaken off*
cervix-icis *neck*
securis-is [f.] *axe*

11. Italian story-tellers and poets invested their own gods with the personalities of the Greek Olympians. By the time Virgil was composing the *Aeneid*, Venus was synonymous with Aphrodite, the goddess of love. She persuades Vulcan, her husband, to forge new weapons for Aeneas, her son.

> **dixerat et niveis hinc atque hinc diva lacertis**
> **cunctantem amplexu molli fovet. ille repente**
> **accepit solitam flammam, notusque medullas**
> **intravit calor et labefacta per ossa cucurrit.**

(Virgil, Aeneid VIII,387-90)

dixerat *(Venus) had spoken*	**solitus-a-um** *familiar*
niveus-a-um *snow-white*	**notus-a-um** *well-known*
hinc *here*	**medullae-arum** *marrow*
lacertus-i *arm*	**intro-are-avi** *enter*
cunctans-tis *hesitating*	**calor-is** *glow*
amplexus-us *embrace*	**labefactus-a-um** *shaken, trembling*
mollis-e *soft*	**os, ossis** [n.] *bone*
foveo-ere *enfold*	**curro-ere, cucurri** *run*
repente *suddenly*	

12. Virgil shows Augustus winning the battle of Actium with the help of all the gods of Rome.

> **hinc Augustus agens Italos in proelia Caesar**
> **cum patribus populoque, penatibus et magnis dis.**

(Virgil, Aeneid VIII,678-9)

hinc *on this side*	**proelium-i** *battle*
Augustus...Caesar *Augustus Caesar*	**penates-ium** *spirits of the household*
agens *leading*	**deus-i** *god*

13. Virgil and his friend Horace were encouraged by Augustus to promote traditional religious values.

> **delicta maiorum immeritus lues,**
> **Romane, donec templa refeceris**
> **aedesque labentes deorum et**
> **foeda nigro simulacra fumo.**

(Horace, Odes III,VI,1-4)

delictum-i *sin*
maiores-um *ancestors*
immeritus-a-um *undeserving*
luo-ere *atone for*
Romane *you Roman(s)*
donec *until*
templum-i *temple*

refeceris (reficio-ere) *you have rebuilt*
aedes-is *shrine*
labens *collapsing*
foedus-a-um *soiled*
niger-gra-grum *black*
simulacrum-i *statue*
fumus-i *smoke*

14. Many of the emperors were given divine status after they died. The emperor Vespasian's dying words show that he did not take this too seriously.

> 'vae,' inquit, 'puto deus fio.'

(Suetonius, Life of Vespasian 23)

vae *oh dear*   **fio-ieri** *become*

Vocabulary

Text

puto-are, putavi, putatum	*think*		
scio-ire, scivi, scitum	*know*		
doceo-ere, docui, doctum	*teach*		
credo-ere, credidi, creditum	*believe*		
nuntio-are, nuntiavi, nuntiatum	*announce*		
cras	*tomorrow*		
hodie	*today*		
simul	*at the same time*		
repente	*suddenly*		
divus-a-um	*divine*	proelium-i	*battle*
niger-gra-grum	*black*	negotium-i	*business*
invisus-a-um	*hateful*	sanguis-inis	*blood*
dulcis-e	*sweet*	ara-ae	*altar*
mollis-e	*soft*	calor-is	*heat*

Exercises

1. Change each sentence to express what was actually said or thought:
- a) **Caesar Romanos victuros esse dicit.**
- b) **Hannibal omnes Romanos inimicos esse credidit.**
- c) **Neronem omnium principum avarissimum fuisse dicunt.**
- d) **poeta sperabat hospites post cenam carmina sua audituros esse.**
- e) **Cicero milites nimium laudatos esse putavit.**

2. Change each sentence into a reported statement, beginning each sentence with **Cloelia dixit** (*Cloelia said that...*):
- a) **amici in Gallia habitant.**
- b) **imperator hodie in amphitheatrum veniet.**
- c) **Antonius epistulam ad Cleopatram misit.**
- d) **orationes validiores quam arma sunt.**
- e) **consilium a senatoribus audietur.**

3. Translate into Latin:
- a) She said that she wanted to go to Rome.
- b) Iulius said that his mother would prepare the dinner.
- c) Clodius said he was a friend of Cicero.
- d) The slaves told the soldiers that Cicero was in Greece.
- e) The soldiers reported the absence of Cicero to Antony.

4. What are the initials **n.b.**, **e.g.** and **p.s.** short for?

5. Identify Latin words which are etymologically linked to: *library*, *computer*, *current*, *rodent* and *quality*.

CHRISTIANITY 13

Grammar

Gerunds

The gerund is a neuter singular noun formed from a verb, e.g. **parandum** (*preparing*), **videndum** (*seeing*). It is not used in the nominative – instead the Romans used the infinitive:

e.g. **videre est credere**   *to see is to believe / seeing is believing*

In other cases, the gerund is used:

e.g. **videndo credimus**   *by seeing we believe*
servus est ad   *the slave is fit for working*
laborandum aptus

The gerund is similar to the gerundive (see chapter 11) except that the gerund is active, and not an adjective but a noun:

accusative	**videndum**	seeing
genitive	**videndi**	of seeing
dative	**videndo**	for seeing
ablative	**videndo**	by seeing

A gerund is sometimes used in place of a gerundive:

GERUNDIVE: **Romae causa videndae venimus**
we came for the sake of Rome-to-be-seen

GERUND: **Romam causa videndi venimus**
we came for the sake of seeing Rome

Note that a gerundive is passive and an adjective, while a gerund is a noun and active.

Practice

With the gerunds from **fugio-ere, laboro-are, pugno-are** and **bibo-ere**, complete each sentence and translate:

1. **servus est aptus ad.........**

2. **servus est aptus ad..........**

3. **miles est aptus ad.........**

4. **miles est aptus ad..........**

se, ipse

se is a <u>reflexive</u> pronoun (i.e. refers to the subject of the sentence, but is never the subject itself: **se** has no nominative). It can mean *him(self)*, *her(self)*, *it(self)* or *them(selves)*. **ipse** is an emphatic form of **is, ea, id** and means *self*:

> e.g. **Caesar ipse dixit**   *Caesar <u>himself</u> spoke*
> **Caesar sibi dixit**   *Caesar spoke <u>to himself</u>*

For the endings of **se** and **ipse**, see pp. 151-2.

A new age

Rome was tolerant of the many different religions practised in the empire, and persecution was rare. The druids in Britain were attacked because they encouraged rebellion and indulged in human sacrifices, often of Roman captives. Christians also were seen as a threat because they refused to practise any rituals other than their own, and thus were perceived to be rejecting the authority of the state. Religious officials and priests (the **flamen, sacerdos**, and **pontifex**) were civic magistrates who looked after the state religion, which existed solely for the well-being of the state. So refusal to recognize the religion was tantamount to insurrection. An outsider's resentment of Christianity was not eased by the exclusion of the rich and comfortable in favour of sinners and destitutes, nor by the cult's existence on the fringe of respectable society. Its secretiveness and lack of moderation were disturbing (you either believed and were a member, or did not and remained outside).

The gospels, once translated into Latin, were accessible to poorer people all over Europe, and gave them something they had rarely felt: a sense of hope. Stoicism had attracted those who had something to lose, and reminded them they might just lose it. The poor had too little to start with, and welcomed the promise of salvation in the next world for those who suffered in this one. For pagans, hardship was something caused by gods who punished forgetfulness as much as any moral misdemeanour, and so they learnt to accept unwanted and unwarranted distress. The Christians, on the other hand, believed that although suffering was not divinely caused, it increased the prospects of salvation. To the bewilderment of pagans, they went out of their way to be poor, abstemious and even martyred. Christianity did not remain for ever the religion of the poor, as later there were a number of rich and powerful people who were converted, including, in the fourth century, emperors themselves. This caused intellectual, literary and most of all political, divisions between Christians and pagans within the ruling classes.

Early Christians discouraged the reading of classical literature. Most of them were unable to read it in any case, and the written language was kept deliberately close to ordinary speech. Educated converts, like Augustine and

Jerome, were conscious of their new loyalty, and joined in the rejection of the classics. Suddenly the polytheistic stories of Virgil and Ovid, who had been held in the highest regard, were reckoned to be blasphemous; Jerome felt guilty because he liked reading Cicero; and the very pleasure of the classics gave educated Christians scope for self-denial. Their quarrel was not really with the books, but the pagans who upheld them, and after this opposition had receded, classical works became acceptable to churchmen as allegorical tales. Before long the full circle had turned, with the monasteries playing a vital role in the survival of pagan Latin literature.

Intellectuals, who had been producing little more than imitations of classical writers and thinkers, were stirred into life with all sorts of difficult questions to ponder, not least the concept and identity of God. A pagan divinity was identified with the phenomenon which it represented. Light, for example, was a mystery to pagans, and they explained it in terms of a sun-god. Christians now inverted the formula: God was the mystery, light the metaphorical representation. This new and complex theology stimulated intellectuals into borrowing ideas from previous philosophers. Plato's theory of forms, which begins (or ends) with corporeal images and leads to the absolute form from which all things are derived, inspired a number of Christian intellectuals, who became known as the *Neoplatonists*.

The political momentum of Christianity overcame paganism and, some would say, the empire too. A distinctive characteristic of Roman administration was essentially a Greek idea which the Romans had put into wider practice: the partially autonomous municipality. In towns all over the empire local magistrates were elected to manage local affairs, including a portion of the taxes. In later years corruption, mismanagement and insecurity in the face of barbarian immigration from the east prompted central government to replace local elections with magistrates of their own choosing, who were obliged to collect the taxes for central government to spend. The leaders of the church filled the vacuum of popular representation, and soon earned more favour than the magistrates: bishops were infinitely preferable to bailiffs. In this way the church replaced the forum as the centre of local affairs, and the self-administered towns began to disappear. It was not very long, of course, before the bishop became the bailiff too, sharing power with a local lord in a manner which underpinned the political structure of the medieval era to follow.

The growth of Christianity was certainly a symptom of the empire's fall. Whether or not it was one of the causes is still hotly disputed by humanists and Christians, with both sides seeming to have more to prove than plain facts. In our attempts to trace the causes of decline, we sometimes overlook how long the empire survived before it finally submitted to old age. It is doubtful whether any single factor was solely responsible for an inevitable end, which occurred for a variety of internal and external reasons, arguably over some hundreds of years. Rome may not have been built in a day, but she did not disappear in one either.

1. Christianity did not allow the worship of any other gods. Since the emperor himself had divine status, this was a difficulty which the enemies of Christ tried to exploit.

> (The chief priests) **miserunt insidiatores qui se iustos simularent, ut caperent eum in sermone, et traderent illum principatui et potestati praesidis. et interrogaverunt illum, dicentes: 'magister, scimus quia recte dicis et doces: licet nobis dare tributum Caesari, an non?' considerans autem dolum illorum, dixit ad eos: 'quid me temtatis? ostendite mihi denarium: cuius habet imaginem et inscriptionem?' respondentes dixerunt: 'Caesaris.' et ait illis: 'reddite ergo quae Caesaris sunt, Caesari: et quae Dei sunt, Deo.' et non potuerunt verbum eius reprehendere coram plebe: et mirati in responso eius, tacuerunt.**

(Luke, *New Testament* 20,20-6) [Trans. Jerome]

insidiator-is *trickster*
iustus-a-um *proper, reasonable*
caperent (capio-ere) *they might catch*
principatus-us *control*
potestas-tatis *power*
praeses-idis *governor*
scio-ire *know*
quia *that* (classical Latin: *because*)

licet *it is allowed*
dolus-i *trick*
temto-are *tempt*
ostendo-ere *show*
ait *he said*
coram [+ abl.] *in the presence of*
miror-ari-atus *wonder at*
taceo-ere-ui *be silent*

2. Christianity's message of salvation gave poor people a measure of hope, something to live (and die) for. The rich were actively discouraged:

> **et iterum dico vobis: facilius est camelum per foramen acus transire quam divitem intrare in regnum caelorum.**

(Matthew, *New Testament* 19,24) [Tr. Jerome]

iterum *again*
facilius (facilis) *more easily*

foramen acus *the eye of a needle*
dives-itis *rich (man)*

3. Sinners were no less welcome to join than respectable citizens, which fostered hostile prejudices. Nero was able to use Christians as scapegoats for the fire of Rome (AD 64) following rumours that he himself had started it.

ergo abolendo rumori Nero subdidit reos et quaesitissimis poenis adfecit quos per flagitia invisos vulgus Christianos appellabat. auctor nominis eius Christus Tiberio imperitante per procuratorem Pontium Pilatum supplicio adfectus erat; repressaque in praesens exitiabilis superstitio rursum erumpebat, non modo per Iudaeam, originem eius mali, sed per urbem etiam quo cuncta undique atrocia aut pudenda confluunt celebranturque.

(Tacitus, *Annals* 15,44,2-3)

ergo *so*	**supplicium-i** *death penalty*
aboleo-ere *destroy*	**in praesens** *for the time being*
rumor-is [m.] *rumour*	**exitiabilis-e** *deadly*
subdo-ere-didi *trump up*	**superstitio-nis** *superstition*
reus-i *defendant*	**rursum** *again*
quaesitus-i *far-fetched*	**erumpo-ere** *break out*
poena-ae *punishment*	**non modo** *not only*
adficio-ere-feci-fectum *afflict, inflict upon*	**quo** *to where*
per flagitia (flagitium-i) *for their crimes*	**cunctus-a-um** *all*
invisus-a-um *hated*	**undique** *from all sides*
vulgus-i *crowd*	**pudendus-a-um** *shameful*
auctor-is *founder*	**confluo-ere** *flow together*
imperito-are *rule*	**celebro-are** *practise*

4. As governor of Bithynia (c. AD 112), Pliny often wrote to the emperor Trajan for guidance on matters of administration. Pliny sought his advice on how to deal with the Christians, and until he heard from the emperor, he decided to treat them as follows:

interim in iis, qui ad me tamquam Christiani deferebantur, hunc sum secutus modum. interrogavi ipsos an essent Christiani. confitentes iterum ac tertio interrogavi supplicium minatus. perseverantes duci iussi. neque enim dubitabam pertinaciam certe et inflexibilem obstinationem debere puniri.

(Pliny, *Letters* X,96)

interim *meanwhile*	**essent (sum, esse)** *they were*
tamquam *as...so to speak*	**confiteor-eri** *admit*
defero-erre *accuse*	**iterum ac tertio** *a 2nd and 3rd time*
modus-i [m.] *method, procedure*	**supplicium-i** *capital punishment*
ipsos (ipse-a-um) *them*	**minatus (minor-ari)** *threatening (them with)*
an *whether*	**duci (duco-ere)** *to be led (to execution)*

Iussi (iubeo-ere) *I ordered*
dubito-are *doubt*
pertinacia-ae *stubbornness*

certe *certainly*
debere puniri *ought to be punished*

5. Pliny reported that anonymous informers had produced lists of Christians.

> **propositus est libellus sine auctore multorum nomina
> continens. qui negabant se esse Christianos aut fuisse, cum
> praeeunte me deos appellarent, dimittendos esse putavi.**

> (Pliny, *Letters* X,96)

propositus est (propono-ere) *was posted*
libellus-i *small book, list*
esse...aut fuisse *that (they) were or had been*
cum *when*

praeeunte (praeeo-ire) *with (me) going first*
appellarent (appello-are) *they called upon*
dimitto-ere *release*
puto-are-avi *think*

6. Pliny found the Christians to be secretive and superstitious, but not threatening any serious harm. He had to extract the information from adherents (the torture of slaves who gave evidence was conventional and commonplace).

> **necessarium credidi ex duabus ancillis, quae ministrae
> dicebantur, quid esset veri et per tormenta quaerere. sed nihil
> aliud inveni, quam superstitionem pravam, immodicam.**

> (Pliny, *Letters* X,96)

necessarius-a-um *indispensable*
ancilla-ae [f.] *maidservant*
ministra-ae *deaconess*
quid esset veri *what was the truth*
quaero-ere *investigate*

et per tormenta *and that through torture*
invenio-ire, inveni *find*
quam *than*
pravus-a-um *depraved*
immodicus-a-um *excessive*

7. The emperor Trajan's reply to Pliny:

> **conquirendi non sunt. si deferantur et arguantur, puniendi
> sunt.**

> (Pliny, *Letters* X,97)

conquiro-ere *search for*
defero-erre *charge*

arguo-ere *convict*
punio-ire *punish*

8. Jerome, the scholar and monk who translated the Bible into Latin (c. AD 400), wrote of a dream in which his loyalties were tested.

> **interrogatus condicionem, Christianum me esse respondi: et ille qui residebat, 'mentiris,' ait, 'Ciceronianus es, non Christianus; ubi thesaurus tuus, ibi et cor tuum.'**

(Jerome, *Letter* XXII,30)

respondeo-ere, respondi *reply*
ille qui residebat i.e. the judge
mentiris (mentior-iri) *you lie*
ait *he said*

thesaurus-i *library*
ibi *there*
cor-dis [n.] *heart, soul*

Vocabulary

Text

tamquam	as if, as it were
rursum	again
undique	from all sides
iterum	again
nihil, nil	nothing
taceo-ere, tacui, tacitum	be quiet
iubeo-ere, iussi, iussum	order
trado-ere, tradidi, traditum	hand over
accipio-ere, accepi, acceptum	receive
invenio-ire, inveni, inventum	find
invisus-a-um	hateful
cunctus-a-um	all
solitus-a-um	accustomed
modus-i	manner, method
simulacrum-i	image
scelus-eris	crime
numen-inis	deity, spirit
lux-cis	light

Prepositions (and prefixes)

With the accusative:

ad	*to* (**acc-, add-, aff-, agg-, all-, ann-, app-, ass-, att-**)
adversus	*against*
ante	*before, in front of* (**ante-**)
in	*in, on, into* (**ill-, imm-, inn-, irr-**)
inter	*among, between* (**inter-**)
per	*through, thorough* (**per-**)
post	*after, behind* (**post-**)
sub	*underneath* (**sub-, succ-, suff-, sugg-, summ-, supp-, surr-**)
trans	*across* (**trans-**)

With the ablative:

a, ab	*away, from, by* (**a-, ab-, au-**)
cum	*with, together* (**cum-, coll-, com-, con-, corr-**)
de	*concerning, down* (**de-**)
e, ex	*out, from* (**e-, ex-**)
in	(as above)
prae	*in front of, before* (**prae-, pre-**)
pro	*before, in front of* (**pro-**)
sub	(as above)

Please note:

Remember the general distinction between prepositions with the accusative which imply motion and those with the ablative which describe a location only.

Exercises

1. Translate into Latin:
  a) Pliny (**Plinius**) himself spoke to the Christians.
  b) Marcus had soldiers with him in the amphitheatre.

c) I saw the image of the emperor himself.
d) Nero gave all the gifts to himself.
e) The gladiator handed over his sword to the soldier.

2. What are the meanings of **modus vivendi, modus operandi** and **nil desperandum**?

3. Identify Latin words which are etymologically linked to *courage, trade, interrogation, sermon* and *contribution*.

4. What are the meanings of **per se, inter se** and **ipso facto** ?

5. Make a list of English words which are derived directly or indirectly from a combination of any of the prepositions in the list above with either of these words:

fero (*I carry*)   **facio** (*I make, do*)

6. Match the English words with their ancestors:

fragilis	*count*
radius	*chattel*
dignitas	*frail*
caput	*dainty*
computo	*ray*

SUGGESTIONS FOR FURTHER READING

Carcopino, J., *Daily Life in Ancient Rome* (Penguin, 1991).

Crawford, M., *The Roman Republic* (Fontana, 1992).

Deighton, H.J., *A Day in the Life of Ancient Rome* (Bristol Classical Press, 1992).

Dowden, K., *Religion and the Romans* (Bristol Classical Press, 1992).

Flower, B., and Bosenbaum, E., *Apicius, The Roman Cookery Book* (Harrap, 1958).

Fowler, W.W., *The Religious Experience of the Roman People* (Macmillan, 1911).

Frere, S.S., *Britannia* (Routledge, 1987).

Gardner, J.F., *Being A Roman Citizen* (Routledge, 1993).

Gardner, J.F., and Wiedemann, T., *The Roman Household: a sourcebook* (Routledge, 1991).

Grant, M., *The World of Rome* (Weidenfeld and Nicolson, 1960).

Jenkyns, R.H.A., (ed.), *The Legacy of Rome: A New Appraisal* (Oxford, 1990).

Kennedy, G., *Art of Rhetoric in the Roman World* (Princeton, 1972).

Ogilvie, R.M., *The Romans and their Gods in the Age of Augustus* (Chatto and Windus, 1969).

Pomeroy, S.B., *Goddesses, Whores, Wives and Slaves: Women in Classical Antiquity* (Shocken, 1975).

Richmond, I.A., *Roman Britain* (Penguin, 1963).

Rose, H.J., *A Handbook of Greek Mythology* (Methuen, 1933).

Scullard, H., *Roman Festivals* (Thames & Hudson, 1981).

Shelton, J., *As The Romans Did* (OUP, 1988).

Wallace-Hadrill, A., *Augustan Rome* (Bristol Classical Press, 1993).

Wells, C., *The Roman Empire* (Fontana, 1992).

White, K.D., *Country Life in Classical Times* (Elek, 1977).

Wiedemann, T., *The Julio-Claudian Emperors* (Bristol Classical Press, 1989).

Wilkinson, L.P., *The Roman Experience* (Elek, 1975).

————— *Golden Latin Artistry* (CUP, 1963).

Williams, G., *The Nature of Roman Poetry* (OUP, 1970).

Oxford Classical Dictionary (2nd edn, 1970).

Bowder, D., *Who Was Who in the Roman World* (Phaidon, 1980).

Radice, B., *Who's Who in the Ancient World* (Penguin, 1971).

Translations

Caesar	*The Conquest of Gaul*, S.A. Handford (Penguin).
Catullus	*The Poems of Catullus*, G. Lee (Oxford World Classics).
Cicero	*Selected Political Speeches* and *Selected Works*, M. Grant (Penguin); *Selected Letters*, D.R. Shackleton-Bailey (Penguin).
Horace	*The Complete Odes and Epodes*, W.G. Shepherd; *The Satires*, N. Rudd (Penguin).
Juvenal	*The Satires*, N. Rudd (Oxford World Classics).
Livy	*The Early History of Rome,* and *The War with Hannibal*, A. de Selincourt (Penguin).
Pliny	*The Letters of the Younger Pliny*, B. Radice (Penguin).
Ovid	*The Metamorphoses* (prose), M. Innes (Penguin); *The Metamorphoses* (verse), A.D. Melville (Oxford World Classics).
Sallust	*The Jugurthine War and the Conspiracy of Catiline*, S.A. Handford (Penguin).
Seneca	*Letters from a Stoic*, R. Campbell; *Four Tragedies and Octavia*, E. Watling (Penguin).
Suetonius	*The Twelve Caesars*, R. Graves (Penguin).
Tacitus	*The Annals of Imperial Rome*, M. Grant (Penguin); *The Agricola and the Germania*, H. Mattingly, rev. S.A. Handford (Penguin).
Virgil	*The Aeneid*, C. Day Lewis (Oxford World Classics).

APPENDICES

A Glossary Of Grammatical Terms

ablative	name of a case of nouns, pronouns and adjectives (*by, with, from, in, on, than*)
accusative	name of a case of nouns, pronouns and adjectives (usually the object)
active	one of two *voices* of verbs, the other being passive; it means that the subject is doing the action (e.g. *she writes the book* is active, *the book is written by her* is passive)
adjective	words which qualify nouns: adjectives *agree* with the nouns they qualify in case, number and gender
adverb	words which qualify verbs, adjectives or other adverbs (e.g. *he spoke so quickly*)
article	the definite article is *the*, the indefinite article *a* (*an*)
case	form of the noun, pronoun or adjective which, by its ending, defines the function of the word in the sentence. The cases: nominative, accusative, genitive, dative and ablative. Also: the vocative (for a person being addressed) and the locative (*at...*)
clause	a main clause contains a subject and a verb, and could serve as a sentence by itself. A subordinate clause also has a subject and a verb, but could not serve as a sentence. A subordinate clause is introduced by words such as *while, that, because, when, if, who* or *though*
comparative	form of an adjective or adverb which indicates a comparison (e.g. *bigger, more quickly*)
conjunction	words which have fixed endings and are used to link clauses and sentences (e.g. *and, but, however, when, if, though, because, since*)
co-ordinative	that which has the function of joining like to like (e.g. co-ordinative conjunctions are *and, but, or*)
dative	name of a case of nouns, pronouns and adjectives (*to, for*)
declension	traditional word for categories of nouns with similar case endings: five declensions in all, e.g. **femina, servus, civis, gradus, res**. To decline a noun is to list its different case-endings
deponent	verbs which have a passive form but an active meaning (e.g. **loquor** *I speak*)
future	the tense of a verb describing action yet to happen (e.g. *I shall..., he will...*)
future perfect	the tense of a verb describing action yet to happen but projecting forward to a moment when the action is completed (e.g. *he will have eaten supper...*)

gender	there are three genders: masculine, feminine and neuter. A *common* noun has one form for both male and female (e.g. **bos, bovis** *an ox*)
genitive	name of a case of nouns, pronouns and adjectives (*of*)
imperative	the form of a verb which expresses a command
imperfect	the tense of a verb describing past action which was continuous or repeated
indicative	the form of a verb denoting a fact rather than a possibility (subjunctive) or a command (imperative)
indirect object	name of a noun when used as a secondary object (e.g. *he gave the book to me*), usually expressed by the dative in Latin
indirect speech	describes a person's statement or thoughts when reported (e.g. *he said that he was hungry*; the direct speech was *I am hungry*)
infinitive	form of a verb which is usually expressed in English with *to* placed in front (e.g. *to be or not to be*)
interrogative	asks a question: distinguish between *who is the man?* (where *who* is an interrogative pronoun) and *he is the man who...* (where *who* is a relative pronoun)
intransitive	a verb which has no object (e.g. *she waits*)
locative	name of a case (rarely used) to describe where something is
mood	the mood of a verb may be indicative, subjunctive or imperative
nominative	name of a case of nouns, pronouns and adjectives which indicates the subject
noun	name of a person, place, thing or abstract idea
object	the noun or pronoun affected by the verb (e.g. *he kicks the ball, she sees the mountain*)
participle	a form of a verb with the function of an adjective (e.g. *the finished chapter, the moving play*), often functioning as the equivalent of a subordinate clause (e.g. *I saw the man sitting* [*as he sat*] *on the bench, I knew the lady* [*who was*] *struck by lightning*). A participle is the only kind of adjective which can have a direct object (e.g. *John, saying these words...*)
passive	see **active**
perfect	the tense of a verb describing a completed, as distinct from a continuous or repeated, action in the past
person	the persons of a verb are expressed by the pronouns *I..., you..., he..., she..., it..., we..., they...*
plural	more than one (as opposed to singular)
prefix	an addition to the front of a word (e.g. *pre-, in-, per-*)
preposition	a word placed before a noun or pronoun (e.g. *in, with, by, from, to*), and determining its case
present	the tense of a verb describing action which is happening now or during the current period

148

principal parts	the four parts of a verb from which all the other parts are formed (e.g. **paro, parare, paravi, paratum**)
pronoun	a word used in place of a noun (e.g. *he, she, them*)
singular	describes only <u>one</u> (as opposed to plural)
subject	the active subject is the <u>doer</u> of the action of the verb, the passive subject is on the receiving end of the verb's action
subjunctive	the mood of a verb to describe potential action (as opposed to indicative)
subordinative	that which has the function of joining something greater to something less (e.g. subordinative conjunctions are *if, because, although, when, while*, etc.)
superlative	the form of an adjective or adverb which expresses the maximum meaning (e.g. *most, biggest, most unusual*)
tense	the time of the action of a verb (present, future, imperfect, perfect, future perfect, pluperfect)
transitive	a verb which takes a direct object
verb	a word describing an action or a state: every sentence must have (or imply) one
vocative	name of a case of nouns, pronouns and adjectives where a person is addressed
voice	a verb has two voices: active and passive

Grammatical Tables: Nouns
Five declensions

1st	
	woman
SINGULAR	
nom.	femina
acc.	feminam
gen.	feminae
dat.	feminae
abl.	femina
PLURAL	
nom.	feminae
acc.	feminas
gen.	feminarum
dat.	feminis
abl.	feminis

2nd			
slave	*master*	*boy*	*wine*
SINGULAR			
servus	magister	puer	vinum [n.]
servum	magistrum	puerum	vinum
servi	magistri	pueri	vini
servo	magistro	puero	vino
servo	magistro	puero	vino
PLURAL			
servi	magistri	pueri	vina
servos	magistros	pueros	vina
servorum	magistrorum	puerorum	vinorum
servis	magistris	pueris	vinis
servis	magistris	pueris	vinis

3rd					
	father	*citizen*	*leader*	*tribe, nation*	*elegance*	*time*
SINGULAR						
nom.	pater	civis	dux	natio	suavitas	tempus [n.]
acc.	patrem	civem	ducem	nationem	suavitatem	tempus
gen.	patris	civis	ducis	nationis	suavitatis	temporis
dat.	patri	civi	duci	nationi	suavitati	tempori
abl.	patre	cive(-i)	duce	natione	suavitate	tempore
PLURAL						
nom.	patres	cives	duces	nationes	—	tempora
acc.	patres	cives	duces	nationes	—	tempora
gen.	patrum	civium	ducum	nationum	—	temporum
dat.	patribus	civibus	ducibus	nationibus	—	temporibus
abl.	patribus	civibus	ducibus	nationibus	—	temporibus

4th		
	step	*hand*
SINGULAR		
nom.	**gradus**	**manus**
acc.	**gradum**	**manum**
gen.	**gradus**	**manus**
dat.	**gradui**	**manu**
abl.	**gradu**	**manu**
PLURAL		
nom.	**gradus**	**manus**
acc.	**gradus**	**manus**
gen.	**graduum**	**manuum**
dat.	**gradibus**	**manibus**
abl.	**gradibus**	**manibus**

5th
thing
SINGULAR
res
rem
rei
rei
re
PLURAL
res
res
rerum
rebus
rebus

Pronouns

	I/me	*you* (s.)	*we/us*	*you* (pl.)	*himself, herself, themselves*
nom.	**ego**	**tu**	**nos**	**vos**	–
acc.	me	te	nos	vos	**se**
gen.	mei	tui	nostri/nostrum	vestri/vestrum	sui
dat.	mihi	tibi	nobis	vobis	sibi
abl.	me	te	nobis	vobis	se

	SINGULAR			PLURAL		
	masculine	feminine	neuter	masculine	feminine	neuter
	this, he, she, it			*these, they, them*		
nom.	**hic**	**haec**	**hoc**	**hi**	**hae**	**haec**
acc.	hunc	hanc	hoc	hos	has	haec
gen.	huius	huius	huius	horum	harum	horum
dat.	huic	huic	huic	his	his	his
abl.	hoc	hac	hoc	his	his	his

	SINGULAR			PLURAL		
	masculine	feminine	neuter	masculine	feminine	neuter
	that, he, she, it			*those, they, them*		
nom.	**ille**	**illa**	**illud**	**illi**	**illae**	**illa**
acc.	illum	illam	illud	illos	illas	illa
gen.	illius	illius	illius	illorum	illarum	illorum
dat.	illi	illi	illi	illis	illis	illis
abl.	illo	illa	illo	illis	illis	illis

	that, he, she, it			*those, they, them*		
nom.	**is**	**ea**	**id**	**ei**	**eae**	**ea**
acc.	eum	eam	id	eos	eas	ea
gen.	eius	eius	eius	eorum	earum	eorum
dat.	ei	ei	ei	eis	eis	eis
abl.	eo	ea	eo	eis	eis	eis

	who, which					
nom.	**qui**	**quae**	**quod**	**qui**	**quae**	**quae**
acc.	quem	quam	quod	quos	quas	quae
gen.	cuius	cuius	cuius	quorum	quarum	quorum
dat.	cui	cui	cui	quibus	quibus	quibus
abl.	quo	qua	quo	quibus	quibus	quibus

	he himself, she herself, itself			*they themselves*		
nom.	**ipse**	**ipsa**	**ipsum**	**ipsi**	**ipsae**	**ipsa**
acc.	ipsum	ipsam	ipsum	ipsos	ipsas	ipsa
gen.	ipsius	ipsius	ipsius	ipsorum	ipsarum	ipsorum
dat.	ipsi	ipsi	ipsi	ipsis	ipsis	ipsis
abl.	ipso	ipsa	ipso	ipsis	ipsis	ipsis

Adjectives

bonus-a-um *good*						
	masculine	feminine	neuter	masculine	feminine	neuter
SINGULAR				PLURAL		
nom.	**bonus**	**bona**	**bonum**	**boni**	**bonae**	**bona**
acc.	bonum	bonam	bonum	bonos	bonas	bona
gen.	boni	bonae	boni	bonorum	bonarum	bonorum
dat.	bono	bonae	bono	bonis	bonis	bonis
abl.	bono	bona	bono	bonis	bonis	bonis

	omnis *all, every*		ingens *huge*		**maior** *greater*	
	masc./fem.	neuter	masc./fem.	neuter	masc./fem.	neuter
SINGULAR						
nom.	**omnis**	**omne**	**ingens**	**ingens**	**maior**	**maius**
acc.	omnem	omne	ingentem	ingens	maiorem	maius
gen.	omnis		ingentis		maioris	
dat.	omni		ingenti		maiori	
abl.	omni		ingenti		maiore	
PLURAL						
nom.	omnes	omnia	ingentes	ingentia	maiores	maiora
acc.	omnes	omnia	ingentes	ingentia	maiores	maiora
gen.	omnium		ingentium		maiorum	
dat.	omnibus		ingentibus		maioribus	
abl.	omnibus		ingentibus		maioribus	

Comparison of adjectives

Regular:

cruel	**saevus**	**saevior**	**saevissimus**
sad	**tristis**	**tristior**	**tristissimus**
easy	**facilis**	**facilior**	**facillimus**
quick	**celer**	**celerior**	**celerrimus**

Irregular:

good	bonus	melior	optimus
bad	malus	peior	pessimus
much, many	multus	plus*	plurimus

* **plus** in the singular is used as a neuter noun

Verbs
Active indicative

	parare	monere	mittere	audire
	to prepare	*to warn*	*to send*	*to hear*
PRESENT				
1.	paro	moneo	mitto	audio
2.	paras	mones	mittis	audis
3.	parat	monet	mittit	audit
4.	paramus	monemus	mittimus	audimus
5.	paratis	monetis	mittitis	auditis
6.	parant	monent	mittunt	audiunt
FUTURE				
1.	parabo	monebo	mittam	audiam
2.	parabis	monebis	mittes	audies
3.	parabit	monebit	mittet	audiet
4.	parabimus	monebimus	mittemus	audiemus
5.	parabitis	monebitis	mittetis	audietis
6.	parabunt	monebunt	mittent	audient
IMPERFECT				
1.	parabam	monebam	mittebam	audiebam
2.	parabas	monebas	mittebas	audiebas
3.	parabat	monebat	mittebat	audiebat
4.	parabamus	monebamus	mittebamus	audiebamus
5.	parabatis	monebatis	mittebatis	audiebatis
6.	parabant	monebant	mittebant	audiebant
PERFECT				
1.	paravi	monui	misi	audivi
2.	paravisti	monuisti	misisti	audivisti

3.	paravit	monuit	misit	audivit
4.	paravimus	monuimus	misimus	audivimus
5.	paravistis	monuistis	misistis	audivistis
6.	paraverunt	monuerunt	miserunt	audiverunt
FUTURE PERFECT				
1.	paravero	monuero	misero	audivero
2.	paraveris	monueris	miseris	audiveris
3.	paraverit	monuerit	miserit	audiverit
4.	paraverimus	monuerimus	miserimus	audiverimus
5.	paraveritis	monueritis	miseritis	audiveritis
6.	paraverint	monuerint	miserint	audiverint
PLUPERFECT				
1.	paraveram	monueram	miseram	audiveram
2.	paraveras	monueras	miseras	audiveras
3.	paraverat	monuerat	miserat	audiverat
4.	paraveramus	monueramus	miseramus	audiveramus
5.	paraveratis	monueratis	miseratis	audiveratis
6.	paraverant	monuerant	miserant	audiverant

Passive indicative

PRESENT				
1.	paror	moneor	mittor	audior
2.	pararis	moneris	mitteris	audiris
3.	paratur	monetur	mittitur	auditur
4.	paramur	monemur	mittimur	audimur
5.	paramini	monemini	mittimini	audimini
6.	parantur	monentur	mittuntur	audiuntur
FUTURE				
1.	parabor	monebor	mittar	audiar
2.	paraberis	moneberis	mitteris	audieris
3.	parabitur	monebitur	mittetur	audietur
4.	parabimur	monebimur	mittemur	audiemur
5.	parabimini	monebimini	mittemini	audiemini
6.	parabuntur	monebuntur	mittentur	audientur

IMPERFECT			
1.	parabar	monebar	mittebar	audiebar
2.	parabaris	monebaris	mittebaris	audiebaris
3.	parabatur	monebatur	mittebatur	audiebatur
4.	parabamur	monebamur	mittebamur	audiebamur
5.	parabamini	monebamini	mittebamini	audiebamini
6.	parabantur	monebantur	mittebantur	audiebantur

PERFECT			
1.	paratus sum	monitus sum	missus sum	auditus sum
2.	paratus es	monitus es	missus es	auditus es
3.	paratus est	monitus est	missus est	auditus est
4.	parati sumus	moniti sumus	missi sumus	auditi sumus
5.	parati estis	moniti estis	missi estis	auditi estis
6.	parati sunt	moniti sunt	missi sunt	auditi sunt

FUTURE PERFECT			
1.	paratus ero	monitus ero	missus ero	auditus ero
2.	paratus eris	monitus eris	missus eris	auditus eris
3.	paratus erit	monitus erit	missus erit	auditus erit
4.	parati erimus	moniti erimus	missi erimus	auditi erimus
5.	parati eritis	moniti eritis	missi eritis	auditi eritis
6.	parati erunt	moniti erunt	missi erunt	auditi erunt

PLUPERFECT			
1.	paratus eram	monitus eram	missus eram	auditus eram
2.	paratus eras	monitus eras	missus eras	auditus eras
3.	paratus erat	monitus erat	missus erat	auditus erat
4.	parati eramus	moniti eramus	missi eramus	auditi eramus
5.	parati eratis	moniti eratis	missi eratis	auditi eramus
6.	parati erant	moniti erant	missi erant	auditi erant

Subjunctive

PRESENT ACTIVE				
1.	parem	moneam	mittam	audiam	sim (sum/esse)
2.	pares	moneas	mittas	audias	sis
3.	paret	moneat	mittat	audiat	sit

4.	paremus	moneamus	mittamus	audiamus	simus
5.	paretis	moneatis	mittatis	audiatis	sitis
6.	parent	moneant	mittant	audiant	sint

IMPERFECT ACTIVE

1.	pararem	monerem	mitterem	audirem	essem
2.	parares	moneres	mitteres	audires	esses
3.	pararet	moneret	mitteret	audiret	esset
4.	pararemus	moneremus	mitteremus	audiremus	essemus
5.	pararetis	moneretis	mitteretis	audiretis	essetis
6.	pararent	monerent	mitterent	audirent	essent

PERFECT ACTIVE

1.	paraverim	monuerim	miserim	audiverim	fuerim
2.	paraveris	monueris	miseris	audiveris	fueris
3.	paraverit	monuerit	miserit	audiverit	fuerit
4.	paraverimus	monuerimus	miserimus	audiverimus	fuerimus
5.	paraveritis	monueritis	miseritis	audiveritis	fueritis
6.	paraverint	monuerint	miserint	audiverint	fuerint

PLUPERFECT ACTIVE

1.	paravissem	monuissem	misissem	audivissem	fuissem
2.	paravisses	monuisses	misisses	audivisses	fuisses
3.	paravisset	monuisset	misisset	audivisset	fuisset
4.	paravissemus	monuissemus	misissemus	audivissemus	fuissemus
5.	paravissetis	monuissetis	misissetis	audivissetis	fuissetis
6.	paravissent	monuissent	misissent	audivissent	fuissent

PRESENT PASSIVE

1.	parer	monear	mittar	audiar	
2.	pareris	monearis	mittaris	audiaris	
3.	paretur	moneatur	mittatur	audiatur	
4.	paremur	moneamur	mittamur	audiamur	
5.	paremini	moneamini	mittamini	audiamini	
6.	parentur	moneantur	mittantur	audiantur	

IMPERFECT PASSIVE

1.	pararer	monerer	mitterer	audirer	
2.	parareris	monereris	mittereris	audireris	

3.	pararetur	moneretur	mitteretur	audiretur	
4.	pararemur	moneremur	mitteremur	audiremur	
5.	pararemini	moneremini	mitteremini	audiremini	
6.	pararentur	monerentur	mitterentur	audirentur	

Perfect passive: paratus sim,   monitus sim, etc.
Pluperfect passive: paratus essem,   monitus essem, etc.

Irregular Verbs

	esse	**posse**	**velle**	**ferre**	**ire**
	to be	*to be able*	*to wish*	*to carry*	*to go*
PRESENT					
1.	sum	possum	volo	fero	eo
2.	es	potes	vis	fers	is
3.	est	potest	vult	fert	it
4.	sumus	possumus	volumus	ferimus	imus
5.	estis	potestis	vultis	fertis	itis
6.	sunt	possunt	volunt	ferunt	eunt
FUTURE					
1.	ero	potero	volam	feram	ibo
2.	eris	poteris	voles	feres	ibis
3.	erit	poterit	volet	feret	ibit
4.	erimus	poterimus	volemus	feremus	ibimus
5.	eritis	poteritis	voletis	feretis	ibitis
6.	erunt	poterunt	volent	ferent	ibunt
IMPERFECT					
1.	eram	poteram	volebam	ferebam	ibam
2.	eras	poteras	volebas	ferebas	ibas
3.	erat	poterat	volebat	ferebat	ibat
4.	eramus	poteramus	volebamus	ferebamus	ibamus
5.	eratis	poteratis	volebatis	ferebatis	ibatis
6.	erant	poterant	volebant	ferebant	ibant

PERFECT				
1.	fui	potui	volui	tuli	ii
2.	fuisti	potuisti	voluisti	tulisti	isti
3.	fuit	potuit	voluit	tulit	iit
4.	fuimus	potuimus	voluimus	tulimus	iimus
5.	fuistis	potuistis	voluistis	tulistis	istis
6.	fuerunt	potuerunt	voluerunt	tulerunt	ierunt
FUTURE PERFECT				
1.	fuero	potuero	voluero	tulero	iero
2.	fueris	potueris	volueris	tuleris	ieris
3.	fuerit	potuerit	voluerit	tulerit	ierit
4.	fuerimus	potuerimus	voluerimus	tulerimus	ierimus
5.	fueritis	potueritis	volueritis	tuleritis	ieritis
6.	fuerint	potuerint	voluerint	tulerint	ierint
PLUPERFECT				
1.	fueram	potueram	volueram	tuleram	ieram
2.	fueras	potueras	volueras	tuleras	ieras
3.	fuerat	potuerat	voluerat	tulerat	ierat
4.	fueramus	potueramus	volueramus	tuleramus	ieramus
5.	fueratis	potueratis	volueratis	tuleratis	ieratis
6.	fuerant	potuerant	voluerant	tulerant	ierant

Verbs: principal parts

	PRESENT	INFINITIVE	PERFECT	SUPINE
FIRST CONJUGATION				
love	amo	amare	amavi	amatum
give	do	dare	dedi	datum
praise	laudo	laudare	laudavi	laudatum
beg	oro	orare	oravi	oratum
prepare	paro	parare	paravi	paratum
SECOND CONJUGATION				
teach	doceo	docere	docui	doctum
have	habeo	habere	habui	habitum

order	iubeo	iubere	iussi	iussum
warn	moneo	monere	monui	monitum
laugh	rideo	ridere	risi	risum
sit	sedeo	sedere	sedi	sessum
hold	teneo	tenere	tenui	tentum
fear	timeo	timere	timui	–
see	video	videre	vidi	visum
THIRD CONJUGATION				
do, drive	ago	agere	egi	actum
drink	bibo	bibere	bibi	–
fall	cado	cadere	cecidi	casum
beat, kill	caedo	caedere	cecidi	caesum
discover	cognosco	cognoscere	cognovi	cognitum
run	curro	currere	cucurri	cursum
say	dico	dicere	dixi	dictum
learn	disco	discere	didici	–
lead	duco	ducere	duxi	ductum
carry on	gero	gerere	gessi	gestum
read, choose	lego	legere	legi	lectum
send	mitto	mittere	misi	missum
chase, seek	peto	petere	petivi	petitum
place, put	pono	ponere	posui	positum
rule	rego	regere	rexi	rectum
write	scribo	scribere	scripsi	scriptum
conquer	vinco	vincere	vici	victum
live	vivo	vivere	vixi	victum
MIXED CONJUGATION				
capture, take	capio	capere	cepi	captum
make, do	facio	facere	feci	factum
throw	iacio	iacere	ieci	iactum
FOURTH CONJUGATION				
hear	audio	audire	audivi	auditum
open	aperio	aperire	aperui	apertum
feel	sentio	sentire	sensi	sensum

come	venio	venire	veni	ventum
know	scio	scire	scivi	scitum
IRREGULAR VERBS				
be	sum	esse	fui	—
be able	possum	posse	potui	—
carry	fero	ferre	tuli	latum
go	eo	ire	ii	itum
wish	volo	velle	volui	—

Imperatives

	singular	plural	
paro-are	para	parate	*prepare!*
video-ere	vide	videte	*see!*
mitto-ere	mitte	mittite	*send!*
audio-ire	audi	audite	*hear!*

Some commonly used imperatives have lost the final vowel from the singular form:

facio-ere	fac	*do!*
dico-ere	dic	*say!*
fero, ferre	fer	*bring!*

Gerundives (adjectives)

parandus-a-um *(ought-)to-be-prepared*
agendus-a-um *(ought-)to-be-done*
   etc.

Gerunds (nouns)

acc.	parandum	*preparing*
gen.	parandi	*of preparing*
dat.	parando	*for preparing*
abl.	parando	*by preparing*

Participles

INFINITIVE		PRESENT	FUTURE	PAST
parare	*prepare*	parans	paraturus	paratus
amare	*love*	amans	amaturus	amatus
monere	*warn*	monens	moniturus	monitus
videre	*see*	videns	visurus	visus
mittere	*send*	mittens	missurus	missus
dicere	*say*	dicens	dicturus	dictus
audire	*hear*	audiens	auditurus	auditus
venire	*come*	veniens	venturus	ventum*

* **venio** is intransitive and does not govern a direct object, so the passive cannot be used in the usual way (although there is the impersonal passive: **ventum est** *it was come*). Several compounds of **venio-ire** are transitive and so do have a straightforward passive (e.g. **circumventus-a-um** *surrounded*, **inventus-a-um** *found*).

The Cases: a summary of uses
Nominative

Subject: **gladiator leones videt**
the gladiator sees the lions

Complement: **gladiator declaratus est victor**
the gladiator was declared victor

Accusative

Object: **gladiator leones videt**
the gladiator sees the lions

Object of motion: **gladiator in amphitheatrum venit**
the gladiator comes into the amphitheatre

Accusative
and infinitive: **senator servum in villa esse dicit**
the senator says that the slave is (the slave to be) in the villa

Length of time: **multos annos manebat**
he stayed for many years

Exclamation: **me miserum!**
wretched me!

Adverbial: **multa dicit**
he says much (many things: neuter plural)

With passive
verbs: **togam indutus**
having put on a toga

Two accusatives **quid aliud pauper deam rogat?**
with verbs of:
asking, hiding *what else does a poor man ask from a goddess?*
and *teaching* **vos philosophiam docebo**
I will teach you philosophy

dominus servum vinum celavit
the master hid the wine from the slave

Genitive

Possessive:	**epistula Ciceronis**	
	the letter of Cicero	
Partitive:	**magna pars exercitus**	
	a great part of the army	
	nemo mortalium omnibus horis sapit	
	no mortal (no one of mortals) is wise at all times	
	quid novi?	
	what news?	
Character:	**cuiusvis hominis est errare**	
	any man can make a mistake	
Quality and quantity:	**vir fortitudinis**	
	a man of courage	
	puer decem annorum	
	a boy of ten years	
Value:	**salutem suam plurimi habet**	
	he regards his safety highly	
Judicial:	**proditionis accusatus**	
	accused of treachery	
Cause of emotion:	**miseret te captivorum**	
	you pity the captives	
Memory:	**tui memini, sed mei oblita es!**	
	I remember you, but you have forgotten me!	
With prepositions:	**causa amicorum**	
	for the sake of friends	
	ars gratia artis	
	art for art's sake	
With adjectives	**plenus vini**	
	full of wine	
	cupidus auri	
	eager for gold	

Dative

Indirect object:	**mihi epistulam Cicero dat** *Cicero gives the letter to me*
	haec vobis dico *I say this (these things) to you*
	Italiam militibus Hannibal monstrat *Hannibal points out Italy to his soldiers*
Possession:	**ei nomen Marcus est** *his name is Marcus*
	Graecis philosophia est *philosophy belongs to the Greeks*
Disadvantage:	**mihi epistulam Cicero adimit** *Cicero takes the letter from me*
Helping and pleasing:	**Iulius nobis bene servit** *Julius serves us well*
	placet mihi te audire *it is pleasing to me to hear you*
Obstructing and displeasing:	**pater nobis irascitur!** *father is angry with us!*
	Antonius Ciceroni invidet *Antonius envies Cicero*
Believing and trusting:	**tibi credo** *I believe you*
Persuasion:	**dux mihi imperat** *the leader orders me*
Agent:	**elephantus tibi videndus est!** *the elephant should be seen by you!*
Predicative:	**Claudia mihi auxilio erat** *Claudia was a help to me*
	haec res fuit dedecori *this matter has been a disgrace*

With adjectives:	**ille servus <u>laboribus</u> utilis est** *that slave is fit for work*
	gratum <u>mihi</u> est vinum *the wine is pleasing to me*

Ablative

Separation:	**<u>Roma</u> venit** *he is coming from Rome*
Agent:	**puella ab <u>amicis</u> visa est** *the girl was seen by her friends*
Accompaniment:	**cum <u>imperatore</u> ambulabam** *I was walking with the emperor*
Instrument:	**<u>gladio</u> interfectus est** *he was killed with a sword*
Cause:	**<u>ira</u> commotus** *moved by anger*
Ablative Absolute:	**hostibus victis Romani redierunt** *after the enemy had been defeated, the Romans returned*
	Augusto duce erat pax *with Augustus as leader there was peace*
Comparison:	**puella sapientior <u>puero</u> est** *the girl is wiser than the boy*
Manner:	**audacia impetum fecit** *he attacked with boldness*
Respect:	**arte rudis** *bereft of skill*
A point of time:	**meridie Romam advenimus** *we arrived in Rome at midday*
Within a period of time:	**Romam duodecim <u>diebus</u> advenerunt** *they reached Rome within twelve days*
After prepositions:	**in <u>agris</u> laborat** *he works in the fields*
Measure of difference:	**discipulus <u>multo</u> doctior magistro est** *the student is much more learned than the master*

Price:	**Socrates emit <u>morte</u> immortalitatem** *Socrates bought immortality with his death*
	servum <u>magno</u> vendidit *he sold the slave at a high price*
With adjectives:	**dignus <u>meliore vita</u>** *deserving of a better life*
	<u>curis</u> liber *free from cares*

Index of Grammatical Endings

Endings are in alphabetical order, with the last letters first:

> Line 1: NOUNS declensions numbered [1-5]
> Line 2: ADJECTIVES [i] like bonus or pulcher
>   [ii] like tristis, celer or ingens
> Line 3: VERBS all conjugations, unless numbered [I-IV]

Endings are singular unless marked 'pl.', and genders are abbreviated to 'm.', 'f.', and 'n.'. Verbs are active unless marked 'passive' and indicative unless marked otherwise.

- a
NOUNS	nom./abl. [1], n. nom./acc. pl. [2,3,4]
ADJS	nom./abl. f. [i], n. nom./acc. pl.
VERBS	imperative [I]

- e
NOUNS	abl. [3,5], vocative [2]
ADJS	n. nom./acc. [ii], m. vocative [i]
VERBS	imperative: [II,III]
	present infinitive
	they...occasional perfect
	you...occasional passive: future, imperfect, present subjunctive, imperfect subjunctive

- ae
NOUNS	gen./dat., nom. pl. [1]
ADJS	f. gen./dat., f. nom. pl. [i]

- isse
VERBS	perfect infinitive

- i
NOUNS	gen. [2,5], nom. pl. [2], dat. [3,4,5], occasional abl. [3]
ADJS	m. n. gen. [i], m. nom. pl. [i], dat./abl. [ii]
VERBS	*I*...perfect
	you...perfect
	imperative [IV]
	present passive infinitive

- mini
NOUNS	a few nouns like **nomen** (**nomini**: dat.) and **homo** (**homini**)
VERBS	*you*...pl. passive: present, future, imperfect, present subjunctive, imperfect subjunctive
	imperative passive pl.

- am
NOUNS	acc. [1]
ADJS	f. acc. [i]

	VERBS	*I*...future [III,IV], imperfect, pluperfect, present subjunctive [II,III,IV]
- em	NOUNS	acc. [3,5]
	ADJS	acc. [ii]
	VERBS	*I*...present subjunctive [1], imperfect subjunctive, pluperfect subjunctive
- um	NOUNS	acc. [2,4], n. nom. [2], gen. pl. [all]
	ADJS	m. n. acc., n. nom. [i], gen. pl. [all]
- o	NOUNS	dat./abl. [2], occasional nom. [3]
	ADJS	dat./abl. [i]
	VERBS	*I*...present, future [I,II], future perfect imperative (rare) *let him/her, let them*
- ar	NOUNS	occasional nom. [3] (e.g. **nectar**)
	VERBS	*I*...present subjunctive passive [II,III,IV], future passive [III,IV]
- er	NOUNS	occasional nom. [2,3]
	ADJS	nom. [i,ii]
	VERBS	*I*...present subjunctive passive [I] occasional present passive infinitive
- or	NOUNS	nom. [3]
	ADJS	nom. [comparative form of all adjectives]
	VERBS	*I*...present passive imperative passive (rare) *let him/her, let them*
- mur	VERBS	*we*...passive: present, future, imperfect, present subjunctive, imperfect subjunctive
- tur	VERBS	*he/she/they*...passive: present, future, imperfect, present subjunctive, imperfect subjunctive
- as	NOUNS	acc. pl. [1], nom. (abstract nouns e.g. **suavitas** [3])
	ADJS	f. acc. pl. [i]
	VERBS	*you*...present [I], imperfect, pluperfect, present subjunctive [II,III,IV]
- es	NOUNS	nom./nom. pl./acc. pl. [3,5]
	ADJS	nom. pl./ acc. pl. [ii]
	VERBS	*you*...present [II], future [III,IV], present subjunctive [I] imperfect subjunctive, pluperfect subjunctive

169

- is   NOUNS   dat./abl. pl. [1,2], gen. [3], occasional acc. pl. [3]
      ADJS   dat/abl. pl. [i], gen. [ii], nom. [ii], occasional acc. pl. [ii]
      VERBS   *you*...active: present [III,IV], future [I,II], future
               perfect, perfect subjunctive, all tenses in plural; passive:
               present, future, imperfect, present subjunctive, imperfect
               subjunctive

- os   NOUNS   acc. pl. [2], occasional nom. [3]
      ADJS   m. acc. pl. [i]

- us   NOUNS   nom. [2,4], gen. [4], nom./acc. pl. [4], n. nom./acc. [3]
      ADJS   m. nom. [i], n. nom./acc. of comparative form (also:
               comparative adverb)
      VERBS   *we*...all active tenses

- bus   NOUNS   dat./abl. pl. [3,4,5]
      ADJS   dat./abl. pl. [ii]

- at   VERBS   *he/she*...present [I], imperfect, pluperfect, present subjunctive
               [II,III,IV]

- et   VERBS   *he/she*...present [II], future [III,IV], present subjunctive [I],
               imperfect subjunctive, pluperfect subjunctive

- it   VERBS   *he/she*...present [III,IV], future [I,II], perfect, future perfect,
               perfect subjunctive

- nt   VERBS   *they*...all active tenses

- u   NOUNS   abl. [4], n. nom./acc. [4], occasional dat. [4]
      VERBS   supine (rare)

Notes on the Authors

Aurelius Augustinus (ST AUGUSTINE)	b. AD 354 in Numidia, north Africa; scholar and rhetorician; was converted to Christianity in 386; his surviving works are in bulk six times those of Cicero, and include *Confessiones*, *De Trinitate* and *De Civitate Dei*.
Gaius Octavius (AUGUSTUS)	b. 63 BC, great-nephew of Julius Caesar; emerged from civil wars during the 1st century BC as the sole source of authority; on the pretext of restoring the republic, he in fact established the imperial dynasty; his work *Res Gestae* is a subjective account of his achievements; d. AD 14.
Gaius Valerius CATULLUS	b. Verona, Italy, c. 84 BC into a wealthy family; extant works include erotic and satirical lyrics, hymns and epyllia (short epics); d. c. 54 BC.
Gaius Julius CAESAR	b. c. 102 BC into a wealthy family; successful general, politician and diplomat, who became dictator; extant works are *De Bello Gallico* and *De Bello Civili*; assassinated in 44 BC.
Marcus Tullius CICERO	b. Arpinum, Italy, 106 BC, into an equestrian family; extant work includes political and legal speeches, letters, treatises on rhetoric, and on political and ethical philosophy; his style became the model for subsequent writers of Latin prose; d. 43 BC.
Quintus Horatius Flaccus (HORACE)	b. Venusia, Italy, 65 BC; son of a freedman; enjoyed Augustus' patronage; extant work includes *Odes*, *Epistles* and *Satires*; d. 8 BC.
JEROME	b. Dalmatia, c. AD 345; ordained priest in 379; commissioned by the pope to revise the Latin version of the New Testament; settled in Palestine where he learned Hebrew and translated the whole Bible into Latin; d. c. AD 420.
Decimus Junius Juvenalis (JUVENAL)	b. c. AD 60; his sixteen *Satires* survive, of which the last is incomplete; d. after AD 130.
Titus Livius (LIVY)	b. Padua, Italy, 59 BC; his major work *Ab Urbe Condita Libri* comprised 142 volumes, of which 35 survive; d. AD 17.

Marcus Valerius Martialis (**MARTIAL**)	b. Bilbilis, Spain, c. AD 40; extant are 14 books of epigrams, containing over 1500 poems; d. c. AD 104.
Cornelius **NEPOS**	b. c. 99 BC; biographer of generals, kings, historians, poets and orators; his work *De Viris Illustribus* survives.
Publius Ovidius Naso (**OVID**)	b. Sulmo, Italy, 43 BC into an equestrian family; his erotic poetry provoked the anger of Augustus and he was banished to the Black Sea; extant are amatory poems, the *Metamorphoses*, the *Fasti*, and poetical letters; d. c. AD 17.
PETRONIUS	1st century AD; a member of Nero's literary circle; extant are fragments of his comic novel the *Satyricon*.
Titus Maccius **PLAUTUS**	b. Sarsina, Italy, c. 254 BC; a writer of comedies; 20 plays survive him; he used Greek New Comedy as a model for his work, and in turn influenced later writers including Shakespeare; d. 184 BC.
Gaius Plinius Secundus (**PLINY** the Elder)	b. Como, Italy, AD 23/24; devoted much of his life to studies and writing; his sole extant work is the *Naturalis Historiae*; uncle of Pliny the Younger; killed by the eruption of Vesuvius, AD 79.
Gaius Plinius Caecilius Secundus (**PLINY**)	b. Como, Italy, c. AD 61; provincial governor, lawyer; his published letters offer a unique picture of life in the early imperial period; d. c. AD 113.
Marcus Fabius Quintilianus (**QUINTILIAN**)	b. Calagurris, Spain, c. AD 40; a teacher of rhetoric and oratory; his book *The Elements of Oratory* survives; d. c. AD 100.
Gaius Sallustius Crispus (**SALLUST**)	b. Amiternum, Italy, 86 BC; a supporter of Julius Caesar; two works are extant: *Bellum Catilinae* and *Bellum Jugurthinum*; d. c. 34 BC.
Lucius Annaeus **SENECA**	b. Cordoba, Spain, c. 4 BC; philosopher and political adviser to Nero; committed suicide (AD 65) after being accused of complicity in a plot against Nero's life; his prolific output included moral essays, letters, and adaptations of several Greek tragedies.
Gaius **SUETONIUS** Tranquillus	b. c. AD 69; biographer of Julius Caesar and first eleven emperors of Rome.

Cornelius **TACITUS**	b. c. AD 55. Orator and historian; he married the daughter of Agricola, a governor of Britain; extant works include: *Dialogues de Oratoribus*, *De Vita Agricolae*, and *Annales*; d. c. AD 118.
Publius Terentius Afer (**TERENCE**)	b. Carthage, Africa, c. 195 BC; brought to Rome as a slave, but his literary skill quickly found him freedom and patronage; six of his comedies survive; his Latinity was much respected by medieval scholars; d. c. 159 BC.
Marcus Terentius **VARRO**	b. Reate, Italy, 116 BC; scholar and antiquarian; two of his books survive; *On Agriculture* and *On The Latin Language*; d. 27 BC.
Gaius **VELLEIUS PATERCULUS**	b. Campania, Italy, c. 19 BC; his *History of Rome* covers the period from legendary beginnings to the 1st century AD; d. post AD 30.
Publius Vergilius Maro (**VIRGIL**)	b. Mantua, Italy, 70 BC; member of Augustus' literary circle; extant works are the *Eclogues*, the *Georgics* and the *Aeneid*; d. 19 BC.

Index of Characters

[For authors, see separate index]

Aeneas   Legendary ancestor of Romans; a prince who escaped the destruction of Troy and settled in Italy.

Agricola   AD 40-93, governor of Britain; father-in-law of the historian, Tacitus, who wrote a biography of him.

Agrippina   AD 15-59, wife of Claudius; mother of Nero; murdered on Nero's instructions.

Alexander   356-23 BC, king of Macedonia who conquered territories as far east as India.

Antony   82-30 BC, lieutenant of Caesar; triumvir with Octavian and Lepidus (43 BC); with Cleopatra was defeated at Actium (31 BC) by Octavian.

Aphrodite   Greek goddess of love; equivalent of Roman Venus.

Apollo   God of sun, archery, healing and prophecy (same name in Greek and Latin).

Ares   Greek god of war; equivalent of Roman Mars.

Ariadne   Helped Theseus slay the Minotaur and eloped with him, only to be abandoned on the island of Naxos.

Aristotle   384-22 BC, influential philosopher and literary critic; Plato's pupil and Alexander the Great's tutor.

Artemis   Greek goddess of hunting and childbirth; equivalent of Roman Diana.

Ascanius   Son of Aeneas; otherwise known as Iulus.

Athene   Greek goddess of protection, warfare, skill and wisdom;

174

equivalent of Roman Minerva.

Atticus　　　　　　109-32 BC, close friend and correspondent of Cicero.

Bacchus　　　　　　Roman god of wine; identified with Greek Dionysus.

Boudicca　　　　　　Queen of the Iceni tribe (East Anglia) whose rebellion was crushed by Suetonius; d. AD 61.

Britannicus　　　　　AD 41-55, son of the emperor Claudius; poisoned, probably on Nero's orders.

Brutus
(Lucius Iunius)　　　Helped to expel the Tarquins; founded the republic and was one of the first two consuls.

Brutus
(Marcus Iunius)　　 85-42 BC, Caesar's assassin; raised an army but was defeated by Antony and Octavian at Phillipi, where he committed suicide.

Caratacus
(Caractacus)　　　　Leader of the south-eastern Britons against the Roman invasion during the reign of Claudius; retreated to the west, then to the north, where the local queen handed him over to the Romans.

Cassius　　　　　　 Supporter of Pompey in the civil war against Caesar; later pardoned, but played a leading part in the assassination of Caesar (44 BC); fought against Antony and Octavian at Philippi, where he took his own life (42 BC).

Catiline　　　　　　d. 62 BC, aristocratic reformer whose unscrupulous methods did not succeed; his conspiracy against the government was crushed during Cicero's consulship.

Cato　　　　　　　 234-149 BC, tried to retain traditional Roman values of simplicity and austerity in the face of Greek and eastern influences; orator and writer.

Cato　　　　　　　 95-46 BC, great-grandson of the elder Cato and critic of Caesar; famed for his Stoic beliefs and adherence to traditional Roman values.

Claudius   10 BC-AD 54, Roman emperor who succeeded Caligula (AD 41) and preceded Nero; Britain was annexed as a province during his reign.

Cleopatra   Queen of Egypt, mistress of Caesar; later, wife of Antony; after Antony's death, she took her own life.

Clodia   Sister of Publius Clodius (below); probably the 'Lesbia' of Catullus' poems; like Catullus, Caelius became infatuated with her, but the relationship soured and ended in the famous court case with Cicero speaking for Caelius (*Pro Caelio*).

Clodius   Caused a political scandal by appearing in women's clothes at the festival of Bona Dea, held in the house of Caesar; though finally acquitted, his alibi was destroyed by Cicero; killed by Milo, whom Cicero subsequently defended (*Pro Milone*). d. 52 BC.

Cloelia   A Roman girl given as hostage to Porsenna, king of the Etruscans; she escaped by swimming across the Tiber, but was handed back to Porsenna, who released her out of admiration for her bravery.

Clytemnestra   Wife of Agamemnon; she killed him on his return from Troy, to avenge his sacrifice of their daughter Iphigenia.

Coriolanus   Early republican figure, who withdrew from Rome after being accused of tyranny; as leader of the Volscians, he would have defeated Rome, had not the entreaties of his mother and wife prevailed (491 BC).

Cupid   Love god; child of Venus.

Diana   Goddess of hunting and childbirth; identified with Greek Artemis.

Dido   Founder and queen of Carthage; received Aeneas when he was washed up on the shores of north Africa, and fell in love with him; took her own life when he left her.

Epicureans   Philosophical sect which originated in Greece and became popular in Rome; encouraged adherents to avoid life's problems and potential sources of stress.

Fulvia   Married Clodius and later Mark Antony; enemy of Cicero; d. 40 BC.

Hannibal   247- c. 182 BC, Carthaginian general who all but defeated Rome; recognized by later Romans as the greatest of their enemies.

Hephaestus   Greek god of the forge; equivalent of Roman Vulcan.

Hera   Greek goddess and wife of Zeus; equivalent of Roman Juno.

Hermes   Greek messenger god; equivalent of Roman Mercury.

Homer   Composer of the Greek epic poems, the *Iliad* and the *Odyssey*; earliest known Greek literature; was deliberately echoed and imitated by subsequent Greek and Roman poets.

Horatius Cocles   Legendary Roman who defended a bridge under attack from the Etruscans, while his comrades destroyed the bridge behind him; despite his wounds and armour, he swam to safety.

Jason   Leader of the Argonauts who sailed to Colchis to find the Golden Fleece; Medea, daughter of the king, helped him steal it, but he deserted her after his return to Greece.

Julia   39 BC-AD 14, daughter of Augustus; her third husband was Tiberius (11 BC); she was banished by her father (2 BC) for licentious conduct.

Juno   Goddess and wife of Jupiter; identified with Greek Hera.

LATIN *Better Read Than Dead*

Jupiter   Father of the gods; identified with Greek Zeus.

Laocoon   Trojan prince and priest; he protested against the proposal to drag the Wooden Horse (which concealed Greeks) into Troy; killed by two serpents immediately after his objections had been heard.

Lares   Spirits of farm-land and dwelling-places.

Lavinia   Daughter of Latinus, an Italian king; married to Aeneas.

Lepidus   Triumvir with Antony and Octavian; d. c. 13 BC.

Lesbia   See Clodia.

Livia   58 BC-AD 29, wife of Augustus; mother of Tiberius.

Maharbal   Carthaginian general under Hannibal; in command of the cavalry.

Marius   157-86 BC, Marius acquired a good military reputation in Africa; the bitter enmity between him and Sulla began the civil conflicts which recurred during the 1st century BC.

Mars   God of war; identified with Greek Ares.

Medea   Daughter of the king of Colchis, who helped Jason steal the Golden Fleece, but was deserted by him when she accompanied him back to Greece.

Menander   342-291 BC, Greek comic playwright.

Mercury   Messenger god; identified with Greek Hermes.

Minerva   Goddess of handicrafts; identified with Greek Athene.

Minicius Macrinus Contemporary of Pliny the Younger.

Narcissus   Freedman who became secretary to Claudius.

Neptune   God of the sea; identified with Greek Poseidon.

Nero   AD 37-68, emperor (54-68) famed for his persecution of Christians; executed many senators in fear of conspiracies, but was popular with poorer people, whose taste for the theatre and horse-racing he shared.

Oedipus   King of Thebes, who killed his father and married his mother; his story was dramatized by Sophocles and later by Seneca.

Pallas   Highly influential freedman; secretary to Claudius, then to Nero.

Paris   Son of King Priam of Troy; while a guest of Menelaus, king of Sparta, Paris abducted his wife, Helen, which caused the Trojan War; traditionally an unheroic and cowardly figure.

Penates   Spirits of the store-cupboard.

Philip   King of Macedonia 359-336 BC; father of Alexander the Great; overran Athens and the other Greek states, bringing them under Macedonian control, where they remained until the arrival of the Romans at the end of the 3rd century BC.

Plato   c. 429-347 BC, Greek philosopher, disciple of Socrates and teacher of Aristotle; his theory of forms had a profound influence on subsequent philosophy and Christian theology.

Pompey   106-48 BC, general and politician; his successes brought first a share in power (triumvirate) and then rivalry with Caesar; after losing the battle of Pharsalus to Caesar he fled to Egypt where he was killed.

Pontius Pilate	Procurator of Judea AD 26-36, during whose administration Jesus Christ was crucified.
Poseidon	Greek god of the sea; equivalent of Roman Neptune.
Prasutagus	King of the Iceni, husband of Boudicca; d. AD 61.
Ptolemy	The name of all the Macedonian kings of Egypt.
Romulus	Brother of Remus; legendary founder of Rome.
Semele	Daughter of Theban king, Cadmus, who bore Dionysus from a union with Zeus.
Sophocles	c. 496-406 BC, Greek writer, producer and actor of tragedies, including *Oedipus Tyrannus* and *Antigone*.
Stoics	Philosophical sect which originated in Greece, and became popular in Rome; encouraged adherents to confront life's problems without fear.
Sulla	138-78 BC, first of the military dictators in the first century BC; his regime was harsh and cruel to those who opposed him, and in Italy sowed the seeds of civil hostility which remained until the rise of Augustus.
Tarquinius Collatinus	Consul during the republic's early days.
Tarquinius Superbus	Last king of Rome (trad. date of removal: 510 BC); he enlisted the support of the Etruscans, but failed to return to power.
Thallus	A scribe working under the emperor Augustus.
Theseus	Athenian hero who killed the Cretan minotaur and escaped with Ariadne, the daughter of the king of Crete; he abandoned her on Naxos.
Thucydides	c. 460-400 BC, Athenian general and historian of the

conflict between Athens and Sparta (*The Peloponnesian War*).

Tiberius 42 BC-AD 37, Roman emperor; stepson and successor to Augustus; a reclusive figure, who is much criticised by the historian Tacitus.

Tiro Personal secretary and librarian to Cicero.

Venus Goddess of love; identified with Greek Aphrodite.

Vespasian AD 9-79, emperor; a realist and pragmatic ruler of Rome.

Vesta Hearth goddess; identified with Greek Hestia.

Vulcan God of the forge; identified with Greek Hephaestus.

Zeus Father of the Greek gods; equivalent of Roman Jupiter.

A Summary of Dates and Events

BC

753	Romulus founds Rome (traditional date).
510	Tarquinius Superbus expelled from Rome: the beginning of the republic.
390	Gauls sack Rome.
280-75	Pyrrhus invades Italy: 'Pyrrhic victory' leaves him with little, and withdraws.
241	Romans gain first overseas province: Sicily.
218	Hannibal begins his campaign against Rome.
201	Carthage is defeated.
197	Spain is absorbed into Roman dominion.
191	Rome begins war in east against Antiochus of Syria.
168	Roman victory against Macedonians secures annexation of Greek states.
129	Annexation of western Asia Minor.
111-106	Wars in North Africa against Jugurtha, king of Numidia.
90-88	War of the Allies: all Italians granted citizenship.
87-1	Civil war between factions of Sulla and Marius.
81-79	Sulla is appointed dictator.
73-1	Spartacus leads slave revolt in Italy.
70	Trial of Verres, ex-governor of Sicily, for extortion; Cicero speaks for the prosecution.
63	Cicero is consul; the conspiracy of Catiline is suppressed.
60	First triumvirate: Caesar, Pompey and Crassus.
58	Caesar begins campaign in Gaul.
55-4	Caesar's two excursions to Britain.

53	Crassus' army destroyed at Carrhae in Mesopotamia: Crassus is killed.
49	Caesar crosses Rubicon and marches towards Rome; Pompey withdraws to Greece.
48	Caesar defeats Pompey at Pharsalus, and is appointed dictator.
44	Caesar is assassinated.
43	Second triumvirate: Mark Antony, Octavian and Lepidus; Cicero is proscribed and executed.
42	Second triumvirate defeat republicans led by Brutus and Cassius at Philippi.
40	Antony takes control of eastern half of the empire, Octavian remains in Rome; tension between the two grows: civil conflict continues.
31	Antony and Cleopatra are defeated by Octavian at Actium.
30	Suicide of Cleopatra and Antony; Egypt is annexed.
27	Octavian assumes the title Augustus.
AD **14**	Death of Augustus, who is succeeded by Tiberius. Legions on Rhine and Danube mutiny.
37	Caligula succeeds Tiberius.
41	Claudius succeeds Caligula.
43	Invasion of Britain.
54	Nero succeeds Claudius.
61	Prasutagus, king of the Iceni tribe, dies: his territory is plundered by Romans, which ignites a rebellion led by his widow Boudicca. The uprising is later put down by Suetonius.
64	Fire in Rome.
65	Conspiracy to assassinate Nero results in widespread executions and suicides (including Seneca's).
131-5	Uprising of Jews in Palestine: suppressed by emperor Hadrian, who forbids Jews ever to enter Jerusalem.

212	Roman citizenship is extended to all free people in the empire.
251	Incursions of the Goths and other barbarians begin.
286	The emperor Diocletian chooses to rule with a colleague, Maximian. Diocletian rules in the east, Maximian in the west.
306	Constantine becomes ruler of the western empire and the first Christian emperor.
323	Constantine fights and defeats his partner, Licinius, and becomes sole ruler of empire.
330	Constantine transfers capital of empire to Byzantium, and renames the city Constantinople.
361	Julian is emperor and tries to restore Roman state religion.
379	Theodosius is emperor and bans all pagan rites.
395	Empire permanently divided into eastern and western halves.
410	Alaric and Visigoths sack Rome.
451	Romans defeat Attila the Hun.
455	Vandals sack Rome.
476	Odoacer, a Germanic chieftain, becomes leader of the west.
527-65	Justinian is emperor of the eastern Roman empire, and appoints a commission of jurists to produce a codification of Roman laws.

A Guide to Pronunciation

a	(short) as in 'c<u>u</u>p'
a	(long) as in 'f<u>a</u>ther'
ae	as in 'f<u>i</u>ne'
au	as in 'h<u>ou</u>se'
b	as in English (**bs** and **bt** are pronounced 'ps' and 'pt')
c	as in 'c<u>a</u>t' (not 'chair' or 'ceiling')
ch	like English 'k', with a sharper expulsion of breath
d	as in English
e	(short) as in 'm<u>e</u>t'
e	(long) as in 'm<u>a</u>te'
ei	as in 's<u>ay</u>'
eu	not a diphthong, but two sounds 'e-oo'
f	as in English
g	as in 'g<u>o</u>t' ('gn' at the beginning of a word is pronounced 'n', and in the middle of a word 'ngn')
h	as in English
l	as in English
i	(short) as in 'l<u>i</u>p'
i	(long) as in 'k<u>ee</u>p'
i	(consonant: sometimes written as a 'j') like English 'y'
m	as in English at the beginning or in the middle of words; a final 'm' should be pronounced with the lips open, as a nasalisation of the preceding vowel.
n	as in English
ng	as in 'a<u>ng</u>er' (not 'hangar')
o	(short) as in 'n<u>o</u>t'
o	(long) as in 'n<u>o</u>te' (as pron. by Scots and Welsh)
oe	as in '<u>oi</u>l'
p	as in English
ph	as in 'p', with a sharper expulsion of breath
qu	as in 'q<u>u</u>it'
r	always trilled with the tip of the tongue

s	as in 'gas' (not 'has')
t	as in English (and even closer to French 't')
th	as in 't', with a sharper expulsion of breath
u	(short) as in 'pull'
u	(long) as in 'pool'
v	(sometimes written as a 'u') like English 'w'
x	as in English
y	(short) as in French 'tu'
y	(long) as in French 'sur'
z	as in English

The English words used above are to be pronounced according to the received manner, except where stated otherwise. For a detailed account, see *Vox Latina* by W.S. Allen (Cambridge, 1975).

Numbers

1	I	unus	11	XI	undecim
2	II	duo	12	XII	duodecim
3	III	tres	13	XIII	tredecim
4	IV	quattuor	14	XIV	quattuordecim
5	V	quinque	15	XV	quindecim
6	VI	sex	16	XVI	sedecim
7	VII	septem	17	XVII	septemdecim
8	VIII	octo	18	XVIII	duodeviginti
9	IX	novem	19	XIX	undeviginti
10	X	decem	20	XX	viginti

21	XXI	unus et viginti	101	CI	centum et unus
22	XXII	duo et viginti	126	CXXVI	centum viginti sex
29	XXIX	undetriginta	200	CC	ducenti-ae-a
30	XXX	triginta	300	CCC	trecenti-ae-a
40	XL	quadraginta	400	CCCC	quadringenti-ae-a
50	L	quinquaginta	500	D	quingenti-ae-a
60	LX	sexaginta	600	DC	sescenti-ae-a
70	LXX	septuaginta	700	DCC	septingenti-ae-a
80	LXXX	octoginta	800	DCCC	octingenti-ae-a
90	XC	nonaginta	900	DCCCC	nongenti-ae-a
98	IIC	octo et nonaginta			
99	XCIX	undecentum	1000	M	mille, *indecl.*
100	C	centum			(*plural:* milia)

Money

10 **asses**	=	1 **denarius**
4 **sestertii**	=	1 **denarius** [A **sertertius** (sesterce) was a silver coin, abbreviated to HS]

50 BC: A soldier was paid HS 900 per annum.
A labourer was paid HS 1,000 per annum.

c. AD 100: Pliny bequeathed HS 2,000,000 to support 100 freedmen.
HS 400,000 was the capital needed to become a knight.

Early 4th century AD: Farm labourers and mule-drivers were paid 25 denarii [HS 100] per day. A primary teacher needed fifteen students to earn the same. A painter (artist) was paid 150 denarii [HS

600] per day, while a painter (decorator) was paid 75 denarii [HS 300]. Pork cost 12 denarii [HS 48] per pound (equivalent of 12 oz. today).

The temple of *Juno Moneta*, from which the words *money* and *mint* are derived, served as the mint in Rome.

Roman names

Praenomen	Nomen	Cognomen
individual name	*gens/clan*	*familia*
Marcus	**Tullius**	**Cicero**
Publius	**Vergilius**	**Maro**
Gaius	**Iulius**	**Caesar**

In addition to these names a prominent Roman might assume another name (**agnomen**), perhaps the name of the family which adopted him, or an honorary title:

Coriolanus	**(Gnaeus Marcius)**
Africanus	**(Publius Cornelius Scipio)**
Magnus	**(Gnaeus Pompeius)**

Praenomina are often abbreviated:

A.	Aulus	P.	Publius
C.	Gaius	Q.	Quintus
Cn.	Gnaeus	S(ex).	Sextus
D.	Decimus	Ser	Servius
L.	Lucius	Sp.	Spurius
M.	Marcus	T.	Titus
M'.	Manius	Ti(b).	Tiberius

Daughters had no peculiar **praenomina**, but were called by the name of the **gens** in which they were born. If there were two, they were distinguished as **maior** and **minor**; if more than two, by **tertia**, **quarta** etc.

Latin and English

Latin and English belong to separate groups of the Indo-European family of languages. English is a Germanic language, beginning life relatively recently when the Anglo-Saxons left the continent to settle in Britain. Latin is an Italic language, and from Latin developed the Romance languages (French, Italian, Portuguese, Spanish and Romanian). There is another group in western Europe, the Celtic languages, which include Welsh, Cornish, Breton and Gaelic. The Italic, Germanic and Celtic groups have a certain amount in common, such as widely-used and recent additions like *computer* or *telephone*, and also words which have been part of man's basic vocabulary for thousands of years: English *mother* and *father* are much closer to Latin **mater** and **pater** (pronounced *mutthair, putthair*) than modern pronunciation might suggest; our word *wool* does not appear to be similar to Latin **lana**, but a connection is offered by Welsh *gwlan*. These are cognate words, related by virtue of a common Indo-European ancestor. Most similarities between English and Latin, however, have come about through derivation, directly from Latin or through French. For example, *two* and **duo** are cognates, *dual* and *duet* are derivatives. The derivation of Latin words has been happening since the Romans were first in occupation of northern Europe, as a result of conquest, trade, religious influence, science, learning and, most recently, technological innovation.

At the time of the Roman occupation of Britain, a few words passed from Latin into the British languages and were later taken up by the Anglo-Saxons. Other words were borrowed by Anglo-Saxons while they were still on the continent. The German tribes were not under direct Roman rule, but many came into contact with Rome either through trade or military service. Some of the words to pass into English during this period are: *street (straet)* **strata via**; *wine (win)* **vinum**; *port* **portus**. Welsh, as a British language, was more directly influenced by Roman occupation, and thus contains many Latin words (e.g. Welsh equivalents of the above examples: *ystrad, gwin* and *porth*). Welsh *ffenestr (window)* survives from **fenestra**, but *fenester*, which appeared in old English, is no longer with us.

Many of the Latin words which passed into English after the Romans left Britain had military or commercial meanings, and, after the arrival of Christianity, religious ones. Besides words of a purely religious character, the Church introduced words of a learned and scientific nature (during this period all learning, science and scholarship remained within churches and monasteries). Examples of Latin words taken into English from AD 450 until the Norman Conquest are: *monk (munuc)* **monachus**; *minster (mynster)* **monasterium** (*monastery* appears much later); *purse (purs)* **bursa**; *camel* **camelus**; *heretic (eretic)* **haeriticus**; *creed (creda)* **credo**; *pope (papa)* **papa**; *saint (sanct)* **sanctus**; *note (not)* **nota**; *paper* **papyrus**; *school (scol)* **schola**; *-chester, -caster* and *-cester* **castra** (*a city*); *cup* (*cupp*) **cuppa.**

Some of these words have not survived, or were replaced at a later date by others which were reborrowed from Latin, directly or through Old French. In the period after the Conquest up until the Renaissance, many French words derived from Latin passed into English. There are also words derived directly from Latin: *admit, arbitrator, cause, client, collect, combine, complete, conclude, confide, conviction, diocese, discuss, eccentric, equal, equator, expedition, explicit, imaginary, immortal, import, legitimate, library, locust, memorandum, prima facie, psalm, requiem, simile, subpoena*, etc. With some words, it is difficult to know whether they came to English through French or directly from Latin (e.g. *distant, impression, execution*), although to some extent this must have varied according to the period and education of individual users. Several words taken from French were later refashioned on Latin models (e.g. suffixes *-tioun, -cioun* and *-sioun* became *-tion* and *-sion*), while others kept the French form, such as *custody* (*custodie*) from **custodia**, and *family* (*familie*) from **familia**.

During the sixteenth and seventeenth centuries, as a result of the Renaissance, scholars and writers coined a large number of new words modelled on Latin originals (not all of which survived), and imported several whole Latin words. Moreover, some existing English words which had been derived from Latin through Old French were at this time sidelined in favour of words more closely modelled on the Latin originals. As time passed, the new formations developed marginally different meanings from the old ones: *purvey* and *provide* (**provideo**), *strait* and *strict* (**strictus**), *count* and *compute* (**computo**), *sure* and *secure* (**securus**), *ray* and *radius* (**radius**), *poor* and *pauper* (**pauper**).

During the Renaissance, the meanings of certain words which had previously been derived from Latin were altered to bring them into line with the meanings of their classical models: in the fourteenth century, an *oration* was a petition, but was later used to mean a formal speech, similar to **oratio**; likewise *discipline* in the thirteenth century meant correction, but in the sixteenth century took on the original Latin sense of control over conduct (**disciplina**); *prefer* was used in the sixteenth century to mean put something forward, on the model of **praefero**, but the word had already appeared two centuries earlier to mean set before others, the usage which is more common today.

Not content with making new words and giving new meanings to ones already in use, scholars of the period also tampered with the spelling of words derived through French: *doute* became *doubt* (**dubium**), *dette* became *debt* (**debitum**), and *receit* became *receipt* (**receptum**). Some of these changes had already occurred in France before the words entered English, for example *caitiff* became *captif* (*captive*) on the model of **captivus**.

In the sixteenth and seventeenth centuries, several Latin words passed into English in their classical form, and some arrived later. Here are a few examples:

16th century: **aborigine, alias, area, circus, delirium, exit, genius, junior,**

miser, radius, species, vertigo, virus.

17th century: **agenda, apparatus, arena, census, curriculum, gratis, premium, rabies, series, specimen, squalor, status, veto.**

18th century: **alibi, bonus, deficit, extra, ultimatum.**

19th century: **consensus, ego, omnibus, referendum.**

20th century: **computer*, facsimile*, video.**

* These words had been used before the twentieth century, a *facsimile* being a likeness, and *computer* a person who counts.

Before the Renaissance, English absorbed Latin nouns and anglicized them. But words imported later came complete with their plural forms, with the result that we now have *curriculum* and *curricula*, *agendum* and *agenda*, and yet *circuses* not **circi**, *spectators* not **spectatores**, and *areas* not **areae**.

Some Latin imports remain in English as the same parts of speech they were in Latin (e.g. *creator* and *genius* are nouns, *stet* a verb). Others change their function (e.g. *alias*, *alibi* and *interim* were Latin adverbs and are now nouns). There are also Latin verbs which survive in English as nouns: *recipe*, *affidavit*, *deficit*, *exit*, *veto*, *caveat*, *ignoramus* and *video*. Latin gerundives (e.g. *memorandum*, *agenda*, *dividend*, *reverend*), almost always kept the orginal Latin sense of obligation (**agenda**: *things which must be done*).

Suffixes were formed from Latin models, such as -*ate*, which was an adjectival ending (e.g. *obstinate*, *desperate*), but now is more commonly used for verbs (e.g. *liberate*, *frustrate*). This ending comes from the past participle **liberatum, frustratum.** There are many other suffixes too, including the adjectival endings -*ible* and -*able* from -**ibilis** and -**abilis**, and some are added to non-Latin stems (e.g. *laughable*, *comfortable*). Prefixes figure in the importing of whole words, and are also added separately (e.g. *post-*, *trans-*, *inter-*, *contra-*, *sub-*, *pre-*). For a list of prepositions and prefixes, see p. 143.

Today, Latin's influence is often seen in technical subjects, in jargon

LATIN *Better Read Than Dead*

or pompous affectation. This might be expected of a language which has long been the vehicle for learning, science, law and officialdom. Yet Latin has also given us countless everyday words, and in the entire history of English, no other language has had, or continues to have, as much influence on our vocabulary.

192

Answers to Exercises

Chapter one
Practice A

1. **puella equum fugat** *the girl chases the horse*
2. **servum dominus fugat** *the master chases the slave*
3. **nautam femina fugat** *the woman chases the sailor*
4. **deus (dea) poetam fugat** *the god (goddess) chases the poet*

Practice B

1. **agricola cum tauro ambulat** *the farmer walks with the bull*
2. **equus in villa est** *the horse is in the villa*
3. **puella tauri faenum equo dat** *the girl gives the hay of the bull to the horse*
4. **poeta agricolae taurum deo dat** *the poet gives the bull of the farmer to the god*

Exercises

1. a) Accusative: *the farmer chases the slave*
   b) Nominative: *Augustus has a bull*
   c) Accusative: *Tiberius sees the woman*
   d) Ablative: *Julius is in Britain*
   e) Ablative: *the poet walks with the sailor*
   f) Genitive: *Tiberius' villa is in Italy*
   g) Accusative: *Julius chases Tiberius into Britain*
   h) Dative: *the sailor gives the bull to the god*
2. a) **agricolam** *the daughter walks towards the farmer*
   b) **equum** *the master gives the horse to the slave*
   c) **Britannia** *the sailor sees Augustus in Britain*
   d) **amico** *Julius walks with a friend*
   e) **Augusti** *Augustus' daughter has a horse in Italy*
3. In memory; forever.
4. Duet, dual, etc.
5. Annual, urban, omnibus, initial, unit, ligament, etc.

Chapter two
Practice

1. **agricolae taurum vident** *the farmers see the bull*
2. **agicolas taurus videt** *the bull sees the farmers*
3. **amici poetae taurum non vident** *the friends of the poet do not see the bull*
4. **nauta deam videt** *the sailor sees the goddess*

Exercises

1. a) Accusative: *Julius comes into the forum*
   b) Ablative: *the son is in the villa*
   c) Ablative: *the woman is with the girls*
   d) Ablative: *Tiberius walks out of the villa*
   e) Genitive: *Augustus' son is in Italy*
   f) Accusative: *the slave is drinking wine!*

2. a) **dat** *the girl gives water to the horse*
   b) **audit** *the goddess hears the poet*
   c) **capiunt** *the Carthaginians do not capture Rome*
   d) **laudat** *the master praises the daughter*
   e) **ducit** *the slave leads the bull to water*
   f) **vident** *the sailors see the poet in the forum*

3. a) **servus feminam videt**
   b) **agricola filios laudat**
   c) **filia Iulium audit**
   d) **Hannibal Italiam capit**
   e) **servus dominum orat**
   f) **puellae poetam amant**
   g) **Augustus imperium habet**

4. **exit** is singular and **exeunt** plural.

5. **loco**: ablative (*in the place of a parent*); **domini**: genitive (*in the year of the Lord*); **toto**: ablative (*in all*); **via**: ablative (*by way of*); **infinitum**: accusative (*forever*); **annum**: accusative (*each year*).

6. **videt, urbs, mittit, bellum, facit, bibit.**

Chapter three

Practice

1. **bonus** *the good man does not drink the wine*
2. **bonis** *the girl gives hay to the good horses*
3. **bonum** *the slave sees the good wine*
4. **bonas** *Augustus praises the good women*

Exercises

1. a) nom. neut. sing.: *wine is pleasing*
   b) acc. fem. sing.: *the poet sees the beautiful woman*
   c) gen. masc. sing.: *the slave does not love the master's cowardly son*
   d) abl. masc. pl.: *the farmer walks with the slaves*
   e) abl. fem. sing.: *there are many men in the villa*

2. a) **femina donum filiis dat** *the woman gives a gift to her sons*
   b) **nautae laeti amicum vident** *the happy sailors see their friend*
   c) **puella equos habet** *the girl has horses*
   d) **vir aquam cum servis bibit** *the man drinks water with the slaves*

194

e) **tauri in villam agricolam fugant** *the bulls chase the farmer into the villa*

f) **Augustus filios pios audit** *Augustus listens to his dutiful sons*

3. a) **Marcus est filius pius**

b) **Iulia poetam gratum audit**

c) **servi multi in foro ambulant**

d) **multa dona sunt Augusto**

e) **domini servos ignavos non laudant**

f) **agricola taurum iratum non fugat**

4. All are neuter plural.

5. Alexander the Great.

6. Knave.

7. Magnanimous, magnify, magnate, etc. Multiply, multiple, multilingual, etc. Avarice, avaricious, etc.

Chapter four

Practice

1. **vos non video**

2. **te amo**

3. **faenum est mihi**

4. **nostrum vinum bibis!**

Exercises

1. *Throw*: imperfect; *stood*: imperfect; *opened*: perfect; *was trying*: imperfect; *going to give*: future; *said*: perfect.

2. a) Nominative: *Augustus was the first princeps*

b) Dative: *Julius was my father*

c) Nominative: *we slaves are pleasing to Augustus*

d) Accusative: *the poet does not love me, but the beautiful woman*

e) Nominative: *Augustus is a friend to (of) the fatherland*

f) Genitive: *the cowardly slave is drinking your wine*

3. a) **magister te non videt**

b) **Augustus acerbum vinum non bibit**

c) **vos avari (estis), nos irati sumus**

d) **taurus nostrum superbus virum saevum fugat**

e) **non mihi erunt servi avari**

4. **ambitio**: ambition; **avaritia**: avarice; **vitia**: vice, etc.

5. Before midday; after midday; among other things; the course (record) of life.

6. The seventh, eighth, ninth and tenth months (before the addition of July and August).

Chapter five

Practice A

(a) We prepare; (b) we shall send; (c) you (pl.) advise; (d) he/she sends; (e) he/she (has) heard; (f) you (s.) (have) advised; (g) you (pl.) were preparing; (h) you (pl.) will hear.

Practice B
1. **audiebant** *the boys were not listening to the teacher*
2. **misit** *the man sent the slave into the amphitheatre*
3. **mittet** *the woman will send her husband*
4. **monebit** *the slave will warn Nero*

Exercises
1. a) **agricolae taurum viderunt** *the farmers saw the bull*
   b) **dona sunt puellae** *they are the gifts of the girl*
   c) **fortuna nobis est saeva** *fortune is cruel to us*
   d) **Augustum-ne vos audivistis?** *did you hear Augustus?*
   e) **filias Augusti ego laudabam** *I was praising the daughters of Augustus*
   f) **magistri pueros in forum ducent** *the teachers will lead the boys into the forum*
2. a) **sedebit** *the slave will sit in the kitchen*
   b) **spectabant** *the boys were watching the games in the amphitheatre*
   c) **dicet** *Augustus will speak to us in the forum*
   d) **vidit** *the woman saw (has seen) the girls in the garden*
   e) **audiverunt** *the farmers (have) heard the plan of Augustus*
   f) **erat** *the poet was not pleasing to Julia*
3. (a) **spectabant**; (b) **ducet**; (c) **vidit**; (d) **audivit**; (e) **monebit**; (f) **veniebat**.
4. a) **feminae consilium audivimus**
   b) **Augustus ad amphitheatrum venit**
   c) **dominus avarus, servi ignavi sunt**
   d) **dei vinum acerbum non bibent**
   e) **agricola in agro femina in horto laborat, sed servus vinum in culina bibit**
5. Pram.
6. Tilling/tending.
7. Culinary (**culina**): of the kitchen, cooking; puerile (**puer**): childish.
8. Preparation; oration; spectator; data; navigation; exculpate; laudatory; admonition; vision; habit; doctor; retention; session; mission; petition; reduction; diction; direction; inscription; audition; convention, etc.
9. Original: execution of one in every ten soldiers; modern: almost complete destruction.

Chapter six
Practice A
(a) 3rd; (b) 4th; (c) 3rd; (d) 5th.

Practice B
(a) **loci**; (b) **temporis**; (c) **meridiei**; (d) **anni**.

Practice C
1. **patris** *the horse is in father's villa*
2. **cives** *the leader sends the citizens to the fields*
3. **manibus** *the girl sees the gift in the hands of the boy*
4. **ducem** *the citizens do not fear the leader*

Exercises
1. a) **servi <u>canes</u>** [acc.] **fugant** *the slaves chase the dogs*
   b) **cives <u>ducem</u>** [acc.] **laudabant** *the citizens were praising the leader*
   c) **pater <u>matrem</u>** [acc.] **culpat** *the father blames the mother*
   d) **gladiator ducem <u>gemitu</u>** [abl.] **audiebat** *the gladiator listened to the leader with a groan*
   e) **dux <u>hostium</u>** [gen.] **ad Africam navigabat** *the leader of the enemy sailed towards Africa*
2. a) Nominative: *the soldiers chased the boys from the camp*
   b) Nominative: *the crimes of the slave were great*
   c) Accusative: *the slave saw the gift of Cicero*
   d) Accusative: *Marcus heard the groans of the enemy*
   e) Nominative: *the sisters of Iulius live in Gaul*
3. a) **pueri cum patre ambulant**
   b) **corpora gladiatorum vidimus**
   c) **canes cenam nostrum (nostri/nostram) spectabant**
   d) **fratres epistulam ad senatum mittent**
   e) **magna sunt munera deorum**
   f) **vos, o senatores, rem publicam amabatis!**
4. They are all related to: **pendo, pendere, pependi, pensum** (weigh, hang).

Chapter seven
Practice A
1. **pueri a matre monentur** *the boys are warned by the mother*
2. **canis a Augusto in villam fugatur** *the dog is chased by Augustus into the villa*
3. **gladiatores a femina laudantur** *the gladiators are praised by the woman*
4. **senator a civibus auditur** *the senator is heard by the citizens*

Practice B
1. **victi** *the enemy were conquered by Caesar*
2. **doctus** *the boy was taught by Seneca*
3. **missa** *the letter was sent by the mother*
4. **datum** *wine was given to Britannicus by a slave*

Practice C

1. **missae** *the girls, who were sent into the fields, did not see their mother* (lit. *the girls having been sent into the fields did not see their mother*)
2. **visum** *the bull saw the soldier in the field and chased him* (lit. *the bull chased the soldier having been seen in the field*)
3. **laudato** *the teacher praised the boy and gave him a gift* (lit. *the teacher gave a gift to the boy having been praised*)

Exercises

1. a) **laudati** *the boys were praised by the teacher*
   b) **amata** *the girl was loved by the poet*
   c) **audita** *the songs (poems) were heard by the emperor*
   d) **ducti** *the gladiators were led into the amphitheatre*
   e) **monitus** *Caesar was warned by his wife*
   f) **visum** *the wine was seen by the slave*
2. a) **cena a servo paratur** *the dinner is prepared by the slave*
   b) **gladiatores in amphitheatrum a milite ducuntur** *the gladiators are led into the amphitheatre by the soldier*
   c) **epistula a senatore scribitur** *the letter is written by the senator*
   d) **canes a femina culpantur** *the dogs are blamed by the woman*
   e) **gladiator a pueris spectatur** *the gladiator is watched by the boys*
   f) **munera a Iulio matri dantur** *gifts are given by Iulius to his mother*
3. a) **cena in culina parata est**
   b) **Roma numquam capta est**
   c) **hostes a Caesare victi sunt**
   d) **puellae a matre laudatae sunt**
   e) **epistula a senatore scripta est**
   f) **taurus in horto visus est**
4. **dictus**: addict, predict, edict, contradict, etc.
   factus: effect, defect, infect, etc.
   latus: translate, prelate, relate, collate, etc.
   missus: submission, permission, etc.
5. Relinquish, relic; computer, reputation, etc.

Chapter eight

Practice

1. a) *if I were a horse, I would eat hay* [3]
   b) *the citizens come to the amphitheatre to see the games* [4]
   c) *the teacher asks where Marcus is* [2]
   d) *the slaves should come to the fields at once* [1]

Exercises

1. a) **huius** *Fulvia is his (this man's) wife*

b) **hoc** *Caesar walks with him (this man)*
c) **haec** *she (this woman) is the sister of Clodius*
d) **hi** *they (these men) were led into the amphitheatre*
e) **haec** *the poet gave these (things) to the woman*
2. a) **ille** *he (that man) will come into Italy with an army*
   b) **illam** *Cicero did not love her (that woman)*
   c) **illos** *we saw them (those men) in the amphitheatre*
   d) **illorum** *we could hear their (those men's) groans*
   e) **illum** *do you want to see him (that man)?*
3. a) **eos** *the bull chased them*
   b) **ei** *Pliny used to give books to her*
   c) **eis** *Hannibal was seen by them*
   d) **id** *that is cruel*
   e) **eius** *have you heard his brother?*
4. a) **quis** *who sent the letter?*
   b) **cuius** *whose dog is in the amphitheatre?*
   c) **quibus** or **quo** *by whom were the Romans captured?*
   d) **quam** *the woman whom the poet loved used to live in this villa*
   e) **cui** *the girl to whom the poet was speaking was in the garden*
5. a) *the women, when they saw the men, were laughing*
   b) *the Greeks, as they say, are impudent*
   c) *I am not so foolish as to do that*
   d) *the emperor orders us to watch the games*
   e) *I am coming to see you*
   f) *when Caesar had reached Rome, he saw his wife*
   g) *when you see, you will know*
   h) *although these men are slaves, they are friends of Rome*
6. **veho-ere** *(carry)*; **volo, velle** *(want)*; **simul** *(at the same time)*.
7. French: le, la, les *(the)*; il, elle *(he/she)*; ils, elles *(they)*.
   Spanish: el, la, los, las *(the)*; él, ella *(he/she)*; ellos, ellas *(they)*.
   Etc.
8. That is; for this (special purpose); something for something.

Chapter nine
Practice A
1. **laetior**
2. **gratior**
3. **ignavior**

Practice B
1. **bibe** *drink the water*
2. **da** *give me the wine*

Exercises
1. a) **tristi:** dat. or abl. singular (any gender).
   b) **magni:** gen. singular, masc. or neut.; nom. masc. plural.
   c) **multa:** nom. or abl. fem. singular; nom. or acc. neut. plural.
   d) **breve:** nom. or acc. neut. singular.
   e) **facilium:** gen. plural (any gender).
   f) **mollis:** nom. masc. or fem. singular; gen. singular (any gender).
   g) **saevis:** dat. or abl. plural (any gender).
   h) **avidum:** acc. masc. or neut. singular; nom. neut. singular.
2. a) **vinum acerbum**
   b) **gravis res**
   c) **digna**
   d) **opus difficile**
   e) **praemia humilibus superbis**
   f) **imperatores laeti**
   g) **vultu tristi**
   h) **grata utilia**
3. a) **agricola est maior {quam servus**
   {servo
   b) **Cicero erat sapientior {quam Catilina**
   {Catilina
   c) **puellae-ne sunt fideliores {quam pueri?**
   {pueris?
   d) **viro meliori {quam Tiberio} nubere volo**
   {Tiberio}
   e) **poeta gratissimus sed ignavior {quam omnes servi} est**
   {omnibus servis}
4. **omnibus** (dative plural): for everyone.
5. Ancillary; native; optimist.
6. Digit: **digitus-i** (finger); reverberate: **verber-is** (blow, beating).

Chapter ten
Practice
1. acc. masc. sing.: *the master saw the slave as he was taking the wine*
2. abl. neut. sing. + acc. masc. sing.: *the master saw the slave sleeping after the wine had been taken*
3. acc. masc. sing.: *the master saw the slave on the point of taking the wine*

Exercises
1. a) Accusative: *the spectators saw Augustus as he was about to come into the amphitheatre*
   b) Ablative (Absolute): *the senators praised Nero upon hearing the prefect*
   c) Accusative: *I saw the poet as he was writing a letter*

200

   d) Accusative: *Caesar captured the Gauls and brought them to Rome*
   e) Accusative: *the enemy captured and burned the city*
2. a) **audito** *the senators were gloomy after listening to the advice of Caesar*
   b) **ferentem** *Hannibal saw the soldier as he was bringing the letter from the camp of the Romans*
   c) **fugiturus** *the slave heard the woman as he was about to run away*
3. a) **Augustus Antonio occiso princeps creatus/factus est**
   b) **nos visuri/visurae (spectaturi/spectaturae) gladiatores in amphitheatro eramus**
   c) **his dictis Caesar tacitus erat/tacebat**
   d) **servus {in animo cenam parare habens} in villam venit**
         {cenam paraturus}
   e) **vir feminam in agris laborantem vidit**
4. We who are about to die salute you.
5. Ferrous: **ferrum-i** (*steel*); bestial: **bestia-ae** (*beast*); disturb: **turba-ae** (*crowd*); polite: **politus-a-um** (*refined*).
6. An essential condition (lit. *without which not...*).
7. **volo, velle** (*want, wish*); **volito-are** (*fly*).

Chapter eleven
Practice
a) *children should be seen and not heard* [3]
b) *the wine of the master should not be drunk* [4]
c) *the poet should not be praised by soldiers* [1]
d) *the show in the amphitheatre ought to be seen* [2]

Exercises
1. a) **laudandus** *Cicero ought to be praised*
   b) **audienda** *the songs should be heard after dinner*
   c) **laudandos** *Caesar came (comes) into the temple to praise the gods* (lit. *for the gods to-be-praised*)
   d) **bibendum** *wine should not be drunk by slaves*
2. a) **laborandum** *now is the time for working*
   b) **vivendum** *now is the time for living*
   c) **dormiendum** *now is the time for sleeping*
   d) **agendum** *now is the time for doing*
3. a) **hortari milites conatus/conata sum**
   b) **ante meridiem profecti/profectae sumus**
   c) **cena servis paranda est**
   d) **Caesar Gallos hortatus est**
   e) **ex urbe ad Ciceronis villam profecti/profectae sumus**
4. **amanda:** fem. sing. of **amandus-a-um** (*to-be-loved*)
   miranda: fem. sing. of **mirandus-a-um** (*to-be-admired*)

memorandum: neut. sing. of **memorandus-a-um** (*to-be-related*)
referendum: neut. sing. of **referendus-a-um** (*to-be-referred*)
addendum: neut. sing. of **addendus-a-um** (*to-be-added*)
agenda: neut. pl. of **agendus-a-um** (*to-be-done*)

5. When the things which ought to be be changed (**mutandis**) have been changed (**mutatis**).
6. That which had to be shown.

Chapter twelve
Practice
1. **dixit Brutum Ciceronem vidisse**
2. **dixit servos cenam paraturos esse**
3. **Marcus dixit se esse civem Romanum**

Exercises
1. a) **Romani vincent**
   b) **omnes Romani sunt inimici**
   c) **Nero omnium principum avarissimus erat**
   d) **hospites post cenam carmina (mei/mea) audient**
   e) **milites nimium laudati sunt**
2. a) **Cloelia dixit amicos in Gallia habitare**
   b) **Cloelia dixit imperatorem hodie/illo die in amphitheatrum venturum esse**
   c) **Cloelia dixit Antonium epistulam ad Cleopatram misisse**
   d) **Cloelia dixit orationes validiores quam arma esse**
   e) **Cloelia dixit consilium a senatoribus auditum iri**
3. a) **(ea/illa/haec) dixit se Romam ire velle**
   b) **Iulius dixit matrem cenam paraturam esse**
   c) **Clodius dixit se Ciceroni amicum esse**
   d) **servi militibus dixerunt Ciceronem in Graecia esse**
   e) **milites Antonio dixit Ciceronem abesse**
4. **nota bene** (*note well*); **exempli gratia** (*by way of an example*); **post scriptum** (*postscript*).
5. Library: **liber** (*book*); computer: **cum + puto-are** (*calculate or consider things taken together*); current: **curro-ere** (*run*); rodent: **rodo-ere** (*gnaw*); quality: **qualis** (*just like*).

Chapter thirteen
Practice
1. **laborandum** *the slave is fit for working*
2. **bibendum** *the slave is fit for drinking*
3. **pugnandum** *the soldier is fit for fighting*
4. **fugiendum** *the soldier is fit for running away*

Exercises
1. a) **Plinius ipse Christianis dixit**
   b) **Marcus milites secum in amphitheatro habebat**
   c) **simulacrum ipsius imperatoris vidi**
   d) **Nero sibi dona omnia dedit**
   e) **gladiator gladium militi tradidit**
2. Manner of living; manner of working; do not give up (lit. nothing to-be-despaired).
3. Courage: **cor, cordis** (*heart*); trade: **trado-ere** (*hand over*); interrogation: **interrogo-are** (*interrogate*); sermon: **sermo-nis** (*conversation*); contribution: **tributum-i** (*payment*).
4. By itself/themselves; among themselves; by the deed itself.
5. Prefer, infer, suffer, offer, differ (dis-), confer, refer, defer, transfer, interfere, etc. Affect, defect, infect, effect, perfect, prefect, etc.
6. **fragilis** *frail*; **radius** *ray*; **dignitas** *dainty*; **caput** *chattel*; **computo** *count*.

English Translations

1 Early Rome

1. In the beginning the Trojans founded and held the city of Rome.
2. Lavinia the daughter of Latinus was given in marriage to Aeneas.
3. The city was called by the name of its founder.
4. He appoints one hundred senators. They were called fathers.
5. From the beginning kings held the city of Rome.
6. Tarquinius Superbus ruled for twenty-five years.
7. Two consuls were then appointed, Lucius Iunius Brutus and Lucius Tarquinius Collatinus.
8. The children of the consul stood bound to a stake.
9. The bridge almost gave a passage to the enemy, had it not been for one man, Horatius Cocles.
10. Cloelia swam across the Tiber and restored them all safely to their relatives.

2 Carthage

1. The war was the most memorable of all.
2. On the ninth day they reached the summit of the Alps.
3. Hannibal shows Italy to the soldiers.
4. In Rome there was a stampede of people into the forum amid much panic and din.
5. After this battle he set out for Rome and met no resistance; he stopped in the mountains near to the city.
6. You know how to conquer, Hannibal, you do not know how to make use of victory.
7. Dido and the Trojan leader come to the same cave.
8. Does his father begrudge Ascanius the Roman citadels?
9. I do not make for Italy of my own free will.
10. Go, chase Italy with the winds [i.e. sail], seek the lands across the waves.
11. Phoenician Dido, fresh from her wounding, was wandering in a large wood.
12. At last she hurried away and fled back in an unfriendly manner.

3 Greece

1. The Macedonian war took the place of the Carthaginian peace.
2. After the herald's voice had been heard, there was joy.
3. Hannibal, a refugee from his own country, had come to Antiochus.
4. When Greece was captured, she [in turn] captivated her wild conqueror and brought the arts to rustic Latium.
5. In Greece first of all, civilization, literature and even crops are believed to have been discovered.
6. Nowadays I hear too many people praising and admiring the ornaments of Corinth and Athens.
7. But the Roman community never had a plethora of writers, because all the best

204

people preferred action to talking.

8. Others will more delicately fashion bronze statues – [as if they were] breathing – (Oh yes I believe it) and they will bring to life faces from marble.

9. You, Roman, remember to rule the nations with your power (these skills will be <u>yours</u>), and to build an orderly life on a foundation of peace, to spare the conquered and subdue the proud.

10. There are in that number many good, learned and modest men, but also shameless, uneducated and frivolous ones. I make this point about the whole race of Greeks: I concede to them their literature, I grant them their knowledge of many arts. But that nation has never encouraged the sacredness and reliability of evidence [given in court].

11. Laocoon in a rage ran down from the topmost citadel and from afar [cried] 'O wretched citizens, why such madness? Whatever that is, I fear Greeks even when bearing gifts.'

12. Teacher, professor, surveyor, painter, masseur, soothsayer, tight-rope artist, doctor, sorcerer – the hungry Greek chappie is a proper know-all.

13. The whole country is given to acting. You smile, and he [the Greek] roars with laughter; then he weeps if he has seen a friend's tears but he does not grieve.../...if you say 'I am hot', he sweats.

4   O Tempora O Mores

1. At first ambition rather than greed exercised the minds of men.
   At first there grew a desire of [for] money, then of [for] power. Greed ruined trust, decency and other good qualities.
   We can bear neither our vices nor the remedies.

2. Let us live, my Lesbia, and let us love, and let us value all the gossip of austere old men at a halfpenny.

3. At this time, we are contemplating defending Catiline, our fellow-candidate. We have the judges we wanted and the utmost goodwill of the prosecutor.

4. All the common people, with enthusiasm of [for] revolution, approved of Catiline's initiative.

5. Meanwhile he did not remain quiet, but prepared ambush for Cicero by all methods.

6. What times! What moral standards! The senate understands these things, the consul sees them: and still this man lives. Lives? Why, he even comes into the senate.

7. Here, they are here in our midst, senators.

8. How many times indeed have you tried to kill me, the consul!

9. I have saved the life of every citizen by the punishment of five crazed and desperate men.

10. I expected some thanks in your letter.

11. Clodius is hostile to me. Pompey assures [me] that he [Clodius] will do nothing against me. It is dangerous for me to believe [it], [and] I am preparing myself for resistance.

12. Pompey tells us not to worry about Clodius.
13. If only I might see that day when I may give thanks to you because you compelled me to live!
14. Gentlemen of the jury, the whole matter in this case of ours rests with Clodia, a woman not only noble but also notorious.
15. First and foremost I seek from you [an opportunity] to see you.
16. My dear Atticus, I fear that the Ides of March have given us nothing except joyous relief.
17. However, I certainly want to keep my friendship with Antony, and I shall write to him, but not before I see you.
18. As a young man I defended the republic, I shall not abandon it as an old man; I scorned the swords of Catiline: I shall not fear yours.
19. The boy Caesar is outstanding.
20. So Octavius may well call Cicero his father, refer everything [to him], and praise and thank [him], but it will become apparent that his words are at odds with his actions.
21. All posterity will admire what Cicero has written about you, and will curse your action against him; more quickly will the race of men fade away from the world than will Cicero.

5 Augustus

1. The armed forces of Lepidus and Antony surrendered to Augustus who in the name of princeps took charge of everything [which had been] exhausted by civil wars.
2. I did not accept the dictatorship, [which was] offered to me by both the people and the senate.
3. I banished into exile those men who murdered my parent.
4. Some write that three hundred men were slaughtered in the manner of sacrificial victims on the Ides of March at the altar constructed in honour of Divine Julius [Caesar].
5. I re-introduced many precedents of our ancestors.
6. He restored sacred shrines [which had] collapsed with age or been destroyed by fire; these and other [temples] he decorated with most lavish gifts.
7. Now let there be drinking, now let us dance upon the earth with unfettered feet.
8. Indeed not even his friends deny that he practised acts of adultery.
9. He discovered the plans of opponents through the wives of each one.
10. He himself administered justice assiduously, sometimes into the night.
11. He decimated the cohorts, if any had given ground in battle, and fed them with barley.
12. A decree went out from Caesar Augustus that the whole world should be registered.
13. Because Thallus had received five hundred denarii for leaking a letter, Augustus broke his legs.
14. He beat Hylas, a pantomime artist, in the hall of his own house with whips.

15. Here is the man whom you often hear being promised to you, here is Augustus Caesar, offspring of a god, [who] will found a golden age.
16. I sing of arms and the man who, by fate a fugitive from the shores of Troy, first came to Italy and the Latin shores.
17. It was now almost the day when Caesar ordered me to depart from the territories of outermost Italy.
18. Marcus Cicero was by chance recounting a dream of the night before to some friends: a boy with a noble face was sent down from heaven on a golden chain and stood at the doors of the Capitol, and to him Jupiter handed a rod; then, on suddenly seeing Augustus, he declared that he was the one [in the dream].

6   The family

1. I am hurrying to my daughter. I believe she does not know me.
2. At the age of eleven Nero was adopted by Claudius.
3. In his early youth Agricola would have drained [the cup of] philosophical studies too keenly – beyond what was conceded to a Roman and senator – if the good sense of his mother had not restrained his inflamed and burning spirit.
4. Veturia, the mother of Coriolanus, and Volumnia, carrying two small sons, went into the camp of the enemy. When they came to the camp and it was announced to Coriolanus that a huge crowd of women was present, he was at first much more stubborn against the female tears. Then one of his attendants happened to recognise Veturia in the midst of the other women: 'Unless my eyes deceive me,' he said, 'your mother, wife and children are present.'
5. And yet he knew what the barbarian torturer was preparing for him. Nevertheless he removed relatives blocking his path and people delaying his return, just as if he were [a lawyer] leaving the long-winded business of clients, with the case decided, and stretching away towards the Venafran fields or Spartan Tarentum.
6. Why does your personal grief disturb you so? [Look at] what has been taken from us – things which ought to be no less dear to people than their children – the state, our honour, prestige and all our public offices. Yes, it is bad to lose children, bad indeed. But these other [losses] are harder to suffer and endure.
7. The poison pervaded all his limbs in such a way that his voice and breath were taken at the same time. Most people were inclined to forgive the crime, putting it down to long-standing feuds of the brothers and a kingdom [which was] impossible to divide.
8. The mother revives the ash and sleeping embers, by lamplight adding the night to her chores, and puts the maids to work with the time-consuming portion of wool [i.e. to keep them occupied], so that she can keep the bed of her husband chaste and bring up her small sons.
9. Someone was punishing his son because he was buying horses and dogs a little too extravagantly. I said to this man, after the boy had departed, 'Hey, have you never done something which could be criticised by your father? "Have you

done" do I say? Do you not sometimes do what your son, if he suddenly became your father, and you his son, would scold with equal sternness?'

10. This morning I greeted you by chance with your real name, Caecilianus, and did not say 'My master'. Do you want to know how much such licence is costing me? That has taken a hundred farthings away from me.

11. No one attends you for yourself, but for some advantage from you. Previously friendship was sought, now it's [your] loot; lonely old men will change their wills and the attentive visitor will move to another threshold.

7 Society

1. In those days senators were in the fields.

2. 'Raising livestock well.' What second? 'Raising livestock well enough.' What third? 'Raising livestock badly.' What fourth? 'Ploughing.' And when he who had asked had said 'What of money-lending?' then Cato replied 'What about murdering someone?'

3. Happy is he who far from business affairs, like the ancient race of mortals, works his father's land with his oxen, free from all interest repayment; it pleases him to lie now under the old oak tree, now on the clinging grass.

4. For neither old men nor boys easily endure the scarcity of footpaths and the steepness and unevenness of mountains.

5. If an enterprise is small it should be considered paltry; but if large and profitable then it is not to be despised. Of all things, however, from which a living is made, nothing is better than agriculture, nothing more fruitful, nothing sweeter, nothing more worthy of a free man.

6. This [slave] causes canes to break, that one is red from the whip, this one from the strap.

7. In this animal [a lamprey], the Roman knight Vedius Pollio found [new] forms of cruelty, plunging condemned slaves into pools of them.

8. Nothing arouses and stimulates affection as much as fear of loss.

9. It is more profitable to cultivate difficult places with hired hands than with slaves.

10. 'What are you up to?' he said, 'Do you think I am a pack-animal or a ship which transports stone? I have contracted the duties of a man, not a horse. I am no less a free man than yourselves, even if my father did leave me a pauper.' And not content with his abuse he then lifted one foot higher and simultaneously filled the road with an obscene noise and smell.

11. You have assets of 100,000. I offer you the sum of 300,000 sesterces to make up the knights' property qualification.

12. He who was reclining next to me noticed, and asked whether I approved. I said no. 'So what custom do you follow?' he said. 'I serve the same to everyone; for I invite [them] to dinner, not a social grading, and I regard as equal in all things those whom I have made equal at the table and couch.' 'Even freedmen?' 'Even they; for at that time I consider them table-companions, not freedmen.' And he [said]: 'It must cost you a lot.' 'Not at all.' 'How can it

be?' 'Because, of course, my freedmen do not drink the same as I do, but I [drink] the same as the freedmen.'

8 Women

1. Yet I want to hear for what reason women, all agitated, have charged into public [places], and barely keep themselves from the forum and the assembly? Once they ·start to be our equals, they will immediately be our superiors.
2. Do you want to impose this competition on your wives, Romans, that rich [women] want to have that which no other [woman] can [have]; [and that] poor [women], so as not to be despised because of this very thing, overreach themselves beyond their means?
3. You do not allow the lady of your household to have a purple cloak, and your horse will be clothed more lavishly than your wife is dressed.
4. WIFE: I am an object of scorn.

   OLD MAN: Says who?

   WIFE: He to whom you entrusted me, my husband.

   OLD MAN: Oh, more bickering! How many times, pray, have I made it clear to you that you should take care that neither of you come to me with a complaint?

   WIFE: How can I see to that, father?

   OLD MAN: Are you asking me?

   WIFE: If you don't mind.

   OLD MAN: How many times have I pointed out to you that you should humour your husband, not observe what he does, where he goes or what he gets up to.

   WIFE: But you see, he is making love to a prostitute here next door.

   OLD MAN: He has good sense, and I'll warrant he will love her even more because of your interference.

   WIFE: And he drinks there.

   OLD MAN: Will he drink any less on your account? Since he keeps you in gold and well-dressed, and furnishes you properly with maids and provisions, it is better, woman, to keep a balanced judgement.
5. You ask that I should watch out for a husband for the daughter of your brother.
6. More troublesome is that woman who as soon as she reclines at table volunteers a lit crit of Virgil. The teachers duck, the professors are seen off, and not one of the lot of them can get a word in.
7. She has my books, reads them repeatedly, and even learns them by heart.
8. Oh sorrowful and bitter misfortune of the Helvidian sisters! Both have died in

childbirth, both having given birth to daughters. I am afflicted by grief, but I do not grieve beyond measure; it seems sorrowful to me that fruitfulness has taken away most honourable girls in their first flowering.

9. Boudicca, carrying her daughters before her in the chariot, declared that it was indeed customary for Britons to go to war under the leadership of women; in that battle it was a matter of victory or death; that was a woman's decision: the men might live and be slaves if they so wished.

10. Learn what kind of attention improves the face, girls. And in what way your beauty is to be preserved. But it is not unworthy: there should be a concern to please amongst you, since our age has well-groomed men.

9 Education

1. But now at birth a baby is entrusted to some little Greek maid, and some [slave] or other [picked] from the entire staff is allocated to her [as an assistant], very often [an individual who is] quite worthless and unsuitable for any serious task. By the fanciful stories and misconceptions of these people, straight away the tender and impressionable minds are tainted; and no one in the entire household cares a jot what he says or does in the presence of the little master.

2. Let there be another student, whom he may envy; from time to time he should compete, and more often than not think he is successful; he should also be encouraged with rewards, which that age-group welcomes.

3. What is it with you, you miserable schoolmaster, hateful creature to boys and girls? Not yet have the crested cocks broken the silence, and already you are disturbing the peace with your harsh growling and wallopings. We neighbours do not ask for sleep all night long: you know, to be awake is neither here nor there, but to lie awake the whole night is no joke. Dismiss your students. Tell me, you chatterbox, do you want to earn what you are paid to make your din – just to keep you quiet?

4. He who teaches you these things is a mutton head, not a master. For our teacher used to say 'Are your things safe? Go straight home; be sure not to look behind you; see that you don't cheek your elders.'

5. Rare is the pay that does not need a court-order of the tribune. But you [parents] impose your strict laws, that the standards of correct speech be met by the teacher, that he read the histories, that he know all the authors like the back of his hand.

6. 'You should attend to these matters,' he says, 'and when the year has turned its cycle, receive the gold which the people demand for a champion.'

7. He did not want to send me to Flavius' school, where great boys born from great centurions went, but dared to take his son to Rome, to be instructed in the arts.

8. Moreover I have begun to declaim Greek with Cassius; however, I wish to have my Latin training with Bruttius.

9. But I seek from you that a clerk may be sent to me as quickly as possible,

preferably a Greek; much of the work in taking notes will then be taken from me.

10   Leisure

1. You will dine well, Fabullus, at my place in a few days if the gods are kind to you and if you bring with you a tasty and large dinner, not forgetting a pretty girl, wine, wit and all your jokes. Bring these and I tell you, dear boy, you'll have a great dinner: your old Catullus' wallet is full – of cobwebs.
2. Whatever is placed [there] you sweep away this way and that. When these things are hidden in your dripping napkin they are handed over to a slave to be taken home, while the whole lot of us do nothing but lie here. If there is any shame, put back the dinner!
3. I am putting on the *Mother-in-law* again for you, which I was never allowed to produce in silence: thus did disaster overtake it. Your good sense, if it will be an aid to our efforts, will prevent that disaster [happening again].
4. For what pleasure do the six hundred mules in *Clytaemnestra* have [for us], or the three thousand bowls in the *Trojan Horse*?
5. A foul shower drenches his face, and his mutilated head spurts much blood from his torn veins.
6. But what pleasure can there be for a refined person when either a weak man is torn apart by a very powerful beast or a magnificent animal skewered with a spear?
7. Indeed nothing is so damaging to good behaviour as sitting idly at some show. For then through the thrills do vices more easily make their stealthy advance.
8. They keep the survivor for another killing. The end for those fighting is death; the job is finished with steel and fire. These things happen while the arena is empty. 'But some person has committed a robbery, has killed a person.' So what? Because he has committed murder, he has deserved to suffer this; but what have you done, poor man, to deserve to watch it? 'Kill, flog, burn! Why does he run on to the blade so timidly? Why doesn't he kill more boldly? Why doesn't he die more willingly?' The show has an interval: 'In the meantime let some fellows have their throats cut, so that at least something is going on.'
9. What good has that man done for us? He produced gladiators worth tuppence, already decrepit, who, had you blown on them, would have collapsed; I have seen better animal-fighters before now. In fact, afterwards they were all flogged.
10. He produced many and various kinds of shows: coming-of-age celebrations, races, theatrical performances, and gladiatorial show[s].

11   Britain

1. Of all these [tribes] by far the most civilized are those who inhabit Kent. This region is entirely by the sea, and they do not differ much from Gallic custom. Those who live inland for the most part do not sow corn, but live off milk and meat, and are clothed in skins. All Britons stain themselves with woad, which produces a sky-blue colour, and with this appearance are more

frightening in battle; their hair is grown long and they shave all parts of their body except their head and upper lip. They share their wives with each other, in groups of ten or twelve, especially brothers with brothers and parents with offspring; but those who are born from these [groups] are considered [to be] the children of those to whom each girl was first escorted [in marriage].

2. There is not the smallest piece of silver on that island nor any hope of resources except from slaves.

3. I shall visit the Britons who are savage to guests.

4. Augustus will be considered a god here and now, once the Britons and threatening Persians have been added to the empire.

5. Divine Julius was first of all the Romans to invade Britain with an army, and although he intimidated the natives with a military victory and occupied the shore, it can be seen that he revealed [Britain] to posterity but did not bequeath it; soon [there were] civil wars and the weapons of the leaders [were] turned against the republic, and there was long neglect of Britain even in peace: Divine Augustus called it policy, Tiberius a doctrine.

6. I had horses, men, weapons and wealth: why [is it] extraordinary if I have let go of these things unwillingly? Just because you wish to rule over everyone, does it follow that everyone should welcome slavery?

7. Under a woman's leadership (you see they do not discriminate between the sexes in matters of authority) they all took up arms.

8. It is believable that the Gauls occupied the neighbouring island. The language is not much different, there is the same boldness in facing dangers and, when these [dangers] have arrived, the same fear in avoiding [them]. However, the Britons display more ferocity, because long standing peace has not yet made them soft. For we have heard that the Gauls were also successful in war; but in due course idleness arrived with peace, and their courage disappeared along with their liberty. This happened to those of the Britons who were conquered some time ago: others remain as the Gauls were.

9. [In Britain] the sky is dirty with frequent rain-clouds and mists; the harshness of chill is absent.

10. Those who recently rejected the Roman language now wanted to be fluent. There was a gradual collapse to the allurements of vices, of colonnades, baths and the sophistication of dinner-parties. The foolish called this civilization, although in fact it was part of their slavery.

12 Religion

1. Each man puts one doorkeeper at his door, and because he is a man he is quite sufficient: those people [i.e. pagans] have placed three gods, Forculus for the gate, Cardea for the hinge and Limentinus for the threshold. So Forculus was unable to look after the hinge and the threshold at the same time.

2. There is a hallway right at the mouth of the entrance to Hades. Here have Grief and vengeful Worries placed their beds; here are Diseases which make

you pale, and gloomy Old Age, and Fear and evil-counselling Hunger and disgraceful Need, shapes terrible to see, and Death and Toil.

3. The harsh mother of the Cupids and the son of Theban Semele and playful Wantonness insist I restore my inclination for passions [which I thought were] finished.

4. Fortuna, delighting in her savage work and persistently playing her wanton game switches her fickle favours, now kind to me now to another.

5. Fortuna, we make you a goddess and place you in heaven.

6. We will endure losses, distress, humiliations, overseas postings, bereavements and divorces – things which do not overwhelm a wise man even if they all come together.

7. Mouse is a syllable. A mouse, however, gnaws cheese; a syllable, therefore, gnaws cheese. There is cause for concern: if I am too careless, a book may gobble up the cheese.

8. Do not ask how the gods are going to end your life or mine, Leuconoe. It's not for us to know. And don't trouble yourself with Babylonian charts..... Be wise, decant some wine, and trim your long-term plans to a brief span. Even while we chat, hateful Time has skipped on. Enjoy the moment – and place as little trust as you can in tomorrow.

9. O Fountain of Bandusia, brighter than crystal, deserving sweet wine and flowers, tomorrow you will be offered a young kid whose forehead reveals the first swellings of horns and foretells mating and jousts – in vain. This offspring of the playful flock is to colour your cool streams with its red blood.

10. He struggles to tear open the knots with his hands, his headband spattered with slaver and black poison, and in the same moment he raises horrendous cries to the stars: just like the bellowing of a wounded bull when it has fled the altar and shaken off the ill-aimed axe from its neck.

11. She finished speaking, and slipping her snow-white arms this way and that she wraps him up in a cuddle. He hesitates. Then suddenly he felt the familiar spark, and the well-known warmth penetrated his innermost core and darted through his trembling bones.

12. On this side Augustus Caesar is leading the Italians into battle, with the senators and the people, with the household gods and the great gods.

13. Though undeserving, you will atone for the sins of your ancestors, Roman, until you have rebuilt the temples, the collapsing shrines of the gods and the statues soiled with black smoke.

14. 'Oh dear!' he said. 'I think I am becoming a god.'

13 Christianity

1. The chief priests sent tricksters to pretend that they were fair-minded, so that they might catch him out in conversation and hand him over to the power and authority of the governor. And they interrogated him, saying 'Master, we know that you speak and teach rightly: is it permitted for us to give a tribute to

Caesar or not?' But he was aware of their trick and said to them: 'Why do you tempt me? Show me a denarius: whose likeness and inscription [is on the coin]?' Answering him they said: 'Caesar's.' And he said to them: 'So give to Caesar what is Caesar's: and what is God's to God.' And they, in the presence of the people, were unable to find fault with his argument: and amazed at his response, they fell silent.

2. And again I say to you: it is easier for a camel to go through the eye of a needle than for a rich man to enter the kingdom of heaven.

3. So to get rid of the rumour, Nero trumped up defendants and with very far-fetched punishments afflicted those whom, hated for their crimes, people called Christians. Christ, the founder of that name, had been put to death when Tiberius was emperor, on the orders of Pontius Pilate the procurator. For a while the deadly superstition was checked, but then broke out again, not only in Judaea, the source of this evil, but also in Rome where from every corner all things sleaze-ridden and shameful ooze together and come into vogue.

4. As for those brought before me on the charge of being Christians, I followed this procedure: I asked them whether they were Christians. Those who freely admitted it were asked a second and third time, and threatened with the death-penalty. If they persisted I had them taken away and executed. For I was in no doubt that at least their stubbornness and inflexible obstinacy ought to be punished.

5. An anonymous leaflet was put in front of me containing the names of many people. Those who denied that they were or had been Christians, and who, with me reciting first, called upon the gods, I thought should be released.

6. I believed it necessary to extract what was the truth from two maidservants – and that through torture – who were called deaconesses. But I found nothing other than a depraved and excessive superstition.

7. They are not to be sought out; but if they are charged and convicted, they are to be punished.

8. When interrogated as to where I stood I replied that I was a Christian, and he who sat [in judgement] said 'You are lying, you are a Ciceronian not a Christian; where your library is, there is your soul.'

GENERAL VOCABULARY

a, ab *by, from*
abnuo-ere-nui *reject*
aboleo-ere-olevi-olitum *destroy*
abstineo-ere-stinui-stentum *restrain*
absum, abesse, afui *be absent*
absumo-ere-sumpsi-sumptum *consume*
ac *and*
accedo-ere-cessi-cessum *approach*
accendo-ere-cendi-censum *stimulate, inflame*
accipio-ere-cepi-ceptum *take possession of, receive*
accumbo-ere-cubui-cubitum *recline, lay oneself down*
accusator-is [m.] *prosecutor*
acer-cris-cre *keen, sharp*
acerbus-a-um *bitter*
acies-ei [f.] *battle-line, sight*
acquiro-ere-quisivi-quisitum *acquire*
acus-us [f.] *needle, pin*
ad [+ acc.] *to, towards*
adcommodatus-a-um *suited*
addo-ere-didi-ditum *add*
adeo *very much, to such an extent*
adficio-ere-feci-fectum *afflict, inflict upon*
adhibeo [2] *apply*
adicio-ere-ieci-iectum *add*
adiungo-ere-iunxi-iunctum *attach*
adiutrix-icis [f.] *assistant*
adorno [1] *decorate*
adsum-esse-fui *be present*
adulescens-ntis [m.] *young man*
adulteria-ae [f.] *adultery*
advenio-ire-veni-ventum *arrive*
adversarius-i [m.] *opponent*
adversus [+ acc.] *against*
aedes-is [f.] *shrine*
aeque *as much, equally*
aequo [1] *make equal*
aes, aeris [n.] *bronze*
aestimo [1] *value, estimate*
aestuo [1] *be hot*
aetas, aetatis [f.] *age, time*
affero-ferre, attuli, allatum *bring*
affirmo [1] *declare*

ager, agri [m.] *field, land*
agmen-inis [n.] *crowd, column*
ago-ere, egi, actum *do, act, perform, lead*
agrestis-e *rustic*
agricola-ae [m.] *farmer*
ait *he/she says*
aliptes-ae [m.] *masseur*
aliquis-quid *someone, something*
aliter *otherwise*
alius-a-ud *other*
alter-era-erum *other (of two)*
altus-a-um *high, deep*
ambitio-nis [f.] *ambition*
ambulo [1] *walk*
amens [adj.] *crazed*
amica-ae [f.] *friend (female)*
amicitia-ae [f.] *friendship*
amiculum-i [n.] *cloak*
amicus-i [m.] *friend (male)*
amitto-ere-misi-missum *let go, lose*
amo [1] *love, like*
amor-is [m.] *love, affection*
amphitheatrum-i [n.] *amphitheatre*
amplexus-us [m.] *embrace*
amplius *more*
an *whether, or*
ancilla-ae [f.] *maidservant*
anima-ae [f.] *soul, life-breath*
animadverto-ere-verti-versum *observe*
animal-is [n.] *animal*
animus-i [m.] *mind, will*
annus-i [m.] *year*
ante [+acc.] *before*
antequam *before*
antiquus-a-um *former, ancient*
aperio [4] *open, reveal*
appareo [2] *be apparent, appear*
appello [1] *call*
aptus-a-um *suited, fit*
apud [+acc.] *among, with*
aqua-ae [f.] *water*
ara-ae [f.] *altar*
aranea-ae [f.] *cobweb*
ardeo-ere, arsi *burn, rage*
arduitas-tatis [f.] *steepness*
argentum-i [n.] *silver*

arguo-ere-ui-utum *show, prove*
arma-orum [n.] *weapons*
aro [1] *plough*
ars, artis [f.] *art, skill*
artus-us [m.] *limb*
arx, arcis [f.] *citadel*
as, assis [m.] *farthing (smallest coin)*
aspectus-us [m.] *appearance*
asperitas-tatis [f.] *harshness*
assidue *assiduously*
at *but*
ater-tra-trum *black*
atque *and*
atqui *and yet*
atrium-i [n.] *hall*
atrox, atrocis [adj.] *atrocious*
auctor-is [m.] *founder*
audacia-ae [f.] *boldness*
audacter *boldly*
audeo-ere, ausus sum *dare*
audio [4] *hear*
aufero-ferre, abstuli, ablatum *take off, take away, carry*
augur-is [m.] *soothsayer*
auratus-a-um *adorned in gold*
aureus-a-um *golden*
aurum-i [n.] *gold*
aut, aut...aut *or, either...or*
autem *however, but*
avaritia-ae [f.] *greed*
avarus-a-um *greedy*
avidus-a-um *greedy*
balineum-i [n.] *bath*
beatus-a-um *happy*
bello [1] *go to war*
bellum-i [n.] *war*
bene *well*
benignus-a-um *kind*
bestia-ae [f.] *beast*
bestiarius-i [m.] *animal-fighter*
bibo-ere, bibi *drink*
bonus-a-um *good*
bos, bovis [c.] *ox*
brevis-e *short*
caballus-i [m.] *horse*
cachinnus-i [m.] *laugh*
cado-ere, cecidi, casum *fall*
caedes-is [f.] *killing*
caedo-ere, cecidi, caesum *beat, kill*
caelum-i [n.] *sky, heaven*

caeruleus-a-um *sky-blue*
calamitas-tatis [f.] *disaster*
callis-is [m.] *footpath*
calor-is [m.] *warmth, heat*
camelus-i [m.] *camel*
candidus-a-um *bright*
canis-is [c.] *dog*
cano-ere, cecini, cantum *sing*
capillus-i [m.] *hair*
capio-ere, cepi, captum *take, capture*
captivus-i [m.] *captive*
caput, capitis [n.] *head*
cardo-inis [m.] *hinge*
careo [+ abl.] [2] *lose, lack*
carmen-inis [n.] *song*
caro, carnis [f.] *flesh*
carpo-ere, carpsi, carptum *reap*
carus-a-um *dear*
caseus-i [m.] *cheese*
castigo [1] *punish*
castra-orum [n.] *camp*
castus-a-um *chaste*
casus-us [m.] *fortune, chance*
catena-ae [f.] *chain*
causa-ae [f.] *cause, case*
caveo-ere, cavi, cautum *look out (for)*
cedo-ere, cessi, cessum *yield, give way*
celebro [1] *practise*
celer [adj.] *quick*
cena-ae [f.] *dinner*
ceno [1] *dine*
census-us [m.] *assets*
centum *hundred*
certamen-inis [n.] *competition*
certe *certainly, at least*
cervix-icis [f.] *neck*
ceterus-a-um *other*
cinis-eris [m.] *ash*
circumspicio-ere-spexi-spectum *look around*
citius *more quickly*
civilis-e *civil*
civis-is [c.] *citizen*
clamo [1] *shout*
clamor-is [m.] *shout, cry*
cliens-ntis [m.] *client*
coepi-episse-eptum *begin*
coerceo [2] *restrain*
cogito [1] *think, contemplate*
cognitio-nis [f.] *inquiry*

cognosco-ere-novi-nitum *discover*
cogo-ere-egi, coactum *compel*
cohors-tis [f.] *troop*
colo-ere-ui, cultum *cultivate*
comedo-esse-edi-esum *gobble up*
commendo [1] *improve, enhance*
commoveo-ere-movi-motum *disturb*
communis-e *common, shared*
commutatio-nis [f.] *change*
comoedus-a-um *like a comedian*
competitor-is [m.] *competitor*
comptus-a-um *well-groomed*
computo [1] *count*
concedo-ere-cessi-cessum *concede*
concupisco-ere-pivi-pitum *desire, aspire to*
concursus-us [m.] *rushing together*
concutio-ere-cussi-cussum *strike, shake*
condicio-nis [f.] *circumstances, condition*
conditor-is [m.] *founder*
condo-ere-didi-ditum *found*
confirmo [1] *confirm, assure*
confiteor-eri, confessus sum *admit*
confluo-ere-fluxi *flow together*
coniunx-iugis [m. & f.] *spouse*
conor [1] *try*
conquiro-ere-quisivi-quisitum *search for*
considero [1] *consider*
consilium-i [n.] *plan, policy, advice*
consisto-ere-stiti *stand*
conspicio-ere-spexi-spectum *catch sight of*
consternatus-a-um *agitated*
consto-are-stiti *stand together, agree with*
consuetudo-inis [f.] *custom, habit*
consul-is [m.] *consul*
contemno-ere-tempsi-temptum *despise*
contendo-ere-tendi-tentum *compete*
contentus-a-um *contented*
contineo-ere-tinui-tentum *hold, keep*
contio-nis [f.] *assembly*
contra [+ acc.] *against*
contrarius-a-um *opposite*
convictor-oris [m.] *table companion*
convivium-i [n.] *dinner-party*
copia-ae [f.] *abundance*
copiosus-a-um *abundant*
cor-dis [n.] *heart, soul*
coram [+ abl.] *in the presence of*

cornu-us [n.] *horn*
corpus-oris [n.] *body*
corripio-ere-ripui-reptum *seize, hurry*
cras *tomorrow*
cratera-ae [f.] *bowl*
creber-bra-brum *frequent*
credibilis-e *credible*
credo-ere-didi-ditum [+ dat.] *trust, believe*
credulus-a-um [+ dat.] *trusting*
creo [1] *appoint*
cresco-ere, crevi, cretum *grow*
cristatus-a-um *crested*
crus-uris [n.] *leg*
cubile-is [n.] *couch, bed*
culina-ae [f.] *kitchen*
culpo [1] *blame*
cultura-ae [f.] *tilling*
cum *with* [+ abl.], *when, since, although*
cum...tum *when..then, both..and*
cunctor [1] *hesitate*
cunctus-a-um *all, whole*
cupido-inis [f.] *desire*
cura-ae [f.] *care, anxiety, attention*
curo [1] *attend, see to*
curriculum-i [n.] *course*
curro-ere, cucurri, cursum *run*
currus-us [m.] *chariot*
damno [1] *harm, condemn*
damnosus-a-um *harmful*
damnum-i [n.] *loss*
de [+ abl.] *from, about*
dea-ae [f.] *goddess*
debello [1] *fight against*
debeo [2] *ought, owe*
decedo-ere-cessi-cessum *withdraw, die*
decem *ten*
decimo [1] *select by lot every tenth man*
declamito [1] *declaim*
decrepitus-a-um *decrepit*
decurro-ere-curri-cursum *run down*
deduco-ere-duxi-ductum *bring*
defendo-ere-di-sum *defend*
defero-erre, detuli, delatum *bring down, offer, report*
deinde *then, next*
delectatio-nis [f.] *pleasure*
delego [1] *assign*
delenimentum-i [n.] *allurement*
deligo [1] *tie*
delinquo-ere-liqui-lictum *make a mistake*

217

demitto-ere-misi-missum *send down*
demonstro [1] *show*
denarius-i [m.] *denarius*
deni *in tens*
deposco-ere-poposci *demand, challenge*
descendo-ere-scendi-scensum *come down, fall*
describo-ere-scripsi-scriptum *register, describe*
desero-ere-serui-sertum *leave, abandon*
desideo [2] *stay sitting*
despero [1] *despair of*
destino [1] *determine, destine*
destitutus-a-um *abandoned, lonely*
detineo [2] *keep*
detrecto [1] *refuse*
deus-i [m.] *god*
devenio-ire-veni-ventum *come down*
dico-ere, dixi, dictum *say, speak*
dictatura-ae [f.] *dictatorship*
dies-ei [m. & f.] *day*
differo-ferre, distuli, dilatum *disperse, separate*
difficultas-tatis [f.] *difficulty*
digitus-i [m.] *finger, toe*
dignitas-tatis [f.] *authority*
dignus-a-um [+ abl.] *worthy of, deserving*
digredior-i-gressus sum *depart*
dimitto-ere-misi-missum *release*
dimoveo-ere-movi-motum *remove*
discedo-ere-cessi-cessum *depart*
discerno-ere-crevi-cretum *divide, separate*
discidium-i [n.] *divorce*
disciplina-ae [f.] *knowledge*
discipulus-i [m.] *student*
disco-ere, didici *learn*
discordia-ae [f.] *disagreement*
discumbo-ere-cubui-cubitum *recline*
diva-ae [f.] *goddess*
divello-ere-velli-vulsum *tear apart*
diversus-a-um *different*
dives, divitis [adj.] *rich*
divus-a-um *divine*
do, dare, dedi, datum *give*
doceo [2] *teach*
documentum-i [n.] *example*
doleo [2] *grieve*
dolor-is [m.] *grief*
dolus-i [m.] *trick*
dominus-i [m.] *master*

domus-us [f.] *home*
donec *until*
dono [1] *donate*
donum-i [n.] *gift*
dormio [4] *sleep*
dubito [1] *doubt, hesitate*
duco-ere, duxi, ductum *lead, bring*
ductus-us [m.] *leadership*
dulcis-e *sweet*
duo *two*
duodeni *in twelves*
dux, ducis [m.] *leader*
e, ex [+ abl.] *out of, from*
ecce *oh! look!*
edico-ere-dixi-dictum *make clear*
edictum-i [n.] *decree*
edisco-ere-didici *learn by heart*
edo-ere-didi-ditum *put forth*
educo-ere-duxi-ductum *bring up, out*
efficio-ere-feci-fectum *produce*
egeo-ere-ui [+ abl.] *need, want*
egestas-atis [f.] *need, shortage*
egregius-a-um *outstanding*
emo-ere, emi, emptum *buy*
emollio [4] *soften, mollify*
enim *for, you see*
enitor, eniti, enixa sum *give birth to*
eo, ire, ii, itum *go*
epistula-ae [f.] *letter*
eques-itis [m.] *knight*
equester-tris-tre *belonging to a knight*
equidem *indeed*
equus-i [m.] *horse*
ergo *so, therefore*
eripio-ere-ripui-reptum *take away*
erro [1] *wander, make a mistake*
erumpo-ere-rupi-ruptum *break out*
esuriens [adj.] *hungry*
et *and, also, even*
et...et *both...and*
etiam *also, even*
evenio-ire-veni-ventum *happen, turn out*
evoco [1] *encourage*
exaequo [1] *regard as equal*
excipio-ere-cepi-ceptum *take, follow after*
excudo-ere-cudi-cusum *hammer out*
excutio-ere-cussi-cussum *shake off*
exeo-ire-ii-itum *go out*
exerceo [2] *exercise, employ*

exercitus-us [m.] *army*
exitiabilis-e *deadly*
exitus-us [m.] *end*
expello-ere-puli-pulsum *banish*
exquiro-ere-quisivi-quisitum *discover*
exsecror [1] *curse*
exspecto [1] *expect, wait for*
exstruo-ere-struxi-structum *construct, build*
extemplo *immediately*
extendo-ere-tendi-tentum *stretch out*
fabula-ae [f.] *myth*
facies-ei [f.] *face*
facilis-e *easy*
facinus-oris [n.] *crime*
facio-ere, feci, factum *make, do*
factum-i [n.] *deed*
facultas-tatis [f.] *capability, opportunity*
faeneror [1] *lend money*
faenum-i [n.] *hay*
faenus-oris [n.] *interest payment*
familia-ae [f.] *household*
familiaris-is [m.] *friend, attendant*
famula-ae [f.] *maid-servant*
fatum-i [n.] *fate*
fauces-ium [f.] *jaws, throat, entrance*
faveo-ere, favi, fautum [+ dat.] *be kind*
fecunditas-tatis [f.] *fruitfulness*
felix [adj.] *happy, fortunate*
femina-ae [f.] *woman*
fero, ferre, tuli, latum *carry, bear*
ferocia-ae [f.] *fierceness*
ferrum-i [n.] *steel*
ferula-ae [f.] *cane*
ferus-a-um *wild, savage*
fidelis-e *loyal, faithful*
fides-ei [f.] *trust, trustworthiness*
filia-ae [f.] *daughter*
filius-i [m.] *son*
finio [4] *end, set bounds to*
finis-is [m.] *end*
fio, fieri, factus sum *become, happen, am made*
flagellum-i [n.] *whip*
flagitium-i [n.] *crime*
flagro [1] *blaze, burn*
fleo-ere-evi-etum *weep*
floreo [2] *flourish*
flos-ris [m.] *flower*
foedus-a-um *dirty, soiled*

fons-ntis [m.] *fountain*
foramen-inis [n.] *opening, aperture*
foris-is [f.] *door, gate*
forma-ae [f.] *beauty, shape*
formido-inis [f.] *fear*
formosus-a-um *beautiful*
forte *by chance; perhaps*
fortuna-ae [f.] *fortune*
forum-i [n.] *forum*
foveo-ere, fovi, fotum *warm, cherish*
fragilis-e *fragile*
frango-ere, fregi, fractum *break*
frater-tris [m.] *brother*
frigus-oris [n.] *cold*
frons-ntis [f.] *forehead*
frumentum-i [n.] *corn*
frustra *in vain, not to be*
frustror [1] *deceive*
frux-gis [f.] *fruit*
fugio-ere, fugi *escape*
fugo [1] *chase*
fumus-i [m.] *smoke*
gallus-i [m.] *cock*
garrulus-a-um *chattering*
gaudium-i [n.] *joy*
gelidus-a-um *cool*
gemitus-us [m.] *groan*
gens-ntis [f.] *race*
genus-eris [n.] *kind, race*
geometres-trae [m.] *surveyor*
gero-ere, gessi, gestum *accomplish*
gladiator-is [m.] *gladiator*
gladius-i [m.] *sword*
gradus-us [m.] *step*
Graeculus-a-um *Greek*
gramen-inis [n.] *grass*
grammaticus-i [m.] *teacher*
gratia-ae [f.] *thanks, favour*
gratulatio-nis [f.] *congratulation*
gratus-a-um *pleasing*
gravis-e *heavy, serious,*
gravitas-tatis [f.] *weight, severity*
grex-gis [m.] *flock*
habeo [2] *have, hold*
habito [1] *live, dwell*
haedus-i [m.] *young goat, kid*
harena-ae [f.] *sand, arena*
haud *not*
haurio, haurire, hausi, haustum *drain, drink up*

hecyra-ae [f.] *mother-in-law*
heus *hey!*
hic, haec, hoc *this, he, she, it*
hinc et inde *here and there*
hodie *today*
homo-inis [m.] *man, human being, person*
honestas-tatis [f.] *reputation*
honestus-a-um *honourable*
honor-is [m.] *honour, favour*
hordeum-i [n.] *barley*
horrendus-a-um *dreadful*
hortor [1] *encourage*
hortus-i [m.] *garden*
hospes-itis [m.] *host, guest, stranger*
hostes-ium [m.] *enemy*
hostia-ae [f.] *sacrificial victim*
humanitas-tatis [f.] *civilization, humanity*
humanus-a-um *civilized*
hypomnema-tis [n.] *memorandum*
iaceo-ere-cui *lie down*
iacio-ere, ieci, iactum *throw*
iam *now, already*
ibi *there*
idem, eadem, idem *the same*
igitur *therefore*
ignavus-a-um *idle, cowardly*
ignis-is [m.] *fire*
ignominia-ae [f.] *disgrace*
ignosco-ere-novi-notum [+ dat.] *forgive*
ilex-icis [f.] *oak-tree*
ille, illa, illud *that, he, she, it*
imago-inis [f.] *likeness, bust, statue*
imbecillus-a-um *weak*
imber-bris [m.] *rain-cloud*
imbuo-ere-ui-utum *impress*
immergo-ere-mersi-mersum *plunge*
immeritus-a-um *undeserving*
immodicus-a-um *excessive*
imperito [+ dat.] [1] *rule*
imperitus-a-um *ignorant*
imperium-i [n.] *power*
impero [+ dat.] [1] *command, order*
impleo-ere-evi-etum *fill*
impono-ere-posui-positum *impose*
impudens [adj.] *shameless*
in *in, on* [+ abl.]; *into, against* [+ acc.]
incendium-i [n.] *fire*
incendo-ere-cendi-censum *burn, inflame*
incertus-a-um *uncertain*
incipio-ere-cepi-ceptum *begin*

incito [1] *arouse*
incola-ae [c.] *inhabitant*
incolo-ere-colui *inhabit*
incurro-ere-cucurri-cursum *run into*
inde *then*
indignus-a-um *unworthy*
industria-ae [f.] *effort, attention*
infans [adj.] *infant*
infero-erre, intuli, illatum *bring in, forward*
inficio-ere-feci-fectum *infect, stain*
inflexibilis-e *inflexible*
ingens [adj.] *huge, great*
ingredior-i, ingressus sum *enter, invade*
inicio-ere-ieci-iectum *impose*
inimicus-a-um *hostile, unfriendly*
initium-i [n.] *beginning*
inquam, inquit *I say, he/she says*
insania-ae [f.] *madness*
inscriptio-nis [f.] *inscription*
insidiae-arum [f.] *ambush*
insidiator-is [m.] *trickster*
insociabilis-e *incompatible*
insolens [adj.] *wanton*
instituo-ere-stitui-stitutum *begin, set up*
instratus-a-um *covered*
insula-ae [f.] *island*
intellegentia-ae [f.] *understanding*
intellego-ere-exi-ectum *understand*
inter [+ acc.] *among*
interdum *sometimes, now and then*
interea *meanwhile, sometimes*
interficio-ere-feci-fectum *kill*
interim *sometimes, meanwhile*
intermitto-ere-misi-missum *leave off*
interrogo [1] *interrogate, question*
intestinus-a-um *private, internal*
intro [1] *enter*
invenio-ire-veni-ventum *find*
inveteratus-a-um *long-standing*
invideo-ere-vidi-visum *envy*
invidus-a-um *envious*
invisus-a-um *hated*
invito [1] *invite*
invitus-a-um *unwilling*
ipse, ipsa, ipsum *him/her/itself*
iratus-a-um *angry*
iste-a-ud *that*
istuc *to that, thither*
ita *in such a way*
iter, itineris [n.] *route, passage*

iterum *again*
iubeo-ere, iussi, iussum *order*
iudex-icis [m.] *judge*
iugulo [1] *cut a throat*
iugum-i [n.] *summit, ridge*
iumentum-i [n.] *pack-animal*
ius, iuris [n.] *justice*
iustus-a-um *fair, reasonable*
iuvenis-e *young*
iuventa-ae [f.] *youth, young people*
labefactus-a-um *shaken*
labor-i, lapsus sum *fall*
labos-oris [m.] *toil*
labrum-i [n.] *lip*
lac-lactis [n.] *milk*
lacer-era-erum *mutilated*
lacertus-i [m.] *arm*
lacrima-ae [f.] *tear*
laetitia-ae [f.] *joy*
laetus-a-um *happy*
lanio [1] *tear apart*
lapidarius-a-um *stone-carrying*
largus-a-um *abundant*
lascivus-a-um *playful*
latrocinium-i [n.] *robbery*
laudo [1] *praise*
lectica-ae [f.] *litter*
lectito [1] *read repeatedly*
lego-ere, legi, lectum *read*
letum-i [n.] *death*
levis-e *light*
lex, legis [f.] *law*
libellus-i [m.] *little book, handbill*
libenter *willingly*
liber-a-um *free*
liber-bri [m.] *book*
liberalis-e *noble*
liberi-orum [m.] *children*
libertas-tatis [f.] *freedom*
libertus-i [m.] *freedman*
libet *it is pleasing*
librarius-i [m.] *clerk*
licentia-ae [f.] *wantonness*
licet *although, granted, it is allowed*
limen-inis [n.] *door, threshold*
lingua-ae [f.] *language, tongue*
liquo [1] *strain*
litigium-i [n.] *dispute*
littera-ae [f.] *letter (of the alphabet)*
litterae-arum [f.] *letter, correspondence,*

literature
litus-oris [n.] *shore*
loco [1] *place, contract*
locum-i [n.] *place*
longe *far*
longus-a-um *long*
loquor-i, locutus sum *speak*
luctuosus-a-um *sorrowful*
luctus-us [m.] *grief*
ludibrium-i [n.] *mockery*
ludo-ere, lusi, lusum *play*
ludus-i [m.] *school, game*
lumen-inis [n.] *light*
luo-ere, lui *wash, atone for*
lux-cis [f.] *light, daylight*
macto [1] *slaughter*
madeo-ere-dui *be wet*
magis *rather, more*
magister-tri [m.] *master, teacher*
magnus-a-um *great, large*
magus-i [m.] *sorcerer*
maior [adj.] *greater (senior, ancestor)*
male *badly*
maledictum-i [n.] *abuse*
malesuadus-a-um *evil-counselling*
malo, malle, malui *prefer*
malus-a-um *bad*
mancipium i [n.] *slave*
mando [1] *entrust*
mane *this morning, early*
maneo-ere, mansi, mansum *remain*
manus-us [f.] *hand*
mappa-ae [f.] *napkin*
maritimus-a-um *by the sea*
maritus-i [m.] *husband*
marmor-is [m.] *marble*
mater-tris [f.] *mother*
matrona-ae [f.] *lady, matron*
maxime *especially*
medicus-i [m.] *doctor*
medullae-arum [f.] *innermost core*
melius *better*
memini-isse *remember*
memorabilis-e *memorable*
mens-ntis [f.] *mind*
mensa-ae [f.] *table*
mentior-iri, mentitus sum *lie, cheat*
mercatura-ae [f.] *business, profit*
mercenarius-i [m.] *mercenary*
merces-edis [f.] *pay*

221

mereo-ere-ui-itum *deserve*
meretrix-icis [f.] *prostitute*
mergo-ere, mersi, mersum *sink*
meridies-iei [m.] *midday*
merum-i [n.] *wine*
metus-us [m.] *fear*
meus-a-um *my*
migro [1] *move*
miles-itis [m.] *soldier*
mille *thousand*
minime *not at all*
ministerium-i [n.] *service*
ministra-ae [f.] *deaconess*
minor [1] *threaten*
minus *less*
miror [1] *wonder at*
mirus-a-um *extraordinary*
miser-a-rum *wretched*
mitto-ere, misi, missum *send*
modo *now, recently*
modus-i [m.] *way, method, measure*
mollis-e *soft, delicate*
moneo [2] *warn, advise*
mons-ntis [m.] *mountain*
monstro [1] *show*
morbus-i [m.] *disease*
morior-i, mortuus sum *die*
moror [1] *delay*
mors-tis [f.] *death*
mortalis-e *mortal*
mos, moris [m.] *custom*
mox *soon*
mufrius-i [m.] *mutton-head*
mugitus-us [m.] *bellowing*
muliebris-e *female*
mulier-is [f.] *woman*
multum [adverb] *much*
multus-a-um *much, many*
mulus-i [m.] *mule*
mundus-i [m.] *world*
munus-eris [n.] *gift, show*
murmur-is [n.] *growling*
mus, muris [c.] *mouse*
muto [1] *change*
nam *for*
narro [1] *tell, recount*
natio-nis [f.] *nation*
natus-a-um *born*
natus-i [m.] *son*
nauta-ae [m.] *sailor*

navigo [1] *sail*
navis-is [f.] *ship*
ne *that not, lest*
ne...quidem *not even...*
nebula-ae [f.] *mist*
nec, nec...nec *and not, neither...nor*
necessarius-a-um *indispensable*
nefas [indecl. adj.] *wrong, forbidden*
neglegens [adj.] *careless*
nego [1] *deny, refuse, say that...not*
negotium-i [n.] *affair, business*
nemo-inis *no one*
neque, neque...neque *and not, neither...nor*
nescio-ire-ivi-itum *be ignorant, not know*
neuter-tra-trum *neither*
ni *if not*
niger-gra-grum *black*
nihil, nil *nothing*
nimis *excessively*
nimium *too much*
nisi *except, unless*
niveus-a-um *snow-white*
nobilis-e *noble, well-born, famous*
nodus-i [m.] *knot*
nolo, nolle, nolui *not want, be unwilling*
nomen-inis [n.] *name*
non *not*
non modo *not only*
nondum *not yet*
nonne *surely*
nonnumquam *sometimes*
nonus-a-um *ninth*
nosco-ere, novi, notum *know*
noster-tra-trum *our*
nota-ae [f.] *social grading*
notus-a-um *known*
novem *nine*
nox-ctis [f.] *night*
noxius-a-um *guilty*
nullus-a-um *no one, not any*
numerus-i [m.] *number*
nummus-i [m.] *coin*
numquam *never*
nunc *now*
nuntio [1] *announce*
ob [+ acc.] *because of*
oblivio-nis [f.] *neglect*
obscenus-a-um *foul, offensive*
observo [1] *observe*
obstinatio-nis [f.] *determination*

obstinatus-a-um *stubborn*
obsto [1] *stand in the way of*
occido-ere-cidi-cisum *kill*
occupo [1] *occupy*
octo *eight*
oculus-i [m.] *eye*
odor-is [m.] *smell*
offensio-nis [f.] *trouble, offence*
offero-erre, obtuli, oblatum *offer*
olim *previously, once upon a time*
omnino *altogether, entirely*
omnis-e *all, every*
opera-ae [f.] *task*
opprimo-ere-pressi-pressum *repress, put down, destroy*
ops-opis [f.] *wealth*
opulentus-a-um *lavish*
opus-eris [n.] *work*
ora-ae [f.] *shore*
oratio-nis [f.] *speech*
orbis-is [m.] *world*
orbitas-tatis [f.] *bereavement*
origo-nis [f.] *source*
ornamentum-i [n.] *ornament*
orno [1] *decorate*
oro [1] *beg*
ortus-a-um *born, descended*
os, oris [n.] *mouth, face*
os, ossis [n.] *bone*
ostendo-ere-endi-entum *reveal*
ostento [1] *show*
ostiarius-i [m.] *door-keeper*
otiosus-a-um *inactive*
otium-i [n.] *leisure, inactivity*
paene *almost*
pallens [adj.] *pallid-making*
palum-i [n.] *stake*
pantomimus-i [m.] *pantomime artist*
par [adj.] *equal*
parco-ere, peperci, parsum [+ dat.] *spare*
parens-ntis [m. & f.] *parent*
pareo [2] [+ dat.] *obey*
pariter *in like manner, equally*
paro [1] *prepare*
pars-tis [f.] *part*
partus-us [m.] *birth*
parum *not enough*
parvus-a-um *small*
pasco-ere, pavi, pastum *feed*
pater-tris [m.] *father*

paternus-a-um *belonging to a father*
patior-i, passus sum *suffer, endure*
patria-ae [f.] *country*
pauci-ae-a *few*
paulatim *little by little*
paulo *a little*
pauper-is [adj.] *impoverished*
pax-cis [f.] *peace*
pecunia-ae [f.] *money*
peius *worse*
pellis-is [f.] *skin*
penates-ium [m.] *spirits of the household*
pendo-ere, pependi, pensum *hang, weigh*
penus-i [m. & f.] *provisions*
per [+ acc.] *through, across, by means of*
perditus-a-um *ruined*
perfundo-ere-fudi-fusum *drench*
periculosus-a-um *dangerous*
periculum-i [n.] *danger*
perpetior-i, perpessus sum *endure steadfastly*
persevero [1] *persevere*
pertimesco-ere-ui *fear very much*
pertinacia-ae [f.] *perseverance*
pertinax [adj.] *persistent*
pervado-ere-vasi-vasum *go through*
pervenio-ire-veni-ventum *reach*
pes, pedis [m.] *foot*
peto-ere-ivi-itum *seek*
philosophia-ae [f.] *philosophy*
pictor-is [m.] *painter*
pius-a-um *dutiful*
placeo [2] [+ dat.] *please, satisfy*
plane *clearly*
plebes-ei [f.] *people*
plenus-a-um *full*
plerique *for the most part*
plerumque *very often*
plurimus-a-um *very many*
poena-ae [f.] *punishment, penalty*
poeta-ae [m.] *poet*
politus-a-um *refined*
pono-ere, posui, positum *place, put*
pons-ntis [m.] *bridge*
populus-i [m.] *people*
porticus-us [f.] *colonnade*
porto [1] *carry*
possum, posse, potui *be able*
post [+ acc.] *after*
postea *afterwards*

posteritas-tatis [f.] *posterity*
postulo [1] *demand*
potestas-tatis [f.] *power*
potior-iri, potitus sum [+ abl.] *take possession of*
poto [1] *drink*
prae [+ abl.] *before*
praeceptor-is [m.] *teacher*
praeceptum-i [n.] *maxim, precept*
praeclarus-a-um *magnificent*
praeco-nis [m.] *herald*
praeda-ae [f.] *plunder, loot*
praeeo-ire-ii-itum *go before*
praefero-ferre-tuli-latum *carry before*
praehibeo [2] *supply*
praemium-i [n.] *reward*
praesens *forthwith*
praeses-idis [m.] *governor*
praeter [+ acc.] *besides, except*
praeterea *moreover*
pravus-a-um *depraved*
primo *at first*
primum [adv.] *first*
primus-a-um *first*
princeps-ipis [m.] *leader, emperor*
principatus-us [m.] *control, leadership*
principium-i [n.] *beginning*
priscus-a-um *ancient*
pristinus-a-um *previous*
pro [+ abl.] *in place of, before*
probitas-tatis [f.] *decency*
probo [1] *approve*
procul *from afar*
procurro-ere-cucurri-cursum *run forward*
proditus-a-um *betrayed*
proelium-i [n.] *battle*
proficiscor-i, profectus sum *set out, leave*
profiteor-eri, professus sum *declare*
profugus-i [m.] *fugitive*
progredior-i, progressus sum *advance*
promitto-ere-misi-missum *promise*
prope *almost, near*
propero [1] *hurry*
propinquus-i [m.] *relative*
propono-ere-posui-positum *put forward, display*
propter [+ acc.] *because of*
prosequor-i, prosecutus sum *follow after*
prosperus-a-um *favourable*
prospicio-ere-spexi-spectum *be on the watch*

proximus-a-um *next*
prudentia-ae [f.] *good sense*
pudendus-a-um *shameful*
pudor-is [m.] *shame*
puella-ae [f.] *girl*
puer-i [m.] *boy, slave*
pugna-ae [f.] *battle*
pugno [1] *fight*
pulcher-chra-chrum *beautiful*
pulso [1] *beat*
pulvinar-is [n.] *couch*
punio [4] *punish*
puto [1] *think*
quadrans-ntis [m.] *4th part of an* **as**
quaero-ere-sivi-situm *search for*
qualis-e *just like, as*
quam *than, as, how, which*
quamquam *although*
quando *when, since*
quantus-a-um *how great*
quare *why*
quartus-a-um *fourth*
quattuor *four*
querimonia-ae [f.] *complaint*
qui, quae, quod *who, which*
quia *because, that*
quid *what, why*
quidam, quaedam, quoddam *somebody, something, a certain...*
quidem *indeed*
quies-tis [f.] *rest*
quietus-a-um *quiet, peaceful*
quingenti-ae-a *five hundred*
quinque *five*
quisquam, quidquam *anyone, anything*
quisque, quaeque, quodque *each, every*
quisquis, quidquid *whoever, whatever*
quo *to where, by which*
quod *because, which*
quondam *formerly*
quotiens *how often*
radius-i [m.] *rod, radius*
rapio-ere, rapui, raptum *take, snatch*
rarus-a-um *rare, unusual*
rasus-a-um *shaved*
recens [adj.] *fresh*
recipio-ere-cepi-ceptum *accept*
recte *properly*
recumbo-ere-cubui-cubitum *lie down*

224

reddo-ere-didi-ditum *restore*
redimo-ere-demi-demptum *buy back, set free*
reduco-ere-duxi-ductum *bring back*
refero-erre, rettuli, relatum *bring back, refer*
reficio-ere-feci-fectum *remake*
refugio-ere-fugi *flee back*
regio-nis [f.] *region*
regno [1] *rule, reign*
regnum-i [n.] *kingdom*
rego-ere, rexi, rectum *rule, guide*
regula-ae [f.] *rule*
religio-nis [f.] *scruple, awe, religion*
relinquo-ere-iqui-ictum *leave*
reliquus-a-um *remaining*
remedium-i [n.] *cure*
reor-i, ratus sum *think*
repente *suddenly*
repono-ere-posui-positum *put back*
reprehendo-ere-hendi-hensum *seize, blame*
reprimo-ere-pressi-pressum *check, restrain*
requiro-ere-quisivi-quisitum *search for*
res novae [f.] *revolution*
res publica [f.] *republic*
res, rei [f.] *thing*
reseco-are-secui-sectum *cut back*
resisto-ere, restiti [+ dat.] *resist, oppose*
respondeo-ere-spondi-sponsum *reply*
responsus-us [m.] *reply*
restituo-ere-stitui-stitutum *restore*
retineo-ere-tinui-tentum *keep*
reus-i [m.] *defendant*
rex-gis [m.] *king*
rhetor-is [m.] *professor*
rideo-ere, risi, risum *laugh*
rigo [1] *soak, drench*
rivus-i [m.] *stream*
rodo-ere, rosi, rosum *gnaw*
rubeo [2] *be red*
ruber-bra-brum *red*
rudis-e *impressionable, inexperienced*
rumor-is [m.] *rumour*
rumpo-ere, rupi, ruptum *break*
rursum *again*
rus, ruris [n.] *land, countryside*
sacculus-i [m.] *purse*
saeculum-i [n.] *age, era*
saepe *often*

saepius *quite often*
saevitia-ae [f.] *cruelty*
saevus-a-um *cruel, savage*
sal-is [m.] *salt, wit*
salutator-oris [m.] *visitor*
saluto [1] *greet*
sane *certainly*
sanguis-inis [m.] *blood*
sanies-ei [f.] *slaver*
sapiens [adj.] *wise, discreet*
sapio-ere-ivi *taste*
satis *enough*
saucius-a-um *wounded*
scaenicus-a-um *theatrical*
sceleratus-a-um *accursed, wicked*
scilicet *of course*
scio-ire, scivi, scitum *know*
scribo-ere, scripsi, scriptum *write*
scriptor-is [m.] *writer*
scripulum-i [n.] *a small weight*
scutica-ae [f.] *strap*
se, sese *himself, herself, themselves*
seco-are-ui, sectum *cut*
secundum [+ acc.] *according to, following*
secundus-a-um *second*
securis-is [f.] *axe*
sed *but*
sedeo-ere, sedi, sessum *sit*
sedo [1] *calm, stop*
segnitia-ae [f.] *sluggishness*
semper *always*
senator-is [m.] *senator*
senatus-us [m.] *senate*
senectus-us [f.] *old age*
senex-is [m.] *old man*
sentio-ire, sensi, sensum *perceive, realize*
septem *seven*
sequor-i, secutus sum *follow*
serius-a-um *serious*
sermo-nis [m.] *speech, conversation*
sero-ere, sevi, satum *sow*
servio [4] *serve*
servitus-tutis [f.] *slavery*
servo [1] *keep*
servus-i [m.] *slave*
sescenti-ae-a *six hundred*
sestertiarius-a-um *worth a sesterce*
severus-a-um *austere, strict*
sex *six*
si *if*

sidus-eris [n.] *star*
silentium-i [n.] *silence*
silva-ae [f.] *wood, forest*
simul *at the same time*
simulacrum-i [n.] *statue*
simulo [1] *pretend, imitate*
sin *but if*
sine [+ abl.] *without*
sino-ere, sivi, situm *allow*
solitus-a-um *familiar, customary*
solus-a-um *only*
solutus-a-um *released*
somnium-i [n.] *dream*
sopitus-a-um *sleeping*
soror-is [f.] *sister*
sospes, sospitis [adj.] *safe*
spatium-i [n.] *space*
speciosus-a-um *splendid*
spectaculum-i [n.] *show*
specto [1] *watch*
spelunca-ae [f.] *cave*
spero [1] *hope*
spes-ei [f.] *hope*
spiritus-us [m.] *breath*
spiro [1] *breathe, blow*
splendidus-a-um *bright*
sponte *of one's own free will*
statim *immediately*
sto-are, steti, statum *stand*
strepitus-us [m.] *noise*
studium-i [n.] *pursuit, study*
subdo-ere-didi-ditum *lay under*
subicio-ere-ieci-iectum *suppress, subject*
subinde *then*
suboles-is [f.] *offspring*
subrepo-ere-repsi-reptum *advance slowly*
subverto-ere-verti-versum *upset, overturn*
sudo [1] *sweat*
suffero-erre, sustuli, sublatum *suffer, endure*
sufficio-ere-feci-fectum *supply, be sufficient*
sufflo [1] *blow*
summus-a-um *utmost*
sumo-ere, sumpsi, sumptum *take*
sumptuosus-a-um *extravagant*
superbus-a-um *proud*
superior-ius *upper*
superstitio-nis [f.] *religious belief*
supplicium-i [n.] *death penalty*
supra [+ acc.] *beyond*

suscito [1] *revive*
suus-a-um *his, her, their*
syllaba-ae [f.] *syllable*
taceo [2] *be silent*
tam *so*
tamen *however*
tamquam *as if, as it were*
tandem *at last, pray*
tantus-a-um *such, so great*
taurus-i [m.] *bull*
tellus-uris [f.] *earth, ground*
templum-i [n.] *temple*
tempto [1] *tempt*
tempus-oris [n.] *time*
tenax [adj.] *clinging*
tendo-ere, tetendi, tensum *stretch out, extend*
teneo [2] *hold*
tener-a-um *tender*
tenuis-e *slender*
terreo [2] *frighten*
terribilis-e *terrible*
terror-is [m.] *terror, fear*
tertius-a-um *third*
testamentum-i [n.] *will*
testimonium-i [n.] *evidence*
testor [1] *bear witness*
thesaurus-i [m.] *library, store-house*
timeo [2] *fear*
timide *timidly*
tolero [1] *endure*
tollo-ere, sustuli, sublatum *raise*
tono-are-ui *thunder*
tormentum-i [n.] *torture*
tortor-is [m.] *torturer*
torus-i [m.] *couch*
totus-a-um *whole, all*
trado-ere-didi-ditum *hand over*
trano [1] *swim across*
transeo-ire-ii-itum *go over, across*
transmuto [1] *transfer, switch*
transverbero [1] *transfix, pierce*
trecenti-ae-a *three hundred*
tres *three*
tribunal-is [n.] *tribunal*
tribunus-i [m.] *tribune*
tribuo-ere-bui-butum *give*
tristis-e *sad*
trucido [1] *murder*
tueor-eri, tuitus sum *preserve*

tum *then*
tumultus-us [m.] *noise*
tunc *then, at that time*
turba-ae [f.] *crowd*
turgidus-a-um *swollen*
turpis-e *disgraceful*
tuus-a-um *your*
ubi *when, where*
ullus-a-um *any*
ultra *more, beyond*
ultrix [adj.] *avenging*
unda-ae [f.] *wave*
unde *from where*
undecimus-a-um *eleventh*
undique *from all sides*
unguis-is [m.] *nail*
universus-a-um *all*
unus-a-um *one*
urbs-is [f.] *city*
uro-ere, ussi, ustum *burn*
ut *that, so that, as, when*
uterque, utraque, utrumque *each of two*
utilis-e *beneficial, useful*
utinam *if only*
utor-i, usus sum [+ abl.] *use*
uxor-is [f.] *wife*
vaco [1] *be empty*
vae *oh dear*
validus-a-um *strong*
varius-a-um *different*
veho-ere, vexi, vectum *carry*
vel *or*
vena-ae [f.] *vein*
venabulum-i [n.] *hunting-spear*
venenum-i [n.] *poison*
venio-ire, veni, ventum *come*
ventus-i [m.] *wind*
venus-eris [f.] *love*
venustus-a-um *charming*
verber-is [n.] *beating, blow*
verbero [1] *whip*
verbum-i [n.] *word*
vereor-eri, veritus sum *fear*

vero *indeed, but*
verro-ere *sweep*
verto-ere, verti, versum *turn*
verum *but, however*
verus-a-um *true, real*
vester-tra-trum *your*
vestibulum-i [n.] *hall*
vestitus-a-um *clothed*
vetustas-tatis [f.] *age*
via-ae [f.] *road, way*
vicinus-a-um *neighbouring*
victor-is [m.] *winner, survivor*
victoria-ae [f.] *victory*
video-ere, vidi, visum *see*
vigilo [1] *be awake*
viginti *twenty*
vilis-e *base*
villa-ae [f.] *villa, farm*
vinco-ere, vici, victum *conquer*
vinum-i [n.] *wine*
vir-i [m.] *man, husband*
vires-ium [f.] *resources, strength*
virgo-nis [f.] *maiden*
virtus-tutis [f.] *courage*
viso-ere, visi *visit*
vita-ae [f.] *life*
vitium-i [n.] *vice, defect*
vitrum-i [n.] *glass, woad*
vitta-ae [f.] *headband*
vitupero [1] *despise*
vivarium-i [n.] *pond, aquarium*
vivo-ere, vixi, victum *live*
vivus-a-um *alive, living*
vix *scarcely*
volo, velle, volui *want, be willing*
volo [1] *fly*
voluntas-tatis [f.] *will, inclination*
voluptas-tatis [f.] *pleasure*
vomo-ere-ui-itum *put forth, give out*
vox-cis [f.] *voice*
vulgus-i [n.] *crowd*
vulnus-eris [n.] *wound*
vultus-us [m.] *face*

LATIN

Better Read Than Dead

The Latin texts in this course are available
on cassette from:
Multilingua, 13 Charlotte Street, Bristol BS1 5PP
Please send s.a.e. for an order form